The Legal Rights of Students with Disabilities

The Legal Rights of Students with Disabilities

International Perspectives

Edited by
Charles J. Russo

ROWMAN & LITTLEFIELD PUBLISHERS, INC.
Lanham • Boulder • New York • Toronto • Plymouth, UK

Published by Rowman & Littlefield Publishers, Inc.
A wholly owned subsidiary of The Rowman & Littlefield Publishing Group, Inc.
4501 Forbes Boulevard, Suite 200, Lanham, Maryland 20706
http://www.rowmanlittlefield.com

Estover Road, Plymouth PL6 7PY, United Kingdom

British Library Cataloguing in Publication Information Available

Library of Congress Cataloging-in-Publication Data

Russo, Charles J.
The legal rights of students with disabilities : international perspectives / edited by Charles J. Russo.
p. cm.
Includes bibliographical references and index.
ISBN 978-1-4422-1083-7 (hardback : alk paper) — ISBN 978-1-4422-1085-1 (electronic)
1. Children with disabilities—Education—Law and legislation. 2. Right to education. I. Title.
K3751.R87 2011
371.91'6—dc22

2011010058

∞™ The paper used in this publication meets the minimum requirements of American National Standard for Information Sciences—Permanence of Paper for Printed Library Materials, ANSI/NISO Z39.48-1992. Printed in the United States of America

To my wife,
Debbie,
With my undying love and affection,
Charlie

Contents

Preface

As well established as the right to education is, the rights of children with disabilities in elementary and secondary schools are neither as well defined nor protected. This sorry state of affairs exists even though the United States became the 141st nation to sign the UN Convention on the Rights of Persons with Disabilities (CRPD)[1] of 2006 when President Obama signed it into effect.[2] Subsequently, when UN ambassador Susan Rice formally endorsed his action by signing the Convention at UN headquarters on October 1, 2009, the United States became the sixtieth nation to ratify the Convention.[3]

At the same time, even though signatories profess their adherence to the lofty principles contained in the CRPD, which went into effect in May 2008, and to an array of documents addressing education as a fundamental human right, as of 2006, according to data accompanying the CRPD, "only 45 countries have anti-discrimination and other disability-specific laws."[4] In addition, UNESCO reports that "[n]inety per cent of children with disabilities in developing countries do not attend school. . . ."[5]

In light of the uneven status of the right to education for students with disabilities, this book includes essays by a representative sample of scholars representing ten nations on all six continents addressing commonalities in this important, and timely, issue. The first substantive chapter is an essay by Bronagh Byrne and Laura Lundy, which surveys international documents on the educational rights of students with disabilities. The remaining chapters, on individual countries, all of which were authored by accomplished academics and/or jurists, are from Australia (Sally Varnham and Jim Jackson); Brazil (Nina Ranieri); Canada (Greg M. Dickinson);

China (Ran Zhang); England (Neville Harris); Malaysia (Fatt Hee Tie); New Zealand (Kate Diesfeld and John Hancock); Singapore (Mui Kim Teh); South Africa (Marius Smit and Petra Engelbrecht); and the United States (Charles J. Russo and Allan G. Osborne Jr.).

Based on a common outline, I asked these scholars to examine such issues as the legal/constitutional sources of special education law in their nations; the rights of students with disabilities, including identification and assessment, placement issues, due process rights, dispute resolution, and funding and cost issues; and a section on emerging issues before rounding out with a conclusion. Acknowledging that issues vary from one nation to the next, I asked authors to examine the topics as they saw appropriate while examining the issues as they saw fit from their own points of view.

By granting authors some latitude in addressing their topics, I could draw conclusions in a final chapter that we hope will lead to future dialogue. Further, as noted, recognizing the importance of as far-reaching a representation as possible, I was fortunate to be able to ensure that I had at least one nation on each continent or region of the world represented. The first book of its kind, and a companion volume to earlier texts on the rights of students[6] and teachers,[7] I hope that this collection of essays will enhance a common understanding of the rights of students with disabilities throughout the world. As the world continues to shrink and interdependence grows, then, one of the major challenges facing the global community is ensuring the educational rights of all children, including those with disabilities.

Readers are advised that rather than translate notes and other pertinent terms into English, they are ordinarily preserved in their original languages. I have done this not only because the underlying documents are often unavailable in English but also because translating text might create difficulties for native speakers who wish to research relevant materials. In addition, since each of the nations covered in this book uses slightly different systems of legal citation, I have left references in their original form rather than attempt to standardize them under one rubric. Finally, I have preserved minor variations in the different forms of English used throughout the world so that readers can get a flavor of how our seemingly common tongue is used throughout the world, particularly for scholars whose native language is not English.

Of course, no single book can ever hope to cover the myriad of legal topics, or laws of nations, addressing the educational rights of students with disabilities. Even so, I hope that these well-written and -researched chapters, authored by leading scholars in the field, can serve as up-to-date and ready sources of information to help keep educational leaders, academics, and students abreast of the many changes in the ever-growing area of comparative special education law.

NOTES

1. UN Convention on the Rights of Persons with Disabilities (2006), available at http://www.un.org/disabilities/convention/conventionfull.shtml.

2. http://www.whitehouse.gov/the_press_office/Remarks-by-the-President-on-Rights-of-Persons-with-Disabilities-Proclamation-Signing/.

3. Removing Barriers: A Long Road (2009, Oct. 1). *Paraplegia News* Vol. 63, Issue 10, p. 69; available at 2009 WLNR 20482459.

4. Fact Sheet on UN Convention on the Rights of Persons with Disabilities (2006), available at http://www.un.org/disabilities/convention/facts.shtml.

5. *Id.*

6. Charles J. Russo, Jan de Groof, & Douglas J. Stewart (Eds.). *The Educational Rights of Students: International Perspectives on Demystifying the Legal Issues.* Lanham, MD: Rowman & Littlefield Education (2007).

7. Charles J. Russo & Jan de Groof. *The Employment Rights of Teachers: Exploring Education Law Worldwide.* Lanham, MD: Rowman & Littlefield Education (2009).

Acknowledgments

As with any book, there are a number of people who must be thanked. Four sets of people provided great assistance in helping put this book together. First, many thanks to Tom Koerner at Rowman & Littlefield Education, who was most supportive of this project from its inception to its being published. Thanks also to Patti Belcher at Rowman & Littlefield and to Desiree Reid for copyediting the text and Jehanne Schweitzer, who assisted in production of the text. Second, it almost goes without saying that I am grateful to the authors for their valuable contributions to this book. Third, I would like to thank my assistant, Ms. Elizabeth Pearn at the University of Dayton, for her efforts in copyediting and helping to prepare the manuscript for publication. I would also like to thank Mrs. Ann Raney at the University of Dayton's Curriculum and Materials Center for her invaluable assistance in locating some of the citations used in this book. Fourth, but certainly not least, I would like to express my deepest appreciation and love for my wife, Debbie, for her ongoing love and support in so many ways, without whom none of this work would have been completed.

Introduction

Protections for Students with Disabilities in International Law?

Bronagh Byrne and Laura Lundy

As an economic, social, cultural, and positional good, the benefits of education are beyond doubt. However, these benefits are elusive for many children and young people with disabilities who are faced with extensive barriers in their quest for educational achievement and fulfilment. Educational provisions for students with disabilities generally have been skewed towards the lower end of the vocational and nonacademic spectrum, often in segregated settings. The poor-quality experiences of students with disabilities has been further exacerbated by the "ablist" norms inherent within mainstream education systems and which are expressed through selection or admission procedures, streaming or "grouping" processes, syllabus design; the physical environment in many schools, communicational barriers, low levels of disability awareness, and institutional discourses of disability more generally.[1]

The international human rights framework is a key mechanism through which protections for students with disabilities can be established and associated practices legitimized. Indeed, the right to education is articulated in all international and regional human rights instruments. Education is conceptualised not just as an end in itself but as a means to an end and as a crucial stepping-stone to the realization of other rights. Students with disabilities, as human beings, are entitled to the same rights as their peers who are not disabled. Yet, the explicit identification in international law of children and young people with disabilities as subjects with rights rather than as burdensome "objects" is relatively recent. The need for detailed articulation and effective implementation of the rights of students with disabilities has taken on renewed emphasis with the adoption of the United Nations Convention on the Rights of Persons with Disabilities (CRPD) in 2006. The development of a thematic treaty is indicative of the recognition accorded to the complexity of disability issues and the conclusion reached by the international community that the difference of disability is such that it has not been, and cannot be, effectively addressed by generalist human rights treaties.

The value of international human rights law for signatory states lies in its characterisation as a blueprint for action, as a set of detailed standards agreed to by the international community and a reflection of consensual norms on a range of issues pertinent to all. While the efficacy of human rights law to effect change "on the ground" is largely dependent on the ways in which its provisions are brought to bear in domestic law, the ability of international law to provide often detailed guidance and direction to States, and in providing what is effectively a barometer against which a State's progress can be measured, is significant.

Human rights law can be used to inform the development of new legislation, policies, and programs, as there have been instances where the responses of treaty-monitoring bodies to State parties' reports or impending ratification have prompted legislative reform. For example, Ireland is currently reforming its legislation regarding mental capacity in preparation for its ratification of the CRPD. The transmutation of "need" to a human rights claim can form part of a broader political strategy, both in legitimating the concerns of students with disabilities as human rights claims and in exerting pressure on duty bearers. International law can thus prompt individual States to reflect critically on and improve existing practices with respect to students with disabilities both directly and indirectly. Still, while the normative obligations of State parties are relatively clear, responsibility for translating these onto the domestic plane ultimately rests with individual States.

The aim of this chapter is to provide a critical analysis of international standards with respect to students with disabilities. This chapter sets out the relevant standards, drawing on the observations and comments of treaty-monitoring bodies with regard to the practices of States highlighted in this book. For the purposes of this chapter, the relevant protections are categorized into five key themes: definitions of disability under international law; the right to receive an education; educational placement; funding and resource issues; and dispute resolution. The chapter concludes with a critique of the international framework and an acknowledgment of the limitations of the standards for students with disabilities.

THE INTERNATIONAL HUMAN RIGHTS SYSTEM

On 10 December 1948, member states of the United Nations (UN) adopted the Universal Declaration of Human Rights (UDHR), a non–legally binding statement of the fundamental rights of every human being. In 1966, following much discussion of how human rights should be categorized, the General Assembly of the United Nations adopted two separate, legally binding treaties—the International Covenant on Civil and Political Rights (ICCPR) and the International Covenant on Economic, Social and Cultural Rights (ICESCR). Together these instruments have become known as the International Bill of Rights.

Since 1948, the international community, under the auspices of the United Nations General Assembly, has drafted and adopted a number of other human rights instruments, including the International Convention on the Elimination of All Forms of Racial Discrimination (CERD) (1965), the Convention on the Elimination of All Forms of Discrimination against Women (CEDAW) (1979), the Convention against Torture and Other Cruel, Inhuman or Degrading Treatment or Punishment (CAT) (1984), the Convention on the Rights of the Child (CRC) (1989), the Convention on the Protection of the Rights of All Migrant Workers and Members of Their Families (CMW) (1990) and most recently, the Convention on the Rights of Persons with Disabilities (CRPD) (2006). These treaties constitute the heart of international human rights law.

As a form of "hard law," these treaties can be distinguished from what is known as "soft law." "Soft law" encompasses declarations, statements, rules and standards. Examples include the Declaration of the Rights of the Child (1959), the UN Standard Rules on the Equalization of Opportunities for Persons with Disabilities (1993) and the Salamanca Statement on Special Needs Education (1994). Although these are not legally binding, they reflect international consensus and represent morally binding agreements and/or obligations. Declarations often provide the basis for later development of binding legal instruments. The UDHR, for instance, has been given legal force in ICESCR and ICCPR while the UN Standard Rules has formed the basis for the CRPD.

Each of the core human rights treaties adopted by the UN includes arrangements for monitoring the ways in which the standards contained within these treaties are implemented by States. This supervisory role is exercised by a "committee of independent experts" known as a "treaty monitoring body." When a State ratifies an international treaty, it becomes a "State party" and assumes an obligation to submit periodic reports to the treaty bodies on the measures it has taken to ensure the enjoyment of the rights contained in that particular treaty. Treaties often have established procedures allowing individuals who claim human rights violations under their provisions to submit complaints to the relevant treaty-monitoring body.[2] In addition, it has become increasingly common practice for treaty-monitoring bodies to issue "General Comments" on particular issues. Whilst these General Comments purport to contain authoritative interpretations of treaties, they are not in themselves legally binding.

Human rights are also codified in regional human rights mechanisms. The three major regional human rights systems are the European Convention on Human Rights (1950), which is overseen by the European Court of Human Rights; the African Charter on Human and People's Rights (1981), which is overseen by the African Commission on Human and People's Rights; and the Inter-American System, which stems from the Organisation of American States Charter (1948), the American Declaration of the Rights and Duties of Man (1948) and the American Convention on Human Rights (1969), and is overseen by the Inter-American Commission on Human Rights and the Inter-American Court of Human Rights. Even so, this chapter focuses on the international human rights system.

THE RIGHTS OF STUDENTS WITH DISABILITIES

With limited exceptions, the core UN human rights treaties have not addressed the human rights of students with disabilities expressly. Only the CRC contains explicit references to disability, while other human rights treaties have subsumed disability under "... other status," as demonstrated in Article 2(1) of the ICCPR and Article 2(2) of the ICESCR. The textual invisibility of people with disabilities in human rights treaties has not been "ameliorated by any conscious effort on behalf of the relevant treaty monitoring bodies."[3] Recognition of the need for the UN to play a much greater role in asserting and monitoring the rights of people with disabilities gained increasing prominence in the 1990s. In his 1993 report, Leandro Despouy, UN Special Rapporteur on Disability, commented on the fact that other groups had the benefit of thematic conventions while people with disabilities did not.[4] Moreover, he maintained that all treaty-monitoring bodies should play a role in supervising the application of their respective treaties to people with disabilities. In 1994, the General Assembly of the UN adopted a resolution on human rights and disability, encouraging "all human rights treaty monitoring bodies to respond positively to its invitation to monitor the compliance of States with their commitments under the relevant human rights instruments in order to ensure the full enjoyment of these rights by disabled persons."[5] The General Assembly reiterated this principle in Resolutions 1996/27, 1998/31 and 2000/51.

DEFINING DISABILITY IN INTERNATIONAL HUMAN RIGHTS LAW

The term *disability* has been used generally as a means of identifying the perceived characteristics of a person, or their perceived status based on how well they measure up against societal norms. This has been evident through, for example, the World Health Organisation's classificatory schema.[6] This is in contrast with the social model of disability, which distinguishes between "impairment" as an individual attribute and "disability" as socially created and rooted in the organisation and structures of society.[7] The way(s) in which *disability* is defined has powerful implications for students in determining access and entitlement to resources, services and opportunities through, inter alia, diagnosis and labelling and acceptance or rejection of expressed needs against set criteria. International human rights law has adopted a generalist approach to disability, deferring decisions of which impairments necessitate specific disability protection to nation-states. Until recently, treaty bodies responsible for monitoring ICESCR and the CRC have adopted the approach to disability taken in the nonbinding Standard Rules of 1993. According to this Rule:

> The term "disability" summarizes a great number of different functional limitations occurring in any population in any country of the world. People may be disabled by physical, intellectual or sensory impairment, medical conditions or mental illness. Such impairments, conditions or illnesses may be permanent or transitory in nature.[8]

The Committee on the Rights of the Child has encouraged States' parties to develop a clear definition of disability. For example, in its response to Brazil's most recent periodic report in 2004, the Committee recommended that its government establish an appropriate definition of disability in order to formulate a comprehensive policy for children with disabilities.[9] More recently, the Committee on the Rights of the Child has taken account of the definition of disability set out in the 2006 Convention on the Rights of Persons with Disabilities.[10] While not a concrete *definition* as such, the CRPD states:

> Persons with disabilities include those who have long-term physical, mental, intellectual or sensory impairments which in interaction with various barriers may hinder their full and effective participation in society on an equal basis with others.[11]

The preamble to the CRPD further recognises that disability is an "evolving concept." The social model approach to disability adopted by the CRPD is not new in itself, having emerged in its purest form in the latter half of the twentieth century. What is unique in this context is its explicit articulation in binding international human rights law. In an educational domain, then, students with disabilities *include,* but are not restricted to, those with physical, mental, intellectual and sensory impairments. Crucially, the CRPD approach distinguishes between "impairment" and "disability" by conceptualising the latter as resulting from the *interaction* between impairment on the one hand and barriers constructed by society on the other. Thus disability is not the product of impairment alone. The barriers alluded to by the CRPD may include those which are attitudinal, physical, environmental, social or economic.[12]

THE RIGHTS OF STUDENTS WITH DISABILITIES TO RECEIVE AN EDUCATION

Article 26 of the UDHR proclaims that everyone has the right to education. This was made binding first by Article 13(1) of ICESCR and elaborated upon by Articles 28 and 29 of the CRC. The CRC places a duty on States' parties to progressively provide primary education that is "compulsory and available free to all" and to do so on the basis of equal opportunity.[13] A lesser duty is imposed with respect to secondary education, the development of which is to be encouraged and made available and accessible to every child, but not compulsory. The CRC specifies that *all* children have the right to an education designed to provide them with life skills and which strengthens their capacity to enjoy the full range of human rights.[14] "Education" in this context goes beyond formal schooling to embrace the broad range of life experiences and learning processes which enable all children, individually and collectively, to fully develop their personalities, talents and abilities and to live "a full and satisfying life within society."[15]

While children and young people with disabilities have clear entitlement to these provisions, they are also able to call upon rights that are specifically afforded to people with disabilities. For example, the UN Standard Rules calls upon States to "recognize the principle of equal primary, secondary and tertiary educational opportunities for children, youth and adults with disabilities in integrated settings."[16] In binding international law, the CRC is a key source of rights for children and young people with disabilities since it was the first core human rights treaty to make explicit reference to disability. Article 2 of the CRC prohibits discrimination in the enjoyment of the Convention rights on the grounds of disability. In its first General Comment on the Aims of Education, the Committee stated that:

> [D]iscrimination on the basis of any of the grounds listed in article 2 of the Convention, whether it is overt or hidden, offends the human dignity of the child and is capable of undermining or even destroying the capacity of the child to benefit from educational opportunities.[17]

This provision clearly extends to education and encompasses discriminatory practices in its varied forms. The significance attached by the Committee to the principle of nondiscrimination is reflected in the general guidelines for both initial and periodic State reports, General Comments issued by the Committee and in responses to States' parties. For example, the Committee has expressed concern that in Malaysia, children with disabilities living in remote areas do not have access to the same level of services as children living in other parts of the country.[18] Recognition of the need for substantive equality measures and of the multiple forms of de jure and de facto discrimination experienced by children with disabilities is also evident throughout the Committee's work.[19]

The CRC encompasses a specific article on children with disabilities. Article 23 asserts, inter alia, that children with disabilities should enjoy a "full and decent life,"[20] receive "special care,"[21] and that assistance is provided to ensure that the child has effective access to and receives education "in a manner conducive to the child's achieving the fullest possible social integration and individual development, including his or her cultural and spiritual development."[22] The Committee on the Rights of the Child has made it clear that children and young people with disabilities have the same right to education as all other children and "shall enjoy this right without any discrimination and on the basis of equal opportunity."[23]

The most detailed articulation of the right to education for students with disabilities is contained in the CRPD. Article 24 of the CRPD affirms the right of people with disabilities to education and draws on Article 29 of the CRC in establishing the aims to which education should be directed.[24] Whilst the aims stated in the CRPD are reflective of educational provisions in other mainstream human rights treaties, their explication here makes clear that students with disabilities, like students without disabilities, have the same entitlement to an effective education; have diverse talents and abilities which must be nurtured and maximized; and that they are full and equal members of society.

EDUCATIONAL PLACEMENT

The educational "buzzword" of the twenty-first century for children and young people with disabilities is *inclusion*. Conceptions of inclusion have derived, in part, from a desire to challenge the prevailing orthodoxy of segregated education and in part from a concern with the growing "rights" agenda at both national and international levels. Richard Rieser distinguishes between concepts of integration and inclusion and suggests that integration is merely an issue of location but that inclusion goes further than this and is essentially about the school adapting to meet the needs of the child rather than vice versa.[25] According to this view, an identification of barriers within the school's environment, teaching and learning strategies, and attitudes, which prevent the full participation of children with disabilities, will be required.

This trend towards "mainstream" or inclusive forms of education for students with disabilities has parallels in international law. However, it is only recently that the distinction between integration as mere location and inclusion as meaningful participation has been understood more clearly at this level. In the context of international law, "special education" is used to denote segregated settings. Rule 6 of the 1993 Standard Rules calls upon States to accommodate students with disabilities within "integrated" settings and to provide adequate accessibility and support services to meet the needs of people with a range of disabilities. However, in recognising that not all schools will yet be able to meet the needs of all students with disabilities, the Rules allow for special—that is, segregated—education, the quality of which should "reflect the same standards and ambitions as general education and should be closely linked to it." Special education is viewed as a temporary measure, ultimately aimed at preparing students for education in the general school system. The Rules do recognise that progression to mainstream education may not be possible for some students with disabilities.

A survey carried out for the United Nations Special Rapporteur on Disability on the implementation of the Standard Rules in 2006 highlighted that in many countries practice fell far short of that stipulated in the Rules. In particular, it was highlighted that in many states there was no legislative requirement to include children with disabilities in mainstream settings.[26] The Standard Rules was followed in 1994 by the Salamanca Statement on Special Needs Education.[27] This document, together with the corresponding Salamanca Framework of Action, called for the inclusion of students with disabilities in the mainstream education system as a matter of course, "unless there are compelling reasons for doing otherwise," and urges States to invest greater effort in early identification and intervention strategies. While neither the Standard Rules or the Salamanca Statement are legally binding in that they constitute "soft law," they are considered to have strong moral force and provide practical guidance to States.

The right of students with disabilities to be educated in mainstream education settings can also be inferred from the work of the Committee on the Rights of the Child. While the CRC text itself is silent on issues of educational placement for students with disabilities, the Committee has paid particular attention to this in its General Comment on children with disabilities. In addition to placing emphasis on the need for early identification, the Committee affirms that "inclusive education should be the goal of educating children with disabilities."[28] The Committee on the

Rights of the Child has spelt out in some detail the form inclusion should take, with emphasis upon individual need. To this end, inclusion may range from full-time placement of all students with disabilities into one regular classroom or placement into the regular classroom with varying degrees of inclusion, including a certain portion of special education.[29] The Committee has also stated that:

> All schools should be without communicational barriers as well as physical barriers impeding the access of children with reduced mobility . . . In order to fully exercise their right to education, many children need personal assistance, in particular, teachers trained in methodology and techniques, including appropriate languages, and other forms of communication, for teaching children with a diverse range of abilities capable of using child-centred and individualised teaching strategies, and appropriate and accessible teaching materials, equipment and assistive devices, which States parties should provide to the maximum extent of available resources.[30]

The focus on the substantive content of educational practices in addition to the question of educational placement is reflective of the Committee's dogma that children's rights do not dissipate by virtue of passing through the school gates.[31] The right to education for children with disabilities is quite broad in scope and does not proclaim to be wholly prescriptive. Whilst the "catchall" approach to inclusion enables account to be taken of the diversity of individual need, segregation is still permitted in instances where children with disabilities require a form of support that is not readily available in the mainstream school system. Like many rights, the right of children with disabilities to be educated in regular schools is not absolute, but is, in this context, contingent upon the extent of individual need and the ability of the school to provide support appropriate to these needs.

Under these principles, States' parties are required to demonstrate, when reporting to the Committee on the Rights of the Child, the steps they have taken in order to progressively realize the principle of inclusive education for children with disabilities. In its responses to the most recent reports of the States' parties that are highlighted in this book, the Committee expressed concern regarding: the inadequate legal protection, programmes, facilities and services for children with disabilities in South Africa;[32] the disparities in access to and availability of education for children with disabilities in China;[33] that children with disabilities are not yet fully "integrated" into mainstream schools in Australia,[34] New Zealand,[35] Brazil[36] and Singapore;[37] that children with disabilities in the UK are still unable to "fully enjoy their right to education";[38] and that the United States has not endorsed the Convention on the Rights of the Child.[39]

The CRPD is the first human rights treaty which itself spells out in detail the optimum education to which children and young people with disabilities are entitled. The CRDP thus carries more weight than the General Comments of the Committee on the Rights of the Child on matters which are intended primarily to offer guidance to State parties on the meaning of particular rights. Article 24 of the CRPD requires States' parties to ensure an inclusive education system at all levels. The Article goes further than the CRC and grants a much more empowering and comprehensive entitlement for students with disabilities, reflective in part of the high level of involvement of people with disabilities during the drafting process of the CRPD. In realizing the right to education, States' parties are obliged to ensure that children and young people with disabilities are not excluded from the general education system on the basis of disability;[40] that they are able to access an inclusive, quality and free primary and secondary education on an equal basis with others in the communities in which they live;[41] and that they are provided with support within the general education system to facilitate their effective education.[42]

The CRPD pays particular attention to students who are deaf, blind or deaf-blind, and to this end requires States' parties to take a range of measures to facilitate their full and equal participation in education, including facilitating the learning of Braille, alternative script, augmentative and alternative modes, means and formats of communication;[43] facilitating the learning of sign language and the promotion of the linguistic identity of the deaf community;[44] and ensuring that the education of those who are blind, deaf or deaf-blind is delivered in the most appropriate languages and modes and means of communication for the individual and in environments which maximize academic and social development.[45] Additionally, States' parties are required to take appropriate measures to employ teachers who are qualified in sign language and / or Braille.[46] The need for teachers to receive training in disability awareness and the use of alternative means and formats of communications, educational techniques and materials to support students with disabilities is specified.[47]

Insofar as the CRPD only came into force in 2007, its monitoring body, the Committee on the Rights of Persons with Disabilities, has not yet had the opportunity to elaborate on any aspect of the right to education. The Committee has issued reporting guidelines for States' parties on the CRPD which requires States' parties to provide detail on each of the above issues as well as measures taken to ensure early identification of people with disabilities and their education needs.[48] It is interesting to note that the CRPD, in contrast to the CRC, does not use the terms *special education* or *special needs*. Nor is any reference made to forms of education outside of the general education system other than that effective, individualized support measures must be provided "in environments that maximize academic and social development."[49] These environments must, however, be "consistent with the goal of full inclusion."[50]

FUNDING AND COST

International human rights law recognizes that States' parties may not be able to immediately realise all of the rights contained within a particular treaty. Unlike civil and political rights which are subject to immediate realisation, the extent to which a state is able to realise economic, social and cultural rights will often depend upon the resources it has at its disposal. The right to education, as an economic and social right, is therefore subject to progressive realization. The concept of progressive realisation is reflected in Article 2(1) of the International Covenant on Economic, Social and Cultural Rights and is recognition of the fact that full realisation of economic, social and cultural rights, by their very nature, may take time to implement. Progressive realisation means that States' parties have a specific and continuing obligation "to move as expeditiously and effectively as possible" towards a particular goal.[51]

The right to education for students with disabilities must also be read in light of Article 4 CRC and Article 4(2) CRPD, which require States' parties to take measures "to the maximum of its available resources" with a view to achieving progressively the full realisation of that right. There is a strong presumption on States not to undertake any retrogressive measures in relation to the right to education. If any deliberately retrogressive measures are taken, the State party has the burden of proving that they have been introduced only after careful consideration of all alternatives and that they are fully justified by reference to the totality of the rights provided for and in the context of the full use of the State party's maximum available resources.[52] The Committee on the Rights of the Child has frequently called upon States' parties to prioritise budgetary allocations to the maximum extent of available resources to ensure implementation of the education rights of children and in particular for those children belonging to disadvantaged and vulnerable groups.[53]

The right of students with disabilities to the support they require is also constrained by the notion of "reasonable accommodation" that permeates the CRPD. This is the first time "reasonable accommodation" has been both included and defined in a core human rights treaty. Article 2 of the CRPD defines *reasonable accommodation* as:

> Necessary and appropriate modification and adjustments not imposing a disproportionate or undue burden, where needed in a particular case, to ensure to persons with disabilities the enjoyment or exercise on an equal basis with others of all human rights and fundamental freedoms.

The explicit inclusion and definition of reasonable accommodation is something of a double-edged sword—a crucial component of the CRPD in recognising the ways in which students with disabilities have been disadvantaged by an educational system based on normalized discourse and of the remedies needed to ensure a more level playing field. However, its operationalisation is often contingent upon interpretations of "reasonableness" and the costs incurred in making such accommodations. Implicit, unfortunately, within the understanding of reasonable accommodation put forth in the CRPD is the idea that the particular needs of some students with disabilities may be excessive or "burdensome." In this context, then, the notion of "reasonable accommodation" can itself become a barrier to the full realization of the right to education for children and young people with disabilities on the grounds that to do otherwise would be inherently "unreasonable."

DISPUTE RESOLUTION IN INTERNATIONAL LAW

Under both the CRC and the CRPD, children and young people with disabilities have the right to express their views freely on all matters affecting them and for their views to be given "due weight" in accordance with their age and maturity.[54] Article 12(2) of the CRC requires States' parties to give children and young people the opportunity to be heard in any judicial and administrative proceedings affecting the child, including those relating to education, either directly or through a representative or an appropriate body in accordance with the child's wishes.

Proceedings must be both accessible and age appropriate and particular attention paid to the provision and delivery of child-friendly information, adequate support for self-advocacy, and appropriately trained staff.[55] Children should have the possibility of addressing an ombudsman or a person of a comparable role in schools in order to voice their complaints.[56] Children should know who these persons are and how to access them. Article 7(3) of the CRPD requires children and young people to be provided with disability and age-appropriate assistance to realise this right. The Committee on the Rights of the Child has expressed particular concern that children in the UK have no right to appeal the decisions of a special educational needs tribunal, and it has called on the UK to address this situation.[57] In its General Comment on Article 12, the Committee on the Rights of the Child has said that:

> Investment in the realization of the child's right to be heard in all matters of concern to her or him and for her or his views to be given due consideration, is a clear and immediate legal obligation . . . It is the right of every child

> without any discrimination. Achieving meaningful opportunities for the implementation of article 12 will necessitate dismantling the legal, political, economic, social and cultural barriers that currently impede children's opportunity to be heard and their access to participation in all matters affecting them. It requires a preparedness to challenge assumptions about children's capacities, and to encourage the development of environments in which children can build and demonstrate capacities. It also requires a commitment to resources and training.[58]

Effective enforceability of the right to education for students with disabilities as established in international law is problematic. Unlike regional human rights mechanisms such as the European Convention on Human Rights, where disputes can be assessed by the European Court of Human Rights, international human rights treaties do not have a judicial equivalent. Instead, each human rights treaty is monitored by a body of experts which is responsible for examining the progress made by each State party in meeting their obligations via a periodic reporting process.[59] In dualist systems domestic remedies relating to international human rights obligations are only possible where a human rights treaty has been explicitly incorporated into domestic law.[60] By contrast in monist states, the act of ratifying an international human rights treaty immediately incorporates the treaty into national law.[61]

Some human rights treaties have an individual complaints mechanism in the form of an Optional Protocol. Under such a mechanism, complaints or "communications" can be submitted to the treaty body by, or on behalf of, individuals or groups of individuals claiming a violation of a right(s) under a treaty. Only complaints from individuals whose State has accepted these procedures may be examined by the treaty bodies. In spite of the CRC containing the most comprehensive set of rights for children, generally it has no individual complaints mechanism at present.[62] An individual complaints mechanism to ICESCR was adopted by the UN General Assembly under an Optional Protocol on 10 December 2008; however, this has not yet come into force.[63] Students with disabilities can submit individual complaints relating to Article 24 of the CRPD to the Committee on the Rights of Persons with Disabilities under its Optional Protocol. This came into force for ratifying States on 3 May 2008. A complaint can only be brought forward once all available domestic remedies have been exhausted. Examinations of complaints are held in closed sessions, and suggestions and recommendations, if any, are forwarded to the State party concerned and to the petitioner. Even though a Committee's views are not legally binding, ignoring them exposes a government to domestic and international criticism that it is not complying with its international obligations.

To the extent that it is so new, no individual complaints have yet been examined by the Committee on the Rights of Persons with Disabilities.

From the work of other Committees it is clear that the entire process, from submitting the complaint to adoption of the Committee's views, is lengthy.[64] The Committee's deliberations are confidential, and there is no opportunity to call witnesses or to engage the government in an oral hearing, as would occur in a domestic court. The use of individual complaints mechanisms is also subject to levels of awareness about their existence within States' parties. Nevertheless, individual complaints mechanisms remain important where no other means of effective recourse is available.

MOVING FORWARD: A PARTICIPATIVE APPROACH TO MONITORING

Whilst States parties' obligations to "promote, protect and ensure" the fundamental rights and freedoms of students with disabilities are undoubtedly made clear within the CRPD, the realisation of these obligations will remain elusive on the ground unless effective implementation and monitoring systems are in place. As with all human rights treaties, the CRPD contains a number of monitoring provisions; namely, the State reporting process and an individual complaints mechanism. The CRPD goes further than previous human rights treaties by placing particular emphasis on the role of people with disabilities in the monitoring and implementation process. The inclusion of Article 33 on national implementation and monitoring is a recognition of the need for strong and explicit systems of monitoring so as to ensure a more effective transmission of and engagement with the Convention's standards at the national level. Among its provisions is the requirement for States' parties to "maintain, strengthen, designate or establish within the State party, a framework . . ., to promote, protect and monitor implementation of the Convention."[65] Article 33(3) stipulates that "civil society, in particular persons with disabilities and their representative organisations, shall be involved and participate fully in the monitoring process."

This must be read in light of Article 4(3) of the CRPD, which requires States' parties to actively involve people with disabilities, including children with disabilities, in the development and implementation of legislation and policies to implement the Convention rights. Moreover, it requires such involvement both in processes relating to the implementation of the Convention and "in other decision-making processes concerning issues relating to people with disabilities." It will be interesting to see what kind of "framework" States' parties put in place and how far students with disabilities are involved in the development of legislation and policies pursuant to Article 24 of the CRPD. The deliberate inclusion of these provisions is something of a natural progression given the wider debate on enhancing the effectiveness of treaty monitoring in general and on additional ways in which effect can be given to human rights norms and obligations at the domestic level. It is also reflective of a move towards a participatory approach to monitoring wherein the lived experiences of rights holders become the principal point of departure.[66]

By placing a positive obligation on States' parties to establish such a participatory mechanism, Article 33 presents individual States with a key avenue through which the generalities of the CRPD can be given, translated and applied in "the small places close to home,"[67] not least by promoting dialogue and meaningful engagement between government bodies and civil society. As is the case with other obligations, States' parties are required to specifically report on how they have actively involved people with disabilities, including children and young people, in the monitoring process. This substantial departure from the monitoring norms of other human rights treaties has the potential to firmly embed the visibility of students with disabilities in the domestic arena with respect to human rights claims.

CONCLUSION

International human rights law has come a long way since the Universal Declaration on Human Rights and its failure to address the need for enhanced and dedicated protections for the rights of persons with disabilities in education or elsewhere. While the new CRPD is a welcome development in this respect, it is notable that persons with disabilities were recognised as a group who might require additional dedicated human rights protections thirty years after women and racial minorities, twenty-one years after children and twenty years after migrant workers.

The reticence of States' parties to address the rights of individuals with disabilities could be seen as an interesting manifestation of what might be a general unease about aspects of human rights law. Socioeconomic rights are often entered into by States with a degree of caution or outright qualification; a concern which usually emanates from uncertainty about their access to the resources which are needed to deliver their promises in the international treaties. The concept of progressive realisation, which is a feature of many human rights instruments, ameliorates this by enabling States to commit to continuous improvement rather than specific guarantees in relation to provision. Nonetheless, when the commitments relate to people with disabilities, the human rights provisions are often subject to further additional qualifications on the stated commitments, with phrases such as *reasonable accommodation* further diluting what might already be regarded as a fairly elastic commitment to provision. Moreover, when specific provisions relate to the educational rights of students with disabilities, this approach is noticeably ratcheted up to the point where some might consider that States have committed little more than the bare minimum in attempting to fulfil their obligations. Indeed, these cumulative and additional qualifications appear to be more reflective of a *conditional* approach to human rights for students with disabilities than the oft-proclaimed universality of human rights discourse.

The resource implications of meeting the individual needs of children with disabilities in an educational context are accepted to be a legitimate reason to place limitations on their rights to access education on the same basis as their peers, limitations which would not be deemed acceptable if the basis of the child's difference was their gender or race. The inherent assumption that students with disabilities, by virtue of their support needs, may constitute a "disproportionate or undue burden" risks becoming the Achilles' heel of the CRPD unless addressed appropriately by its Committee. There is a danger that the concept of reasonable accommodation itself becomes a barrier which may "hinder full and effective participation" of children with disabilities "on an equal basis with others."[68] In particular, students with more complex and resource-intensive needs may find themselves once again relegated to the margins of rights talk on the grounds of unreasonableness.

Reducing the problem of rights realisation to the expense of the child with a disability places undue and wholly inappropriate responsibility on students with disabilities: that if a student did not have expensive support needs then States' parties would be more "able" to realize their right to education. As such, in the eyes of human rights law, the student with a disability seemingly becomes the barrier to the development of their own rights discourse. It is crucial that the Committee on the Rights of Persons with Disabilities grants at least as much attention to the interpretive underpinnings of the CRPD and their implications for the realization of the substantive rights, as it does to the substantive issues alone.

So, in effect, while international human rights law provides a useful and comprehensive framework for guiding and assessing domestic law and practice in relation to students with disabilities, the lack of specificity and ubiquitous qualifications in the key texts allow individual States' parties considerable discretion in determining the content of domestic law, policy and practice. If the rights of students with disabilities are to be realised progressively in signatory states, the role of the Committee on the Rights of Persons with Disabilities will be crucial. In its General Comments, the Committee has the opportunity to articulate what the full (as opposed to progressive) realisation of the right would look like. Through its monitoring mechanism the Committee has the ability to cement the potential of the CRPD to influence State practices and induce behavioural change through processes of "coercion," "persuasion" and/or "acculturation."[69] This is a crucial point in the history of disability rights.

Disability commentators have long warned of the prominent role played by structures and institutions in the creation and sustainment of "disablist" practices.[70] The international human rights framework is no exception. In articulating the prescribed and proscribed, the standards contained in the CRPD can ultimately be understood as an "objectification of the dominant vision recognized as legitimate, or . . . of the legitimate vision of the world . . . [as] guaranteed by the [international order],"[71] and, in so doing, contributes to the production of knowledge and discourse in and around disability. It is this naturalization which emerges as part of those deeper structures of domination and oppression to which students with disabilities are often subject. The role of the Committee in reconceptualizing taken-for-granted practices as inherently discriminatory, and in uncovering hidden contradictions within the international human rights framework more generally, it will be key in shaping a positive legacy for the CRPD, lest it becomes a contributory factor in giving the least robust rights to those who stand to benefit the most.

NOTES

1. See Baker, J., Lynch, K., Cantillon, S. and Walsh, J. (2004) *Equality: From Theory to Action*, Hampshire: Palgrave Macmillan; Riddell, S., Tinklin, T. and Wilson, A. (2005) *Disabled Students in Higher Education: Perspectives on Widening Access and Changing Policy*, London: Routledge.

2. Optional Protocols to ICCPR; CAT; CERD; CEDAW; and CRMW.

3. Quinn, G. (2008) Resisting the "Temptation of Elegance": Can the Convention on the Rights of Persons with Disabilities Socialise States to Right Behaviour? In O. M. Arnardottir and G. Quinn (eds.) *The UN Convention on the Rights of Persons with Disabilities*, Leiden: Martinus Nijhoff Publishers, p. 217.

4. Despouy, L. (1993) Human Rights and Disabled Persons, UN publication No.E.92.XIV.4. Para 280/281. Despouy was appointed Special Rapporteur on Disability by the Sub-Commission on Prevention of Discrimination and Protection of Minorities.

5. UN GA Res 1994/27, at para. 6.

6. The World Health Organisation (WHO) introduced an *International Classification of Impairments, Disabilities and Handicaps* (ICIDH) in 1981. The ICIDH defined impairment as "any loss or abnormality of psychological, physiological or anatomical structure or function" (1980: 27), while disability was defined as "any restriction or lack (resulting from an impairment) of ability to perform an activity in the manner or within the range considered normal for a human being" (1980: 28). The third term, *handicap*, was defined as "a disadvantage for a given individual, resulting from an impairment or disability, that limits or prevents the

fulfilment of a role (depending on age, sex, social and cultural factors) for that individual" (1980: 29). WHO revised their classification and developed a more environmental understanding of disability in *Functioning Disability and Health,* ICFDH (2001).

7. Barton, L., Barnes, C. and Oliver, M. (2002) *Disability Studies Today,* Oxford: Polity Press.

8. Standard Rules on the Equalization of Opportunities for Persons with Disabilities, annexed to General Assembly resolution 48/96 of 20 December 1993 (Introduction, at para. 17).

9. Concluding Observations: Brazil, Committee on the Rights of the Child (2004) 37th Session CRC/C/15/Add.241 at para. 51.

10. Committee on the Rights of the Child (2006) General Comment 9: The Rights of Children with Disabilities, CRC/C/GC/9.

11. Article 1, CRPD.

12. Zarb describes barriers such as lack of access to buildings and transport systems; unequal access to education and employment and services; a lack of representation and involvement in local planning and politics—all at local, national and international levels. Zarb, G. (1995) *Removing Disabling Barriers,* London: Policy Studies Institute, at p. 4. Oliver (1990) cites other examples such as "the inability of the general population to use sign language, the lack of reading material in Braille, or hostile public attitudes to people with non-visible disabilities." Oliver, M. (1990) *The Politics of Disablement,* London: Macmillan, at p. vii.

13. Article 13(1) ICESCR; Article 28(1) CRC.

14. Article 29(1) CRC.

15. Committee on the Rights of the Child (2001) General Comment 1: The Aims of Education, CRC/GC/2001/1, at para. 2.

16. Rule 6, Standard Rules 1993, *supra* note 8.

17. Committee on the Rights of the Child (2001) General Comment 1, *supra* note 15, at para. 10.

18. Concluding Observations: Malaysia, Committee on the Rights of the Child (2007) 44th Session, CRC/C/MYS/CO/1, at para. 6.

19. CRC General Comment 9, *supra* note 10, at para. 11.

20. Article 23(1) CRC.

21. Article 23(2) CRC.

22. Article 23(3) CRC.

23. CRC General Comment 9, *supra* note 10, at para. 44.

24. Set out in Article 24(1) CRPD: that is, to "the full development of human potential and sense of dignity and self-worth, and the strengthening of respect for human rights, fundamental freedoms and human diversity," and "the development by persons with disabilities of their personality, talents and creativity, as well as their mental and physical abilities, to their fullest potential."

25. Rieser. R. (2000) "Special Educational Needs or Inclusive Education" in M. Cole, *Education, Equality and Human Rights,* London: Routledge, at p. 151.

26. Global Survey on the Implementation of the Standard Rules on the Equalization of Opportunities for Persons with Disabilities, United Nations, October 2006, p. 47.

27. The Salamanca Statement (UNESCO) was agreed by representatives of ninety-two governments and twenty-five international organisations at the World Conference on Special Needs Education, held in Salamanca, Spain.

28. CRC General Comment 9, *supra* note 10, at para. 48. The Committee on the Rights of the Child draws upon the definition of inclusion set out in UNESCO's Guidelines for Inclusion: Ensuring Access to Education for All (UNESCO 2005). "Inclusion is seen as a process of addressing and responding to the diversity of needs of all learners through increasing participation in learning, cultures and communities, and reducing exclusion within and from education. It involves changes and modifications in content, approaches, structures and strategies, with a common vision which covers all children of the appropriate age range and a conviction that it is the responsibility of the regular system to educate all children . . . Inclusion is concerned with the identification and removal of barriers . . ." (pp. 13 and 15).

29. *Id.*, at para. 48.

30. *Id.*, at para. 44.

31. CRC General Comment 1, *supra* note 14, at para. 8.

32. Concluding Observations: South Africa, Committee on the Rights of the Child (2000) 23rd Session CRC/C/15/Add.122 at para. 32.

33. Concluding Observations: China, Committee on the Rights of the Child (2005) 40th Session CRC/C/CHN/CO/2 at para. 75.

34. Concluding Observations: Australia, Committee on the Rights of the Child (2005) 40th Session CRC/C/15/Add.268 at para. 61.

35. Concluding Observations: New Zealand, Committee on the Rights of the Child (2003) 34th Session CRC/C/15/Add.216 at para. 39.

36. Concluding Observations: Brazil *supra* note 9, at para. 50.

37. Concluding Observations: Singapore, Committee on the Rights of the Child (2003) 34th Session CRC/C/15/Add.220 at para. 40.

38. Concluding Observations: United Kingdom of Great Britain and Northern Ireland, Committee on the Rights of the Child (2008) 49th Session CRC/C/GBR/CO/4 at para. 66.

39. The United States has not ratified the CRC. J. Becker (2002, May 5) "World Summit on Kids, Do We Care? As Leaders Gather at the UN, the U.S. Has Yet to Ratify the World Treaty on Children's Rights," *Newsday*, p. B4.

40. Article 24 (2)(a).

41. Article 24 (2)(b).

42. Article 24 (2)(d).

43. Article 24 (3)(a).

44. Article 24 (3)(b).

45. Article 24 (3)(c).

46. Article 24(4).

47. *Id.*

48. Committee on the Rights of Persons with Disabilities, Reporting Guidelines (2009) CRPD/C/2/3.

49. Article 24 (2)(e).

50. *Id.*

51. Committee on Economic, Social and Cultural Rights General Comment 3 (1990) *The Nature of States Parties Obligations* (Art. 2, para. 1), at para. 9.

52. Ibid.

53. Concluding Observations: Australia, *supra* note 33, at para. 17; Concluding Observations: China, *supra* note 32, at para. 75; Concluding Observations: Malaysia, *supra* note 18, at para. 24; Concluding Observations: New Zealand, *supra* note 34, at para. 15; Concluding Observations: Singapore, *supra* note 36, at para. 15.

54. Article 12(1) CRC, Article 7(3) CRPD.

55. Committee on the Rights of the Child (2009) General Comment 12: The Right of the Child to Be Heard, CRC/C/GC/12, at para. 34.

56. *Id.*, at para. 46.

57. Concluding Observations: United Kingdom of Great Britain and Northern Ireland, *supra* note 37, at paras. 66/67.

58. *Id.*, at para. 135.

59. The Committee on the Rights of the Child, which is the monitoring body of the CRC, and the Committee on the Rights of Persons with Disabilities, the monitoring body of the CRPD.

60. Examples include UK, Ireland, Canada, United States, Australia and New Zealand.

61. Examples include Germany, France and Italy.

62. Work is ongoing to develop a draft Optional Protocol to the CRC that would allow for an individual complaints mechanism.

63. The Optional Protocol to ICESCR will come into force three months following ratification by the tenth State.

64. The Human Rights Committee; the monitoring body of the ICCPR (1966); the Committee on the Elimination of Discrimination against Women; the monitoring body of CEDAW (1979); and the Committee on the Elimination of Racial Discrimination; the monitoring body of CERD (1965).

65. Article 33(2) CRPD.

66. Melish, T. J. (2007) The UN Disability Convention: Historic Process, Strong Prospects, and Why the U.S. Should Ratify, *Human Rights Brief*, 14(2), pp. 37–47, at p. 37.

67. Eleanor Roosevelt, remarks delivered at the United Nations in New York on March 27, 1958.

68. Article 1, CRPD.

69. Goodman, R. and Jinks, D. (2004) How to Influence States: Socialization and International Human Rights Law, *Duke Law Journal* 54(3), pp. 621–703.

70. See for example: Finkelstein, V. (1980) *Attitudes and Disabled People*, New York: World Rehabilitation Fund; Finkelstein, V. (1993) The Commonality of Disability, in J. Swain, V. Finkelstein, S. French and M. Oliver (eds.) *Disabling Barriers—Enabling Environments*, London: Sage; Oliver, M. (1990) *The Politics of Disablement*, London: Macmillan; Oliver, M. (1996) *Understanding Disability: From Theory to Practice*, London: Macmillan.

71. Bourdieu, P. (2000) *Pascalian Meditations*, Cambridge: Polity Press, p. 186.

1

Australia

Sally Varnham and Jim Jackson

Education is an inalienable right of every person to have the opportunity to benefit from schooling that is accessible to all on an equal basis. The education system in Australia is underpinned by this principle as it makes provisions in educational legislation and policy to remove the barriers to educational opportunities so that all people are able to partake equally.

Australia is a federation of six states: New South Wales (NSW), Queensland (Qld), South Australia (SA), Tasmania (Tas), Victoria (Vic), and Western Australia (WA), along with two territories, the Australian Capital Territory (ACT) and the Northern Territory (NT). The Australian Constitution sets out the division of power between the federal, state and territorial governments.[1] It is important to note in this context that the Constitution, unlike the U.S. Constitution, does not contain a Bill of Rights.

The federal system means that there is both state and commonwealth (federal) legislation. While public education is a state matter, as is the registration of nongovernment schools, funding predominantly comes from the Commonwealth government and there are conditions relating to its provision. Disability discrimination is provided for both in Commonwealth legislation, the Disability Discrimination Act 1992 (Commonwealth Lawyer [Cth]) and its recent amendment act, the Disability Discrimination and Other Human Rights Legislation Amendment Act 2009 (Cth), and in state and territory legislation; for example, the Anti-Discrimination Act 1977 (NSW) and the Equal Opportunity Act 1995 (Vic).[2]

Modern education policy and legislation in Australia expressly or implicitly embraces inclusion rather than separation of students with disabilities. The education of children with disabilities and special needs in

Australian schools is a combination of the general principles set out at the beginning of each state and territory education act, with detail being provided for in delegated legislation and policy. These provisions aim to incorporate the right to education, equal opportunity, freedom from discrimination, and the right to participation as provided for in international conventions such as the International Convention on the Elimination of All Forms of Discrimination and the United Nations Convention on the Rights of the Child (UNCROC). Consistent with these principles, recent decades have seen developments in the area of the education of children with special needs in Australia as to the inclusion of students with disabilities within mainstream education pursuant to Article 23.1 of UNCROC: "States parties recognize that a mentally or physically disabled child should enjoy a full and decent life, in conditions which ensure dignity, promote self-reliance and facilitate the child's active participation in the community."

At the same time, there is an increasing recognition of the importance of the views of children in the decision-making process of their education. This principle of participation is set out in general terms in Article 12 of UNCROC, which provides in Article 12(1): "States parties shall assure to the child who is capable of forming his or her own views the right to express those views freely in all matters affecting the child, the views being given full weight in accordance with the age and maturity of the child."

Australia has an indigenous population, the Aboriginal people, whose children operate generally at a disadvantage within the educational system in terms of access to schooling in remote areas and services for those with disabilities and learning difficulties. In addition, as Australian society becomes progressively multicultural, the challenge is to ensure equal opportunity for the children of the "new" Australians whose educational needs relate to both language and cultural differences.

Against this background, this chapter examines special educational needs as provided in the education acts of the Australian states and territories; the Commonwealth Disability Standards for Education 2005; the Disability Discrimination Act 1992 (Cth) as amended by the Disability Discrimination and Other Human Rights Legislation Amendment Act 2009 (Cth) (DDA); cases highlighting issues arising in the context of the education of children with special needs and disability discrimination; and as a constitutional right.

STATE AND TERRITORY EDUCATION ACTS: PROVISION FOR THE EDUCATION OF CHILDREN WITH SPECIAL EDUCATIONAL NEEDS

The original Education Acts of all Australian jurisdictions made little provision for the education of children with special needs. Since this was considered a parental responsibility, such children were excluded from the compulsory attendance provisions with the result that they either did not attend school or were educated in charitable institutions. Progressively, the right of all children, including those with disabilities, to education was recognized, but it was believed that this should be undertaken in separate institutions in the case of children with special educational needs.

Separate schools and institutions were established as some were built for the specific purpose of serving children with disabilities and specially equipped. Since the 1980s, there has been a worldwide recognition of the benefits for all children of inclusion in mainstream schooling of students with special needs. As such, education policy and legislation in Australia is now designed around the philosophy reflected in Article 23.1 of UNCROC.

The education acts of all Australian states and territories make provision to varying degrees for the education of children with special needs, as the education department of each also implements policies to ensure equal educational opportunities for all students. While the legislation of some states and territories still contains provisions for the establishment of special educational facilities, the overriding principle is one of inclusive education, with independent education plans and necessary resourcing required for the education of children with disabilities.

In the early days of the inception of policies of inclusion, there was little recognition and understanding of the measures that were necessary to enhance the removal of barriers to children with disabilities from participating on an equal basis. School administrators were seemingly overwhelmed by their perceptions of the difficulties they would encounter in enrolling children with special needs and making accommodations for them in school life.[3] Consequently, there were some legal actions emanating from complaints to the Human Rights and Equal Opportunity Commission[4] from that time which provide evidence of the problems encountered by these children in their education and participation in the school community and its activities.[5]

The policy of inclusion is implied in the legislation of New South Wales, Victoria, the Australian Capital Territory, Western Australia, and Queensland, all of which begin with broad statements of principles and objects, including the provision of education to all children free of charge in order to assist all students to attain their educational potential.[6] Section 20 of the New South Wales legislation, for example, specifically regulates for aid to be given to government schoolchildren with special needs, including "financial assistance, facilities, courses of study, staff, staff training or distance education," any financial assistance to be paid from the public "purse."[7]

The legislation of other Australian jurisdictions similarly calls for assistance to be provided within government schools for students with disabilities or special needs with no contribution required from their parents.[8] In

Victoria, for instance, the assistance to be provided for children with special needs includes special meals for those who are disadvantaged by their socio-economic background.[9] In some jurisdictions there is a legislative provision requiring the minister or the chief executive to establish special schools and special education for children with special learning needs. In South Australia and Tasmania, the legislation provides definitions for these facilities.[10]

DEFINITION AND INTERPRETATION OF *DISABILITY*

The special educational needs of children are as diverse and wide-ranging as the disabilities that give rise to their special needs, which may be physical, emotional, intellectual or behavioral. This is reflected in the definition of *disability* contained in s4 of the Disability Discrimination Act 1992 (Cth) (DDA), which includes total or partial loss of a person's bodily or mental functions; total or partial loss of a part of the body; the presence in the body or organisms that have caused or are capable of causing disease or illness; a disorder or malfunction that results in the person learning differently from a person without the disorder or malfunction; and a disorder, illness, or disease that affects a person's thought process, perception of reality, emotions or judgment or that results in disturbed behavior.

Following tribunal and judicial determinations of allegations of discrimination in relation to the discipline of children whose behavioral difficulties threatened the safety of the school environment, the following sentence was added to the definition: "To avoid doubt, a disability that is otherwise covered by this definition includes behavior that is a symptom or manifestation of the disability." Thus, it must be considered whether the cases in this area discussed below would now be decided differently.

The educational legislation of the different Australian jurisdictions also contain definitions of disability and/or mechanisms by which students may be assessed. These provisions vary widely in their specificity and breadth. For example, in the Education (General Provisions) Act 2006 (Qld):

> **165 Meaning of person with a disability**
>
> (1) A person with a disability is a person who is decided, in accordance with a policy approved under subsection (2), to be unlikely to attain the levels of development of which the person is capable unless the person receives special education.
>
> (2) The Minister must approve a policy about the criteria to be considered in deciding whether a person is a person with a disability.

Whereas, in Western Australia, the definition in the legislation is all encompassing:

Section 4 *disability* means a condition—

(a) which is attributable to an intellectual, psychiatric, cognitive, neurological, sensory or physical impairment or a combination of those impairments;
(b) which is permanent or likely to be permanent;
(c) which may or may not be of a chronic or episodic nature; and
(d) which results in—
  (i) a substantially reduced capacity of a person for communication, social interaction, learning or mobility; and
  (ii) the need for continuing support services.[11]

Legislation in New South Wales, on the other hand, offers assistance to children in government schools who have special needs other than those arising from physical or intellectual disabilities.[12] Further, the Education Act 1979 (NT) of the Northern Territory still uses the term *handicapped child,* with its definition in s 33 as a child whose educational progress will suffer because of a mental or physical handicap unless the child has access to special educational arrangements.

Assessment of Special Educational Needs

Legislation relating to the assessment of special needs in education varies greatly between the jurisdictions. In the Northern Territory, South Australia, and Tasmania, the chief executive officer[13] may make arrangements for the education of children with developmental disabilities in accordance with prescribed procedures.[14] In some jurisdictions, further provision is made for children to be placed in special education at the request of head teachers[15] or parents.[16] In some states and territories, parents of children who are developmentally disabled are required to comply with the direction of the relevant chief executive officer as to the placement of children into special education. However, where this is the case there is provision for parents to appeal against such a direction.[17] In Victoria, there are no specific special educational provisions, but the Act provides that parents of students with disabilities are not required to contribute to the cost of providing additional support for their children in state schools.[18]

COMMONWEALTH DISABILITY STANDARDS FOR EDUCATION 2005

Section 31 (1A) of the DDA provides for disability standards to be put in place to require persons dealing with individuals with disabilities to make reasonable adjustments in order to eliminate discrimination as far as is possible. In the case of education, these standards were formulated in 2005 and are known as the Commonwealth Disability Standards for Education. It is unlawful for a person to contravene a disability standard.[19] If education providers comply with the standards by making such reasonable adjustments, this provides an answer to an accusation of unlawful discrimination under the Act.[20] It is also an answer to such an allegation that to make any such adjustment would cause "unjustifiable hardship" to the educator.[21]

These standards are of considerable significance in terms of the educational rights of students with disabilities. The standards apply across all levels and sectors of educational providers, from preschool to government and nongovernment providers of compulsory education and tertiary institutes, training organizations, and skill centers. Their objects are expressed as eliminating discrimination in education and training while ensuring equal opportunities for persons with disabilities in education and training in addition to promoting acceptance and recognition that the disabled have the same fundamental rights as others. In substance, the standards provide norms to apply in enrolment and participation as well as for reasonable adjustments to be made to ensure that persons with disabilities have the same education opportunity as those who are not disabled.

The scheme of the standards is as follows. Part Three of the Act requires providers to make reasonable adjustments to assist students with disabilities to be on the same bases as peers without the disabilities in enrolment and participation, which includes the use of facilities or services. What is a "reasonable adjustment" is defined in s 4 of the DDA as one that does not result in "unjustifiable hardship" on those on whom the requirement is imposed; namely, the education provider for the purposes of the Standards. All relevant circumstances, and the interests and views of students and their peers, are to be taken into account in deciding what is "reasonable" in terms of all the affected parties. The obligation to make "reasonable adjustments" has been significantly reinforced by the Disability Discrimination and Other Human Rights Legislation Amendment Act 2009 (Cth), which came into force on 5 August 2009 and significantly amends the DDA as discussed below.

Parts Four, Five, Six, and Seven of the Act set out the standards to be complied with by education providers in terms of enrolment, participation, curriculum development, accreditation, delivery of courses and programs, and student support services to ensure that individuals with disabilities are able to partake in educational opportunities to the fullest extent possible and as far as possible on the same basis as those without disabilities. Part Eight mandates that education providers must develop and implement strategies and measures designed to eliminate harassment and victimization of students with disabilities. The offense provisions contained in ss 37, 38 and 42 of the Disability Discrimination Act 1992 (Cth) are preserved.

Importantly, Part Ten of the Act stipulates that it is not unlawful for education providers to fail to comply with one or more of the standards above if they are able to demonstrate that compliance would result in their incurring "unjustifiable hardship." The "unjustifiable hardship" argument provided for here and contained in the DDA has provided little comfort for school authorities faced with discrimination allegations in relation to accommodation of children with special requirements due to physical disabilities. Still, the DDA has shielded school officials in other contexts, particularly in relation to their responses to children with behavioral difficulties who cause disruptions and threaten the safety of school communities.

DISABILITY DISCRIMINATION ACT 1992 (CTH) AND THE DISABILITY DISCRIMINATION AND OTHER HUMAN RIGHTS LEGISLATION AMENDMENT ACT 2009 (CTH) (DDA)

Disability discrimination legislation, essentially the Commonwealth DDA and equivalent state and territory legislation,[22] have as their aim:

(a) to eliminate, as far as possible, discrimination against persons on the ground of disability in the areas of:
  (i) work, accommodation, education, access to premises, clubs and sport; and
  (ii) the provision of goods, facilities, services and land; and
  (iii) existing laws; and
  (iv) the administration of Commonwealth laws and programs; and
(b) to ensure, as far as practicable, that persons with disabilities have the same rights to equality before the law as the rest of the community; and
(c) to promote recognition and acceptance within the community of the principle that persons with disabilities have the same fundamental rights as the rest of the community.[23]

Section 22 of the Act relates specifically to education, providing that it is unlawful for education providers to discriminate on the basis of individuals' disabilities in the areas of admission as students, access to benefits, expulsions, or subjecting students to other detriments. This section also makes it unlawful discrimination to have curricula or training courses which exclude students with disabilities or subject them to detriment in this context. Further, the Act divides unlawful discrimination on the basis of disability into direct and indirect discrimination.[24]

The direct discrimination prohibition in s 5 states that it is unlawful for discriminators to treat aggrieved persons less favorably in circumstances that are not materially different than they treat or would treat persons without disabilities. In addition, this makes it unlawful discrimination if discriminators fail to make reasonable adjustments where such failures have the effect that aggrieved persons are treated less favorably than individuals without disabilities in situations that are not materially different.

Section 6 provides that indirect discrimination occurs when discriminators require aggrieved persons to comply with requirements or conditions with which they would be or are unable to comply and that have the effect or likely effect of disadvantaging persons with disabilities. In addition, it is indirect discrimination if individuals fail to make reasonable adjustments which would be required to enable compliance for aggrieved persons who would otherwise likely have been disadvantaged. Importantly, the burden of proving the reasonableness of requirements or conditions lies on the discriminators.

There have been recent significant amendments to these provisions in terms of enhancing the protection afforded to disability rights. These were implemented by the Disability Discrimination and Other Human Rights Legislation Amendment Act 2009, which came into force on 9 August 2009. The changes are incorporated within the provisions above, but it is necessary to discuss them separately since the case law discussed below was resolved prior to their implementation and, in fact, the amendments are attempts to respond to the decisions.

Importantly, the amendments to both sections have the effect of creating an explicit duty on education providers to make "reasonable adjustments" that is in line with the tenor of the Commonwealth Standards. Under s 5, in addition to it being unlawful to treat persons less favorably (s 5[1]), it is unlawful to fail to make reasonable adjustments where this failure results in individuals with disabilities being treated less favorably than those who do not need the adjustments in similar circumstances (s 5[2]).

Similarly, under s 6 and in relation to indirect discrimination, it is not only unlawful to require individuals to comply with requirements or conditions with which they are not able to meet and which have the affect of disadvantaging them (s 6[1]). Moreover, it is unlawful in circumstances when persons are unable to comply with requirements or conditions without having reasonable adjustments made on their behalf if the actions of offending parties such as school officials cause individuals to be disadvantaged due to their disabilities (s 6[2]). As amended, this section means that in order to substantiate claims of indirect discrimination, persons must show they are unable to comply with the requirements or conditions and that this is to their disadvantage, as was the case before. However, complainants now no longer have to prove, as previously, that requirements were unreasonable, but the burden of proof of reasonableness is on those requiring compliance—in this case, a school.

An obvious argument in the school context is that children with disabilities who engage in disruptive behavior and fail to comply with behavioral rules could argue that they were unable to comply due to their disabilities. It would be then up to school officials to prove that the rules were reasonable in the circumstances; that is, for the safe and orderly management of educational environments and that they made reasonable adjustments in terms of behavioral plans for children with disabilities, but not to the detriment of this responsibility.

The "unjustifiable hardship" provisions contained in the Commonwealth Standards[25] and in the DDA[26] of the Act are of utmost importance to education providers. These provisions maintain that it is not unlawful for persons to discriminate against other persons if avoiding the discrimination would impose unjustifiable hardship on discriminators. A combination of these provisions requires for determinations to be made as to whether standards have been breached and such breaches amount to direct discrimination or whether the failure of education providers to make reasonable adjustments amounts to direct discrimination. This depends on two inquiries.

The first question considers whether officials made all reasonable accommodations. If not, the second inquiry considers whether making such adjustments would have resulted in an "unjustifiable hardship." The burden of proving that particular adjustments or accommodations would have resulted in "unjustifiable hardship" falls on education providers.[27] Section 11 of the Act sets out the circumstances which may be taken into account in making such determinations; these include the nature of the benefits or detriments which could be accrued by persons who are concerned. Importantly, financial circumstances, particularly the cost to the educator for compliance and the availability of funding to the person with the disability may be taken into account in making determinations as to unjustifiable hardship (ss 11[1][c] & [d]).

AUSTRALIAN CASES HIGHLIGHTING ISSUES RELATING TO THE EDUCATION OF CHILDREN WITH DISABILITIES

The allegations of discrimination made in respect of primary and secondary education in Australia fall loosely within three areas: in relation to enrolment of children with disabilities; failure to provide learning support for students with disabilities in order to ensure, as far as possible, their equality of educational opportunity; and actions taken by school officials in relation to discipline of children with disabilities.

It is important to note that these cases were decided prior to the 2009 amendments to the DDA; the clarification at the end of the s 4 definition of disability, the inclusion of a positive duty in ss 5 and 6 to make reasonable adjustments; and the reversal of the burden of proof in relation to proof of reasonableness of the requirement or condition in s 6.

THE FAILURE OF SCHOOL OFFICIALS TO PERMIT THE ENROLMENT OF STUDENTS WITH DISABILITIES

An early allegation of discrimination under s 22 was *Finney v. Hills Grammar School.*[28] Scarlett Finney was a six-year-old girl with spina bifida. When her parents, the applicants in the matter, applied to enroll her in Hills Grammar School, the application was denied. School officials argued that they lacked adequate resources to meet the child's special needs such as accessibility. The complaint of discrimination was upheld both by Commissioner Innes of the then Human Rights and Equal Opportunity Commission[29] and later by Tamberlin J of the Federal Court on the school's application for judicial review of the Commissioner's decision.

The critical issue in the case related to the school's argument of "unjustifiable hardship." Commissioner Innes undertook a broad consideration of all of the circumstances and a balancing of the benefits and detriments of the student's attendance at the school. He ruled that the benefits were substantial and included those that accrued not only for the child and her family but also importantly for the school and the whole school community. Weighed against this were the obvious detriments such as additional costs and work for the teachers, which he found the school to have "overstated" and which in any event did not amount to "unjustifiable hardship." The Commissioner declared that:

> the concept of "unjustifiable hardship" connotes much more than just hardship on the respondent. The objects of the Act make it clear that elimination of discrimination as far as possible is the legislation's purpose. Considered in this context, it is reasonable to expect that the school should have to undergo some hardship in accepting Scarlett's enrolment. It is clear from the evidence that this would have occurred, as Scarlett required services and facilities not required by other students. The nub of the issue is whether such hardship was unjustifiable.[30]

Tamberlin J of the Federal Court agreed, stating that a finding of "unjustifiable hardship" requires a balancing exercise of the benefits and the detriments, taking all the relevant circumstances into account.

Stephanie Travers by her next friend Wendy Travers v. New South Wales[31] was similarly concerned a child with spina bifida who had been refused enrolment by school officials because of their concerns relating to the accessibility of toilet facilities. The magistrate entered an order in favor of the child, declaring that school officials relied on a misapprehension of the pupil's needs and appropriate accommodation could have been made relatively easily.

FAILURE TO PROVIDE LEARNING SUPPORT FOR CHILDREN WITH DISABILITIES

The following cases are not so much concerned with perceptions of educational officials of the difficulties associated with the physical attendance of children with disabilities at schools as with their failure to make accommodations necessary for students to have equal learning opportunities. Notably, the allegations were of indirect discrimination on the basis that by not providing children with appropriate language support, officials required them to comply with the requirements of the learning environment which they were clearly unable to do.

The Catholic Education Office v. Clarke[32] was a 2004 appeal of the education provider to the Full Federal Court against an order of the Federal Court which upheld a complaint of indirect discrimination pursuant to s 6 DDA. The Court's finding was on the basis that, by not providing Auslan (the Australian language for the deaf) support to a deaf child who was Auslan dependent, officials imposed a "requirement or condition" on him which was not reasonable and with which he was unable to comply in the circumstances.

The facts leading up to the case were that the parents of Jacob Clarke wished to enroll him at MacKillop Catholic College and had discussions with officials about the learning support that would have been provided. The college produced a learning support model for the student but advised him and his parents that there was little prospect of the inclusion of the support in Auslan, despite the parents' offer to make a grant to the school to provide partial funding for Auslan support for their son and other students.

The Full Federal Court (Tamberlin, Sackville J and Stone JJ) upheld the judgment of the lower court. The judges were careful to set aside considerations which could, in their view, be made in an allegation of direct discrimination under s 5 relating to a failure to provide accommodation which may rest on a plea of unjustifiable hardship. The judges saw the principles relating to indirect discrimination under s 6 as requiring that the onus be on the aggrieved person to prove that the "condition or requirement" imposed by the education authority was not reasonable in the circumstances; the test of reasonableness is an objective one which required the balancing of the discriminatory effect against the reasons for the imposition of the condition or requirement and a weighing of all relevant factors. Now, pursuant to the s 6(4) amendments to the DDA, the burden of proof would be reversed, and it would be up to school officials to prove reasonableness of the requirements or conditions. However, the decision would in all probability have been the same.

In later litigation in 2006, in *Hurst v. Queensland*,[33] the allegation of indirect discrimination similarly rested on the failure of school officials to provide Auslan support. The court again ruled in favor of the child on the ground that the student suffered a serious disadvantage. The Full Federal Court of Appeal was of the opinion that in a consideration of whether there was indirect discrimination, the proper question was whether the child would have suffered "serious disadvantage in complying with a requirement or condition, irrespective of whether that person 'can cope' with the requirement or condition."[34] Also, in 2006 the Victorian Civil and Administrative Tribunal (VCAT), in *Beasley v. Victoria Department of Education and Training (Anti-Discrimination)*,[35] decided that the failure to provide Auslan for the student, Dylan Beasley, during times of class discussion amounted to indirect discrimination insofar as his opportunity to participate in valuable interactive class discussion was severely limited.

Most recently in this context, also in the State of Victoria, was the 2009 judgment of the Supreme Court of Victoria on an appeal from VCAT in an action taken under the provisions of the Equal Opportunity Act 1995 (Vic), which are equivalent to the DDA provisions. *State of Victoria v. Turner*[36] concerned Becky Turner, a thirteen-year-old with a brain dysfunction that resulted in a learning disorder manifesting itself in varying symptoms of varying severity. The basis of the complaint of indirect discrimination was that the pupil was unable to comply with the requirement that she access education without the school's provision of a dedicated teacher's aide. The Tribunal had agreed and made various directions around the provision of a teacher's aide for the child, including an award of compensation for her educational loss and her depression.

The appeal of the state on questions of law was heard by Kyrou J. Importantly, he explained that the Tribunal had not erred in its finding of indirect discrimination insofar as it was open to doing so. The judge concluded that the "no full-time teacher's aide" condition was not reasonable in respect of some of the subjects the pupil had undertaken at the schools she attended. Even so, the judge ruled that the Tribunal acted outside of its jurisdiction in making the various orders and so adjourned the proceedings for the parties to make submissions.

The most recent case involving an allegation of indirect discrimination is that of *Phu v. State of NSW (NSW Department of Education and Training)(No 3)*.[37] The complaint was made under the New South Wales state provisions equivalent to ss 6 and 22 DDA, ss 49B(1)(b) and 49L(2)(a) Anti-Discrimination Act 1977 (NSW). Accordingly, the complaint was considered by the Administrative Disputes Tribunal of New South Wales. The Tribunal declined jurisdiction to consider any matters relating to the Disability Standards for Education 2005 as they are formulated under the DDA, and thus any determination was outside the Tribunal's power.

At issue was the status of a child who suffered autism, severe global developmental delay, and other disabilities while attending a special school. The child engaged in serious self-harming behavior leading her father to contend that the school's failure to provide one-on-one support for her during the school day resulted in a detriment to her. The father also claimed that requiring his daughter to complete her education without such support amounted to a condition with which she was unable to comply, therefore amounting to indirect discrimination. The Tribunal restated the requirements to satisfy a claim of indirect discrimination as the imposition of a requirement or condition with which an applicant did not or could not comply, with which a "substantially higher proportion" of persons without the applicant's disability are able to comply, and which is not reasonable in the circumstances.

The Tribunal engaged in a lengthy consideration of all of the measures that school officials introduced, the investigations they undertook towards identifying triggers for incidents of self-harm. The Tribunal also considered the moves educators made towards reducing the triggers by providing behavior management strategies along with the evidence of expert witnesses concerning the value of all of these measures weighed against the provision of one-on-one support. Further, the Tribunal noted the restatement by the Victorian Supreme Court *State of Victoria v. Turner*[38] that the onus is on applicants to prove objectively the unreasonableness of requirements or conditions. Taking all of the factors into account, particularly the steps taken by school officials to take and act on advice relating to supporting the child and mitigating her self-injurious behavior, the Tribunal ruled that the educators did not act unreasonably in denying the child one-on-one care.

DISCIPLINING STUDENTS WHOSE DISABILITIES MANIFEST THEMSELVES IN DISRUPTIVE BEHAVIOR

It is this area that clearly demonstrates the tension between the responsibilities of school officials to ensure safe environments for all members of school communities and their duties in respect of the education of particular children.[39] It is here also that the essential issue becomes whether, if children are excluded from school as a result of behavior that is a manifestation of their disabilities, it can be said that they were discriminated against on the grounds of their disabilities. The following cases demonstrate the considerable difficulty faced by tribunals or courts that are confronted with complaints relating to children who are excluded from schools because of their disturbed behavior when the (mis)behavior can be directly linked to their disabilities.

Section 4 of the DDA contains a broad definition of *disability*, which includes total or partial loss of a person's bodily or mental functions or a part of the body and the presence in the body of organisms causing or capable of causing disease or illness, malfunction, malformation and disfigurement. Importantly for the present purposes is the inclusion of a disorder or malfunction resulting in learning differently from individuals without the disorders or malfunctions and illnesses or diseases that affects their thought processes, perceptions of reality, emotions, or judgment or that results in disturbed behavior.[40] Since the cases below were litigated, a clarification has been inserted at the end of the definition of disability which defines it as including behavior which is a symptom or manifestation of a disability.[41]

L v. Minister of Education Queensland,[42] which was heard by the Anti-Discrimination Tribunal of Queensland, arose as a complaint by the mother of a child with an intellectual impairment who was suspended from a mainstream government school. The girl had been assessed as needing a high level of support due to her behavioral difficulties arising from her disability. School officials put forward two arguments: first, that the girl was suspended as a result of her behavior, a fate which would have befallen any child in the school who behaved in the same manner.

The Tribunal found that the girl's behavior was characteristic of a child with her disability and could not be separated from it. Therefore, the Tribunal maintained that excluding the girl for her behavior affectively amounted to discrimination on the basis of her disability. However, the Tribunal agreed with school officials on their second argument, namely "unjustifiable hardship." The Tribunal decided that while financial considerations alone would not suffice, the circumstances surrounding the girl's behavioral problems were such that there was considerable disruption for the other children and heavy demands on the teachers concerned.[43]

The decision of the High Court of Australia in *Purvis v. New South Wales (Department of Education and Training)*[44] led to significant commentary and the addition of the clarification of the s 4 DDA definition noted above. The case concerned Daniel Hoggan, a ward of state who was in the foster care of the complainants, Mr. and Mrs. Purvis. Insofar as the child was brain damaged at birth, his disability resulted in behavioral problems. The child's application for enrolment was declined by the high school, but he was eventually enrolled following a successful complaint to the then Human Rights and Equal Opportunity Commission (HREOC). Following discussions with all concerned parties, behavioral plans were put in place for the student. When the plans proved unsuccessful, the student's behavior posed a serious safety risk to teachers, teachers' aides, and other children in the school. Following several suspensions from school, the principal chose to exclude the student in light of his concerns for the health and safety of the staff and students at the school. The foster parents complained to HREOC, which found that there was direct discrimination in terms of s 22(2) and s 5 of the DDA. After the school authority's appeal to the Federal Court was successful, the parents sought review from the High Court of Australia.

The High Court was divided, with the majority rejecting the appeal. In its view, there were two questions. First, the High Court wondered how, under the circumstances, school officials would have treated a person without the student's disability. Second, the High Court questioned whether the treatment of the student was less favorable than that afforded persons without disabilities and whether it could have been said that this treatment was due to his disability. The High Court ruled that the student was not treated less favorably by officials on account of his disability. In explaining the Court's separation of the behavior caused by the disability from the disability itself, Gleeson CJ wrote:

> The fallacy in the appellant's argument lies in the contention that, because the pupil's violent behavior was disturbed, and resulted from a disorder, s 5 always requires, and only permits, a comparison between his treatment and the treatment that would be given to a pupil who is not violent. Rather it requires a comparison with the treatment that would be given, in the same circumstances, to a pupil whose behavior was not disturbed behavior resulting from a disorder. Such a comparison requires no feat of imagination. There are pupils who have no disorder, and are not disturbed, who behave in a violent manner towards others. They would probably be suspended, and, if the conduct persisted, expelled in less time than the pupil in this case.[45]

The difficulty of the complainant in this case rested largely on the "comparator" analysis as expressed. However, the recent clarification to the s 4(1) DDA definition arguably renders this decision extinct on this point. It is also important to note that under the previous legislation, school officials were unable to use the "unjustifiable hardship" argument once children are enrolled. Since this has now been changed, this argument may be used in relation to exclusion of a child from school.

Minns v. State of NSW[46] concerned Ryan Minn, a child with severe behavioral difficulties who was at the center of claims that he was directly and indirectly discriminated against by officials at the two state schools he attended. This case similarly related to discipline in the form of suspension and expulsion of the child from school, moves which school officials considered necessary to ensure the safe educational and working environments of all other members of the school community.

The judgment of the Federal Magistrates' Court of Appeal was made after the decisions of the Federal Court and Federal Court of Appeal in *Purvis.* Raphael FM (Federal Magistrate) considered that these courts had adopted the proper construction of "comparator," also approved of later by the majority of the High Court judges as stated in Gleeson J's judgment above. Raphael FM viewed the substance of the allegation of direct discrimination under s 5 DDA in the same manner and decided that it was not proven. The applicant alleged indirect discrimination under s 6 on the basis that the imposition of school behavior rules and discipline policies amounted to the imposition of conditions with which, because of his disability, he was unable to comply, and that this was unreasonable. Raphael FM declared that he had "no difficulty in finding the policies were reasonable"[47] and were designed to enable all students to achieve their potential with a minimum of disruption. He added that school officials had, in fact, modified the policies as far as possible to take account of the applicant's disabilities. Importantly, Raphael FM pointed out that:

> The students could not achieve their potential if most of the teachers' time was taken up with handling Ryan. The playgrounds would not be safe if Ryan was allowed free rein for his aggressive actions. Therefore the claim for indirect discrimination must fail in the manner in which it is put.[48]

In *Zygorodimos v. Department of Education and Training*[49] the Victorian Administrative Appeals Tribunal applied the decision in *Purvis* to an allegation of discrimination made as a result of a child's being moved from one class to another. The child, who was an epileptic and profoundly deaf, was attending a special school for children with hearing impairments. The child demonstrated severely disruptive behavior and was moved from one class in which the teacher was unable to cope to another class. The Tribunal believed the proper comparator was a boy without epilepsy who behaved in the same manner and on this basis, discrimination was not proven.

The 2009 amendments to the Disability Discrimination Act 1992 (Cth)[50] would have significant impact on the reasoning of the tribunals in these cases, were they pursued under that legislation. First, in an allegation of indirect discrimination made under s 6, it is no longer necessary for applicants to prove that a substantially higher proportion of persons without disabilities comply or can comply with imposed requirements or conditions. It is sufficient for findings of indirect discrimination for persons with disabilities to satisfy tribunals that they are unable to comply and that they are disadvantaged by the requirements or conditions.[51] Second, the burden of proof has reversed with the onus now on respondents—in this context, school officials—to prove the reasonableness of the requirements or conditions they are imposing. These changes, in terms of the federal law, at least, significantly enhance the chance of disabled students to succeed in substantiating allegations of indirect discrimination.

THE VIEWS OF THE CHILD

Australian state and federal education and antidiscrimination statutes, by their statements of principles and provisions, are aimed at ensuring that children with disabilities have the same educational opportunities as their peers who are not disabled. Article 12 of the United Nations Convention on the Rights of the Child (UNCROC) requires that children have the right to express their views in all matters affecting them and that their views must be given due weight in accordance with their age and maturity. In addition, Article 13 of UNCROC provides for children to have the right of freedom of expression and to get and to share information.

Even though parents make complaints of discrimination on the part of their children in most cases, since students have allegedly been the victims of discriminatory conduct, it is their rights to equality in education that have been implicated. Many times it may be seen that behind the reports of courts and tribunals on allegations of discrimination against school authorities lies a long history of conflict between them and the parents of specific children. Often this raises the question of the place of the views of children in the analysis.

In all of the reports of the events leading up to the protracted battle between school officials and the foster parents of Daniel Hoggan in *Purvis*, there is little discussion of what he would have wished for his education. It is clear from the student's running away and engaging in violence towards teachers and other students that he found his attendance at high school intensely stressful. It may be in many such cases that the ability of children to contribute to decisions may be limited, but this should not denigrate the fact that unless there are compelling reasons against it, the contribution of the child should rightly be sought and their wishes taken into account in decisions relating to their education.

Along this same line of thought, in the case of Scarlett Finney the Commissioner took evidence from the six-year-old child who expressed the view that she wanted to be able to participate in school life as any other child. Commissioner Innes wrote:

> The opinion of the person with the disability should not be accepted without question as this would place the respondents in very invidious positions. But the person's views should be given weight, alongside the views of experts in the field who have had the chance to assess the individual in question and form an opinion. The greatest barriers which people with a disability face in our community are the negative assumptions made about them by other members of the community.[52]

In *Murphy v. New South Wales*,[53] the facts leading up to the hearing by the Human Rights Commissioner of the complaint of direct discrimination reveal a long history of continued acrimony between school officials and the parents. This relationship resulted in the principal's calling the police and having the mother removed from school while also closing the gate and denying the student access to school. In such situations, vital considerations such as the best interests of the child and their views are seemingly lost as children find themselves in the middle of adults who hold firm views.

The right of children with disabilities to be consulted is now provided for in the Commonwealth Disability Standards for Education 2005. The duty of education providers to gain the views of children is required in the making of reasonable adjustments to accommodate students in the context of admissions or enrolments, participation, or the use of facilities or services (s 3.5) as well as the application of standards for enrolment (s 4.2[3]). In addition, school officials must consult with children on whether their disabilities affect them in their ability to participate in their courses or programs and in their use of school facilities or services (s 5.2[2]). However, the above duties are arguably significantly limited in practice by the alternative duty on the school to consult with "an associate of the student."

CONSTITUTIONAL RIGHTS

Australia has no constitutional bill of rights in which the right to equal treatment and opportunity and freedom from discrimination is enshrined. Still, one state and one territory, Victoria and the Australian Capital Territory, recently passed human rights legislation, including the right of recognition and equality before the law.[54] These Acts apply to the actions of public authorities which carry out functions of a public nature, necessarily including public schools.[55] Nongovernment schools are expressly excluded from Victorian legislation but are expressly included in the Australian Capital Territory.[56]

In *State of Victoria v. Turner*[57] an alternative argument based on provisions of the Charter of Human Rights and Responsibilities Act 2006 (Vic) was put before the Supreme Court of Victoria. The submission on behalf of Becky Turner[58] was based on s 8, which provides for recognition and equality of all persons before the law, and s 32, which provides for the interpretation of all statutory provisions in a manner which is compatible with human rights. The allegation of indirect discrimination on the part of the provider of the student's education was made under s 9 of the Equal Opportunity Act 1995 (Vic), which is the equivalent provision to s 6 of the DDA (Cth), and the order was made by the Tribunal under s 136.

Korou J was unable to apply the Charter in the case at bar because of timing. The issue had been raised before the judge in an appeal on a question of law from the earlier case of the Victorian Civil and Administrative Tribunal, and proceedings to that Tribunal had been commenced before the Charter's inception. In other words, had the judge applied the Charter in this case, it would have had the effect of giving the Charter unintended retrospective operation. Still, the fact that the Charter was argued clearly points to its application to future actions.

CONCLUSION

Provision for equal educational opportunity for children with disabilities is made in Australia federally by the Commonwealth Disability Standards for Education 2005. A breach of any of these standards amounts to disability discrimination under the Federal Disability Discrimination Act 1992 (Cth). Complaints of either direct or indirect discrimination under this Act must be made to the Australian Human Rights Commission for conciliation. If complaints are not resolved, applications may be made to the Federal Magistrates Court or Federal Court of Australia. Alternatively, aggrieved persons may opt to pursue their allegations under state antidiscrimination legislation to a state body or Tribunal designated for that purpose.

There are three situations which have most commonly given rise to allegations of direct or indirect discrimination on the part of education providers. The first, direct discrimination, occurs where it is alleged that there has been a failure on the part of school officials to make accommodations for physical or other disabilities which resulted in detriments to the students concerned. This failure may also give rise to allegations of indirect discrimination where it has rendered children unable to comply with conditions or requirements of education providers. Second, issues have arisen in relation to school discipline, particularly in the form of exclusion, of children whose disability manifests itself in disruptive and antisocial behavior.

In the first of these situations, school officials are required to balance the resourcing of such accommodations with the needs of entire school communities. In the second scenario another layer is added to the factors which educators must take into account; namely, the responsibility for the safety of all members of the school community. Important in this case is the addition to the definition of disability under s 4(1) of the Act, which clarifies that "disability" includes behavior that is a "symptom or manifestation" of the disability. Now, also under s 21 (B) of the DDA, school officials can raise the "unjustifiable hardship" defense in all contexts and use the wide range of circumstances set out in s 11. This includes financial considerations.

As demonstrated by the cases above, rarely are there easy answers. Evidence in Australia, as is the case worldwide, suggests that in addition to the forms of physical and intellectual disabilities long recognized and for which most schools now would have well-established mechanisms for accommodating, there are emerging a wide range of emotional and other disabilities. These new disabilities manifest themselves in all manner of behavioral problems and present a whole new range of challenges for school officials. In ensuring access to equal educational opportunities for all their students along with the safety and well-being of all members of school communities, educational authorities in Australia, as elsewhere, have a delicate balancing act to perform.

BIBLIOGRAPHY

Conroy, M. & Jackson, J. (2005) "Disability and School Education Law: Law and Policy in the UK and Australia" in Harris, N. & Meredith, P. (eds.), *Children, Education and Health*, Ashgate Press, UK.

Dempsey, I. (2003) "The Impact of the Disability Discrimination Act 1992 (Cth) on School Students with a Disability in Australia," *Australia and New Zealand Journal of Law and Education*, 8(1), 17.

Dickson, E. (2006) "Disability Standards for Education and the Obligation of Reasonable Adjustment," *Australia and New Zealand Journal of Law and Education*, 11(2), 23.

Dickson, E. (2008) "The Inclusion and Exclusion of Students with Disability Related Problem Behaviour: The Contrasting Approaches of Australia and the United States of America," *Australia and New Zealand Journal of Law and Education*, 13(2), 49.

Jackson, J. & Varnham, S. (2007) *Law for Educators: School and University Law in Australia*, LexisNexis, Sydney.

Keefe-Martin, M. & Lindsay, K. (2002) "Issues in Australian Disability Discrimination Case Law and Strategic Approaches for the Lawful Management of Inclusion," *Australia and New Zealand Journal of Law and Education*, 7(2), 161.

NOTES

1. s 51 Australian Constitution.

2. The legislation of the other states and territories are the Anti-Discrimination Act 1991 (Qld), the Equal Opportunity Act 1984 (WA), the Equal Opportunity Act

1984 (SA), the Discrimination Act 1991 (ACT) and the Anti-Discrimination Act 1992 (NT).

3. For a comprehensive discussion of the management of the early days of inclusion, see Keefe-Martin, M. & Lindsay, K. (2002) "Issues in Australian Disability Discrimination Case Law and Strategic Approaches for the Lawful Management of Inclusion." *Australia and New Zealand Journal of Law and Education* 7(2), 161–177.

4. The federal body which is responsible for overseeing the implementation and operation of the Disability Discrimination Act 1992 (Cth) and for considering, conciliating and making decisions on complaints of discrimination. From August 2009 this body is known as the Australian Human Rights Commission pursuant to the Disability Discrimination and Other Human Rights Legislation Amendment Act 2009 (Cth). The Commission has major responsibilities under the international Convention on the Rights of Persons with Disabilities ratified by Australia in July 2008.

5. Particularly *Finney v. Hills Grammar School* [1999] HREOCA, *Stephanie Travers by her next friend, Wendy Travers v. New South Wales* [2001] FMCA, discussed below.

6. 6 s 4 Education Act 1990 (NSW), s 1.2.1 Education and Training Reform Act 2006 (Vic), s 18 Education Act 2004 (Act), s 3 School Education Act 1999 (WA), s 5 Education (General Provisions) Act 2006 (Qld).

7. s 20(2) & (3) Education Act 1990 (NSW).

8. For example, s 2.2.6 Education and Training Reform Act 2006 (Vic).

9. s 2.2.20 Education and Training Reform Act 2006 (Vic).

10. For example, s 5 Education Act 1972 (SA) and s 3 Education Act 1994 (Tas).

11. School Education Act 1999 (WA).

12. For example, in addition to children with disabilities and significant learning difficulties, children from non-English-speaking backgrounds, Aboriginal children and children who are disadvantaged because of their social-economic background are included.

13. s 20(1)(c),(d) & (f).

14. Education Act 1979 (NT) s 34 with the help of an advisory committee, s 35(1): Minister may make such provision as he or she considers necessary or desirable, s 35(2): arrangements for education of children and for payment of expenses; Education Act 1972 (SA) s 75A(1): direction that a child be enrolled in special school where it is in the best interests of the child, s 75A(2): a child not to be enrolled other than at nominated school, s 75A(3)(b): the direction may be varied or revoked after consultation with parents; Education Act 1994 (Tas) s 21(a): the Secretary may determine whether or not a child or a person is entitled to be enrolled in a special school, s 21(b): the Secretary may determine the circumstances or manner in which the child or person may be enrolled and s 21(c): the Secretary may determine any other matter relating to the enrolment.

15. For example, ss 36(1)(b) & 36(1)(d) of the Education Act 1979 (NT) and by regulation 59 of the South Australian Education Regulations 1997.

16. For example, ss 36(1)(a), 36(1)(c), 36(2) Education Act 1979 (NT) and s 75A(3)(a) of the Education Act 1972 (SA).

17. s 38(1) Education Act 1979 (NT); s 75C Education Act 1972 (SA).

18. s 2.2.6 Education and Training Reform Act 2006 (Vic).

19. s 32 Disability Discrimination Act 1992 (Cth).
20. s 34.
21. Part Ten Commonwealth Disability Standards for Education 2005.
22. Anti-Discrimination Act 1977 (NSW), Equal Opportunity Act 1995 (Vic), Anti-Discrimination Act 1991 (Qld), Equal Opportunity Act 1984 (WA), Equal Opportunity Act 1984 (SA), Discrimination Act 1991 (ACT), and the Anti-Discrimination Act 1992 (NT).
23. As set out in s 3 Disability Discrimination Act 1992 (Cth).
24. The following sections were substituted by the Disability Discrimination and Other Human Rights Legislation Amendment Act 2009.
25. Part Ten.
26. s 29A.
27. DDA.
28. *Finney v. Hills Grammar School* [1999] HREOCA 14 (20 July 1999).
29. Now known as the Australian Human Rights Commission, pursuant to the Disability Discrimination and Other Human Rights Legislation Amendment Act 2009 (Cth).
30. *Finney v. Hills Grammar School* [1999] HREOCA 14 (20 July 1999).
31. [2001] FMCA 18.
32. [2004] FCAFC 197.
33. [2006] FCAFC.
34. At para. 134.
35. [2006] VCAT 1050.
36. [2009] VSC 66.
37. [2009] NSWADT 282 (12 November 2009).
38. [2009] VSC 66 (4 March 2009).
39. It is important to note that a school in NSW may be prosecuted under relevant occupational health and safety legislation for failing to ensure safety. In order to escape criminal liability for physical or mental harm suffered by a member or members of the school community, a school must be able to demonstrate that it took every practical remedial step and what eventuated was beyond its control. There have been two successful prosecutions under s 8(1) Occupational Health & Safety Act 2000 (NSW) in recent years when the harm was caused by disruptive students with behavioral difficulties—*Barrie Johnson v. New South Wales (Department of Education and Training)*[2006] NSWIRC 109 and *The Crown in the Right of New South Wales (Department of Education and Training) v. Maurice Michael O'Sullivan* [2005] NSW IRC 198.
40. However, in a complaint which preceded this legislation, epilepsy was held not to be covered in the New South Wales legislation: *Kitt v. Tourist Commission* EOC #92-196.
41. Inserted by the Disability Discrimination and Other Human Rights Legislation Amendment Act 2009.
42. (1996) EOC #92-787.
43. (1996) EOC #92-787 at 78,821.
44. [2003] HCA 62.
45. [2003] HCA 62 at para. 11.
46. [2002] FMCA 60 (28 June 2002).

47. [2002] FMCA 260 at para. 257.

48. Above at para. 263.

49. [2004] VCAT 128.

50. Disability Discrimination and Other Human Rights Legislation Amendment Act 2009 (Cth).

51. s 6(1).

52. *Finney v. Hills Grammar School* [1999] HREOCA 14.

53. HREOC decision no. H98/73 (27 March 2000).

54. s 8, Human Rights Act 2004 (Vic) and s 8, Charter of Human Rights and Responsibilities 2006 (ACT).

55. s 4 Human Rights Act 2004 (Vic).

56. ss 40 and 40A Charter of Human Rights and Responsibilities 2006 (ACT).

57. [2009] VSC 66 (4 March 2009).

58. This decision related to an appeal on questions of law from the decision of VCAT that the student had been indirectly discriminated against by the failure of school officials to provide a full-time teacher's aide, thus requiring her to access her education without this necessary assistance. The case is discussed above.

2

Brazil

Nina Ranieri

Special education in Brazil is a constitutional right as well as a combined obligation of the State and families founded in the 1988 Federal Constitution. In legal terms, the National Education Act (NEA) (Law 9.394/1996) defines this right as "a modality of school education," preferably offered in the regular school system to all disabled students. Insofar as being legally considered a "modality of school education," officials have the duty to identify, evaluate, and place students while defining what constitutes an appropriate education. Of course, making this determination requires an extensive interpretation of special education in light of the United Nations Convention on the Rights of Persons with Disabilities (CRPD) (Decree 6.949/2009) and ordinary Brazilian laws.

All of the norms that apply in Brazil, interpreted consistently with the principle of nondiscrimination present in Article 5 of the Federal Constitution in conjunction with the guarantee of equal conditions of access and permanence in school to all that identified in Article 206 I of the Federal Constitution, broadened the original legal scope of special education to what is now considered "inclusive education." The understanding of "inclusive education" as a key term in the application of Brazilian law means full inclusion in regular classes for children with special educational needs, regardless of whether they are disabled, have serious learning difficulties, or are highly gifted.

Under the Brazilian constitution, access to compulsory free education from ages six to seventeen is a right that must be exercised (Article 208, I). In other words, the right to education is more an obligation of parents or guardians on behalf of their children, implying the responsibility of the government not only in providing free education but also guaranteeing quality and supportive services. According to the Brazilian Elementary School Education Census of 2008, in a universe of 53 million children in almost 200,000 educational establishments, only 385,000 students with disabilities are enrolled in regular schools. Unfortunately, data are lacking about those who are not included in either special or regular schools.

This chapter examines the law of special education in Brazil in relation to students with disabilities, namely those with "long-term physical, mental, intellectual or sensory impairments which in interaction with various barriers may hinder their full and effective participation in society on an equal basis with others" (CRPD, Article 1). The chapter offers neither a complete analysis of the legislation nor an exhaustive research of jurisprudence in Brazil, but it describes key fundamental principles governing special education and the schooling rights of students with disabilities, keeping in mind that constitutional law and practice continue to change and evolve. The remainder of this chapter examines constitutional and legal sources of the law of special education in Brazil; the rights of students with disabilities (including matters dealing with identification, assessment, and placement; due process rights; and funding of special education); emerging issues; and a conclusion.

CONSTITUTIONAL AND LEGAL SOURCES OF SPECIAL EDUCATION LAW

In addition to the Federal Constitution of Brazil (CF) (1998), there are five main legal sources for special education, all but the last of which are discussed in the rest of this section. In chronological order, these sources are the Disabled Persons Protection Act (DPPA) (Law 7.853/1989); the Child and Adolescent Statute (ECA) (Law 8.069/1990); the National Education Act (NEA) (1996); the Interamerican Convention for the Elimination of all Forms of Discrimination against Disabled Persons—the Guatemala Convention of 2001 (Decree 3.956/2001), ratified as ordinary law; and the UN Convention on the Rights of Disabled Persons (CRDP) (Decree 6.949/2009), approved by the National Congress under a constitutional amendment designed to assure all human rights treaties a hierarchically superior position in the Brazilian legal system (Forty-fifth Amendment of 2004), meaning that the Convention overrules all applicable ordinary laws.

This chapter does not comment on the CRDP not only because it consolidates the fundamental principles already expressed by international law in conjunction with Brazilian constitutional and ordinary law but also since it is discussed in the overview chapter. There are other legal sources in Brazil deriving from international law and ratified by the National government such as the UN Declaration on the Rights of the Child (1989) and the UNESCO Convention against Discrimination in Education (1960).

State constitutions in Brazil do not deal with special education; neither do laws organizing municipalities (Lei Orgânica do Município, CF Article 29) address special education except for those establishing the obligations of public educational systems, a matter addressed in State statutes. The National Board of Education (CNE), a federal entity that is subordinate to the Ministry of Education, is primarily responsible for the regulation of the NEA. For example, the NEA enacted Resolutions CNE 2/2001 and 1/2002, establishing National Guidelines for Special Education and Teacher Training requirements in Special Education. More recently, Resolution CNE 4/2009 was enacted to establish more concrete details for basic special education.

The DPPA, the ECA, and the NEA are regulated to a large extent by decrees, resolutions, and administrative rules. Decrees and resolutions permit flexibility in updating ordinary laws, adapting them to the alterations required by internally ratified international conventions. Added to this are other ordinary laws enacted to guarantee rights for individuals with disabilities: Law 10.048/2000 demands governmental and private priority in ensuring services and activities such as transportation, education, law enforcement, and calls for judicial involvement; Law 10.098/2000, which established the norms for physical access to public places, including schools; Law 10.436/2002, which introduced the Brazilian language, LIBRAS, as an official means of communication and a compulsory subject in teacher training courses, among others, which increases the complexity of guaranteeing special education to all. This myriad of provisions, while contributing to the development of special education, creates a legal jungle requiring legal experts to enforce the law. Paradoxically, the more legislation that is enacted, the more complex it is to understand and implement rights to special education that is to be enforced by the Public Ministry.

As a preliminary matter, it is important to keep in mind that in Brazil, constitutional provisions as well as federal and state regulations are generally self-executing. This means that government agencies, including educational systems, are immediately bound by the juridical amalgam that guarantees special education. If statutes or regulations are unclear, Brazilian courts have the authority to intervene based on the initiative of the injured parties or the Public Ministry.

THE FEDERAL CONSTITUTION

The guidelines in the Federal Constitution of Brazil protect and promote special education based on the right to equality before the law (Article 5) and the right to be different, which implies the right not to be discriminated against (Article 208, III). This is a reflection of the principle of the dignity of the human person as enshrined in Article 1. This cornerstone is further reinforced in Article 206, I, under the fundamental right to equality of access and permanence in school and guaranteed in Article 205, which characterizes education as "a right for all and the duty of the State and family, promoted and fostered with the cooperation of society, with a view to the full development of the person, his preparation for the exercise of citizenship and his qualification for work." These provisions are interpreted in connection with Article 227, which demands priority in assuring the rights of children and adolescents.

Article 208 of the Federal Constitution also entitles all children, regardless of whether they are disabled, in elementary schools from ages six to fourteen, and at no cost to their parents, to be assisted by means of complementary programs providing school materials, food, and health care. Under this article, government authorities and school officials cannot refuse to provide these services under the penalty of the law.

Explicit guarantees of the education rights of the students with disabilities are described in the NEA (Article 23, XXIV). Further, the principles by which the State ought to be guided in this field are part of the Decennial National Education Plan (Article 214). The actual plan is not being analyzed here because of its vague and imprecise provisions (Law 10.172/2001) that are subject to forthcoming modifications.

THE DISABLED PERSONS PROTECTION ACT (DPPA) (LAW 7.853/1989)

The objectives of the Disabled Persons Protection Act are to prevent and eliminate all forms of discrimination against persons with disabilities while promoting their full integration into society. In order to ensure that these aims are met, the law addresses such practical measures as institutional and personal responsibilities, criminalizing acts that could harm or jeopardize the disabled, and establishing the possibility of using class action lawsuits and public interest actions in order to guarantee equity.

The DPPA is further implemented by Federal Decree 3.298/1999, which affords State and municipal governments the opportunity to enforce the DPPA by carrying it out to its full effect. Under this law, special education is qualified as a right in education (Article 2), formally protected by the Public Ministry, which has the duty to assure the full implementation of the law. In other words, the enforcement of this right is not a decision of the parents, guardians, or students: the prosecutors of the Public Ministry are obliged to take all the legal measures to implement the law.

At this point it is worth noting that the Public Ministry is an independent governmental institution, both on the federal and state levels, whose function is to protect of the rule of law, the national democracy, public interests, and fundamental rights (CF, Article 127). The members of the Public Ministry, public prosecutors, represent society against the union, States, and municipalities demanding the implementation of statutes laws and nationally ratified international treaties (CF, Articles 127 e 129, III), acting on behalf of citizens whose rights have been or could be jeopardized.

In this complex context of judicial activities it is important to remember that the prosecutors do not protect individual rights directly but do so collectively. In other words, the prosecutors usually deal with the representatives of civil society such as union leaders, community leaders, nongovernmental organizations, and the media. In the fledgling Brazilian democracy, which was installed in 1988 under the Federal Constitution, the role of the Public Ministry is crucial in all spheres that impact society, including education and the rights of the disabled.

THE CHILD AND ADOLESCENT STATUTE (ECA) (LAW 8.069/1990)

This law governs the rights of children and adolescents up to the age of eighteen, providing them with "full protection" (Article 4) in their best interest. The spirit of the law is to assure the priority of the rights of children in any circumstances with clear obligations with regard to supporting, caring for, raising, and educating the young (Articles 53 to 55). Under this law, although parents and guardians are the main actors, the ultimate responsibility of guaranteeing an education for children still lies with the State. As with the other statutes, it is the responsibility of the Public Ministry to guarantee its enforcement.

In Brazil homeschooling is forbidden as a result of the strict provisions of this law which views school attendance as a fundamental right in order to ensure intellectual and social development. However, a resolution that was adopted pursuant to the ECA grants a significant legal exception in the case of children and adolescents with extreme disabilities or who need hospital or domestic environments in addition to special education and specialized services (CNE Resolution 4/2009, Article 6).

THE NATIONAL EDUCATION ACT (NEA) (LAW 9.394/1996)

In the light of Articles 58 and 59 on the NEA, special education ensures the delivery of assistance to students through such approaches as special curricula, methods, resources, and teacher preparation, affording children the opportunity to achieve their maximum potential while developing skills for possible professional careers. Besides covering preschool, basic and higher education, work-based training, and adult education or lifelong learning, the provisions of the NEA create an obligation on the part of the State to provide adequate opportunities for all students, in light of their singular and specific needs.

THE GUATEMALA CONVENTION (DECREE 3.956/2001)

The Guatemala Convention of 2001 is by far the most important single source for special education law in Brazil. First, thanks to the framework of the Guatemala Convention, the original concept of special education, as enacted by NEA, now allows for a broader interpretation of the benefit based on the singular needs of students with disabilities. Second, this Convention defines all measures creating physical or moral obstacles to the exercise of the rights of the disabled as discrimination based on disabilities. Third, the Convention declares that distinctions or preferences adopted to promote the social integration and personal development of students with disabilities does not constitute discrimination.

THE RIGHTS OF STUDENTS WITH DISABILITIES

The educational rights of students with disabilities in Brazil are primarily governed by the Constitution and federal acts mentioned above. Even so, states and municipalities retain the authority to enact additional laws and regulations under the general clause of cooperative federalism (Federal Constitution, Articles 19 and 211). As such, state and municipal laws and regulations are subject to the same constitutional and legal limitations as their federal counterparts.

As a Federal State, Brazil consists of twenty-eight separate, but occasionally overlapping, educational systems; each of the twenty-six States has its own educational systems in addition to a separate one of the Union and the Federal District in Brasilia (NEA, Articles 9, 10, 11). Although the NEA allows municipalities to create their own educational systems, they are also free to use the State system in educating their children (Article 11). Yet, considering that there are 5,561 Brazilian municipalities, the total number of educational systems in the country could, potentially, reach the amazing total of 5,589 units. At present, though, there are about 2,500 municipal systems, but only 56 percent of them operate due to lack of funds or specialized human resources.

In short, students with disabilities in Brazil are entitled to the following four basic rights. First, students have a right to a free and inclusive public education, preferably in regular educational systems, whether private or public (CF, Article 205). Second, students have a guarantee to equal conditions of access and permanence in school, giving all children an adequate opportunity depending on their individualized singular needs (CF, Article 206, I). Third, the law requires governmental authorities to grant students priorities in fulfilling their right to education (CF, Article 227). Fourth, students have the right to be protected from all forms of negligence, discrimination, exploitation, violence, cruelty, and oppression (CF, Article 227).

The recent adoption of the CRDP further enhances the rights of students with disabilities in Brazil in two ways. First, the CRDP calls for the eradication of discrimination against students with disabilities. Second, the CRDP mandates the adoption of appropriate measures to guarantee that children adapt reasonably in schools as educational officials must take all measures necessary to speed up the adaptation process or to provide nondiscriminatory equality to students with disabilities.

Five primary legal consequences result from these statutory rights. First, the State has the duty to assure the rights of children and adolescents with disabilities before safeguarding the rights of other groups of the disabled, including the elderly, who also have a legal priority (Law 10.741/2003). Legal priority rights in Brazil create rights to immediate and differential treatment of individuals who are so protected (Article 6 of the Decree 5.296/2004, regulating Laws 10.048 and 10.098/2000).

Second, as stated in the ECA, "full protection," is a corollary of the guarantee of protection from all forms of negligence, discrimination, exploitation, violence, cruelty, and oppression. This includes the obligation of the State to assure the means of rehabilitation for mental and physical impairments when obstacles are present to integration in regular schools (Decree 3.298, Article 17, §§ 1 and 2); rehabilitation also implies that the State has the duty to provide necessary medical and psychological support for students with disabilities.

Third, authorities risk legal liability if they fail to provide compulsory education or provide it irregularly for students with disabilities (CF, Article 208, § 2). The ultimate responsibility for enforcing these provisions rests with the Federal Government, which can take steps when there are local or regional failures in this regard.

Fourth, all the school procedures, including individual assessments, must be consistent with the idea of "inclusive education." This implies that officials must adapt their schools to the specific needs of each student with disabilities, regardless of their number. The law further dictates that academic assessment, based on the NEA's general requirement of school competency evaluation in light of earlier schooling (Article 24, IV, c), is a means used to identify individual needs. As such, school officials have some latitude in deciding how to organize and implement assessments. Educators also have freedom to establish class groupings based on such characteristics as students' ages or actual or intended skill levels in reading, writing, and mathematics by the end of their fundamental schooling of nine years. Students with special needs are also entitled to regression recoupment and to alternative assessments aligned to alternate achievement standards (NEA, Article 24, V).

Fifth, since the ratification of the Guatemala Convention in 2001, although schooling is compulsory for students with disabilities, they are not obliged to accept the distinctions or preferences related to inclusive education. Yet, as noted earlier, nothing is required to be individually eligible for special education apart from having special needs since requirements such as age limitations or parental consent are unnecessary.

IDENTIFICATION, ASSESSMENT AND PLACEMENT ISSUES

Identifying persons in need of special education requires responsible authorities to base their assessment on Decree 5.296/2004 (Article 5, §1, I), which implements Laws 10.048 and 10.098, in the light of the new CRPD. As noted, these definitions of disability status are not strictly related to the concept of "incapacity"; rather, these classifications are grounded in the "special needs" of students who are disabled, have serious learning difficulties, or are highly gifted.

Once identified, special needs students are entitled to be enrolled in regular education as well as in units of Specialized Services for Special Education (AEEs) pursuant to Federal Decree 6.571/2008 and CNE Resolution 4/2009 that are financed by local authorities with federal and state support if necessary. The role of the AEEs parallels that of officials in regular schools by helping to promote the inclusion process. As such, AEE services can also be provided to students in hospitals or domestic environments if needed. Residential placements for regular education are provided only for students with disabilities who are homebound.

Under the provisions of the DPPA, ECA and NEA, federal, State, and municipal authorities have the duty to identify and assure the full exercise of fundamental rights to students with disabilities regardless of whether they attend public or private schools. In locations where there is a lack of free specialized education, disputes have arisen over whether authorities are obliged to place children in private schools at no costs to their families.

In a recent case involving the rights of students with disabilities, the São Paulo State Court, TJSP, extended the protections that they receive further than the Supreme Court of Brazil. In fact, the Supreme Court of Brazil had refused to interpret the Constitution in favor of the tuition reimbursement to private schools for a student who was deaf (Brazilian Supreme Court—RE n° 241.757/MA, 06/29/1999). The opinion of the Court was that private schools cannot receive public funds if they had not fulfilled all of the legal requirements to receive public funds, even if they had already been classified as social assistance schools where special education services were to be delivered. To the contrary, the São Paulo State Court ruled that the rights to education and to equal access, as well as the best interests of children, guaranteed the immediate enrollment of children with special needs (TJSP, Civil Appeal n. 279.484-5/7-00, 01/19/2006; Civil Appeal n. 752.718.5/4-00, 05/21/2008; Civil Appeal n. 564.314.5/5-00, 01/24/2007).

A noteworthy point, in terms of special education, is the novelty of the judicial discussion of general educational rights in the face of due process guarantees in the Federal Constitution and statutes. Perhaps this is due to societal needs of liberties and basic democratic rights that emerged soon after 1988. Yet, it is only after 2000 that there has been an increase of Brazilian Supreme Court cases relating to education rights. Still, most disputes involving education are resolved by State courts but can be appealed to the Supreme Court if they concern constitutional rights.

DUE PROCESS RIGHTS

The Federal Constitution of Brazil generally provides due process standards of fairness and justice (Article 5, XXXVI, LIII, LIV, LV, LVI, LVII, LVIII, LIX). These standards guarantee that the government is limited to exercising power pursuant to the settled maxims of law and under safeguards for the protection of individual rights as prescribed by the Constitution and pertinent ordinary laws. Protected rights include constitutional and legal remedies such as injunctions, popular actions, and civil and criminal actions under the general constitutional clause relating to the access of all protections afforded under the article addressing judicial power (Article 5, XXXV).

Insofar as providing special education is a governmental function, the Public Ministry, both at the federal and State levels, can initiate civil and/or criminal lawsuits against public or private authorities who are either not implementing the DPPA or ECA properly or at all as they relate to students with disabilities. The DPPA and ECA also authorize the Public Ministries to initiate class action suits to have these laws implemented by the responsible authorities.

As reasoned by the federal courts, the Public Ministries have the legal competence to represent and protect individual needs against the State

(Superior Tribunal of Justice [STJ], EREsp n. 466.861/SP, 03/28/2007; EREsp n. 684.594/RS, 12/09/2007, EREsp n. 684.162, 10/ 24/2007). Moreover, the NEA authorizes the prosecutors of the Public Ministries to sue the State to guarantee places in compulsory schooling individually or collectively for students with disabilities (Article 5).

In protecting the rights of the disabled, the Public Ministries can convene public hearings before suing the State and/or private educational authorities to ensure that they comply with the due process provisions of the Federal Constitution and the various statutes. When acting on behalf of public interests, the Public Ministries ordinarily carry out civil investigations (FC, Article 129, III); criminal investigations are under the jurisdiction of police officials. In sum, the Public Ministries carry out the task of due diligence in order to ensure that students with disabilities are afforded their full rights in public schools.

In their official capacity, the Public Ministries investigate programs for students with disabilities; their transitions from special schools and classes to regular schools and classes; the results of the transitions; and the manner in which public authorities encourage their enrollment in regular schools. In the event that school officials refused to admit students with disabilities or cancel their enrollments due to a lack of facilities and human resources, the attitude of the school with regard to the problem is investigated since school authorities could be sued under criminal law (Lei n. 7.853/89, art. 8º).

The Public Ministries can also initiate litigation against public authorities if they do not adequately use technical and financial support for inclusion programs in local education systems; this includes the allocation of public funds to private social schools for students with disabilities. Under these circumstances, prosecutors can verify whether officials are providing appropriate schooling; if there is an increase in enrollments; whether there are school plans for adapting buildings, classrooms, and access to the needs of students with special needs; if they have hired teachers to provide instruction in the LIBRAS sign language; whether there is pedagogical material in Braille and other resources for the visually impaired; and how academic assessments are carried out. In relation to teacher education, the Public Ministries also verify whether courses in pedagogy include training in special education and classes addressing diversity. Additionally, the Public Ministries control how the AEEs serve the needs of students with disabilities; how effectively the administration of AEEs operate; and how public nursery schools are prepared to receive babies with special needs with the aim of providing early education (Law 7.853/89, art. 2º, I, a). Since, unfortunately, there are no quasi-judicial dispute resolution processes available in the Brazilian educational system, the parents and guardians of students with disabilities have priority in filing litigation on their behalf in disputes over whether their needs are being met.

FUNDING AND COST ISSUES

The constitutional framework for funding education in Brazil guarantees public resources as a binding percentage of tax revenue (Article 212 of the Constitution). According to this provision, the Union, or federal government, shall apply no less than 18 percent, while the States, the federal district, and the municipalities are required to supply at least 25 percent of the tax revenues annually for education.

There is a further obligatory allocation of 60 percent of the above-mentioned resources for the universalization of basic education through the temporary Fund for Maintenance and Development of Basic Education, more commonly referred to as the FUNDEB. The resources of this fund are distributed based on the number of students enrolled annually in the public schools maintained by each government entity and premised on a minimum value per student as established by the federal government. Under this plan, the enrollment of each special needs student is considered a "double enrollment" due to the compulsory enrollment in the AEEs as well as regular schools. As such the local government receives twice the amount from the FUNDEB for children with disabilities when compared with their peers who are not disabled (Decree 6.571/2008 and CNE Resolution 4/2009).

At the same time, in order to guarantee social inclusion, municipalities are obliged to allocate public funds first to regular schools and only then to the AEEs and other private social and charitable entities or schools that work with students with disabilities. Otherwise, paradoxically, public funds would stimulate discrimination and not inclusion by maintaining students with disabilities in separate environments, a situation still prevalent in the majority of school systems in Brazil.

In any event, the Union has the duty to supplement the fund in each State and in the federal district whenever the governmental entities fail to provide support that reaches the nationally set minimum per student. The distribution of resources prioritizes enrolments from the first to eighth grades of basic schooling. This synergy is clearly a consequence of the cooperative fiscal federalism that applies to special education. A further example of this cooperation, in addition to FUNDEB, that directly and substantially impacts special education, is the availability of federal funds for state and local governments conditioned on their observing specified rules established by Law 10.845/2004 and by Federal Decree 6.571/2008.

Private schools can also receive public funds (Federal Constitution, Article 213) if they are non-profit-making and reinvest their financial excesses in education only; from the point of view of the law for the purpose of receiving public funds, it does not matter whether these schools are religious, communal, or philanthropic in nature. The NEA (Article 77) adds other conditions for public funding of private schools such that in the case of closures, the funds revert to other non-profit-making religious, communal, or philanthropic schools or the government. The Public Ministry controls the allocation and expenditure of these resources to these schools.

EMERGING ISSUES

In 2009, about 14.5 percent of Brazilians were identified as having disabilities. This percentage continues to increase due to longer life expectancies. Yet, the barriers to inclusion have increased. The most critical issues that need to be addressed when seeking to serve students with disabilities are difficulty of access to most places, the lack of adequate instructional materials, the lack of teacher support in classes, and the lack of suitable public transportation. These barriers affect individuals and students with disabilities of all classes regardless of economic or social backgrounds. Even so, these challenges are especially dire in situations as applied to individuals who are socially and economically vulnerable.

If in the last decade public policy has focused on the rights of the disabled, today it is directed to policies of inclusion through affirmative action such as distance learning at all levels of education, community centers for sports and recreation, and helping the disabled to live as independently as possible.

In the judicial sphere, Brazilian courts are engaged in activism in education by engaging in more flexible and ample interpretations of education law. This is particularly true on the part of the Supreme Court. Since the beginning of 2000, the Court's decisions have been in favor of the effectiveness of the guarantees related to education, especially at the basic level.

A paradigmatic decision from the Supreme Court of Brazil was the vote of Justice Celso de Mello in a case on enrollment in a preschool in the city of Santo Andre in São Paulo State. The case was initiated by the Public Ministry against the municipality over the priority of practical and financial measures in education by the involved government authorities. The fact which provoked the suit was the partial fulfillment of the municipality's obligation in guaranteeing education to all local children at a level well below what was expected (STF, RE n. 410.715/SP, 11/22/2005). The constitutional fundaments of the decision were based on Article 227, which demands priority in assuring the rights of children, including those with disabilities, and called on the municipality to fund education adequately.

CONCLUSION

Special education in Brazil began in the nineteenth century. Yet, it was only in the second half of the twentieth century that education laws governing special education were enacted. An important factor in the development of special education law in Brazil was the fact that it became a signatory to many international covenants on the rights of disabled persons. In the beginning of the twenty-first century, Brazil is one of the relatively few nations in the world with specific legislation on special education. However, Brazilian law has yet to produce the desired results due to reasons such as the relative newness of the laws as well as the fact that many in the population are simply unaware of their rights. Unfortunately, then, exclusion of individuals with disabilities continues to be a grave problem in Brazil.

One of the reasons why the rights of students with disabilities are not complied with in Brazil is the broad spectrum of criteria in the identification of needs for special education, whether on the part of the governmental authorities or school officials. Another challenge is to assure all of these rights in public schools in light of the lack of funding, adequately prepared teachers, and well-defined assessment plans for students. This is why the domain of the Public Ministry includes the protection of public interest through litigation and public hearings, the repercussion of which go beyond the limits of class and individual actions.

Neither access to schooling nor compulsory fundamental education necessarily answer the constitutional principle of equality in education. The right to special education is only assured if schooling aims to prepare students with disabilities as both persons and productive participants in society. In the Brazilian system, special education is a constitutional means of promoting equality that is designed to make the disabled full members of an inclusive society.

LIST OF CASES

Civil Appeal nº 279.484-5/7-00
São Paulo State Court—TJSP
Date of trial: 01/19/2006

Civil Appeal nº 564.314.5/5-00
São Paulo State Court—TJSP

Date of trial: 01/24/2007

Civil Appeal nº 752.718.5/4-00
São Paulo State Court—TJSP
Date of trial: 05/21/2008

Civil Appeal nº 895.089.5/6-00
São Paulo State Court—TJSP
Date of trial: 06/16/2009

Civil Appeal nº 838.687-5/8-00
São Paulo State Court—TJSP
Date of trial: 08/24/2009

EREsp nº 466861 / SP
Brazilian Superior Court of Justice
Date of trial: 03/28/2007

EREsp nº 684594 / RS
Brazilian Superior Court of Justice
Date of trial: 09/12/2007

EREsp nº 684162 / RS
Brazilian Superior Court of Justice
Date of trial: 10/24/2007

REsp nº 984.078 / SC
Brazilian Superior Court of Justice
Date of trial: 10/28/2008

RE nº 241757 AgR / MA
Brazilian Supreme Court
Date of trial: 06/29/1999

RE 410.715 / SP
Brazilian Supreme Court
Date of trial: 11/22/2005

LIST OF RESOURCES

Child and Adolescent Statute (ECA) (Law 8.069/1990) http://www.planalto.gov.br/ccivil_03/Leis/L8069.htm

CNE Resolution 4/2009
CNE Resolution 4/2009, Article 6

Convention on the Rights of Persons with Disabilities (CRPD) (Decree 6.949/2009) http://www.planalto.gov.br/ccivil_03/_ato2007-2010/2009/decreto/d6949.htm

Convention on the Rights of Persons with Disabilities (CRPD) (Decree 6.949/2009), Article 1 http://www.planalto.gov.br/ccivil_03/_ato2007-2010/2009/decreto/d6949.htm

Decree 5.296/2004
http://www.planalto.gov.br/ccivil/_ato2004-2006/2004/decreto/d5296.htm

Disabled Persons Protection Act (DPPA) (Law 7.853/1989) http://www.planalto.gov.br/ccivil_03/Leis/L7853.htm

Disabled Persons Protection Act (DPPA) (Law 7.853/1989), Article 2 http://www.planalto.gov.br/ccivil_03/Leis/L7853.htm

Education Act (NEA) (Law 9.394/1996) http://www.planalto.gov.br/ccivil_03/Leis/L9394.htm

Federal Constitution, Article 5 http://www.planalto.gov.br/ccivil_03/constituicao/constitui%C3%A7ao.htm

Federal Constitution, Article 205 http://www.planalto.gov.br/ccivil_03/constituicao/constitui%C3%A7ao.htm

Federal Constitution, Article 206, I http://www.planalto.gov.br/ccivil_03/constituicao/constitui%C3%A7ao.htm

Federal Constitution, Article 208 http://www.planalto.gov.br/ccivil_03/constituicao/constitui%C3%A7ao.htm

Federal Constitution, Article 208, I http://www.planalto.gov.br/ccivil_03/constituicao/constitui%C3%A7ao.htm

Federal Constitution, Article 208, III http://www.planalto.gov.br/ccivil_03/constituicao/constitui%C3%A7ao.htm

Federal Constitution, Article 227 http://www.planalto.gov.br/ccivil_03/constituicao/constitui%C3%A7ao.htm

Federal Decree 3.298/1999
http://www.planalto.gov.br/ccivil/decreto/d3298.htm

Federal Decree 6.571/2008
http://www.planalto.gov.br/ccivil_03/_Ato2007-2010/2008/Decreto/D6571.htm

Interamerican Convention for the Elimination of All Forms of Discrimination against Disabled Persons—the Guatemala Convention (Decree 3.956/2001) http://www.planalto.gov.br/ccivil_03/decreto/2001/D3956.htm

Law 10.048/2000
http://www.planalto.gov.br/ccivil/leis/L10048.htm

Law 10.098/2000
http://www.planalto.gov.br/ccivil_03/Leis/L10098.htm

Law 10.172/2001
http://www.planalto.gov.br/ccivil_03/leis/leis_2001/l10172.htm

Law 10.436/2002
http://www.planalto.gov.br/ccivil_03/Leis/2002/L10436.htm

National Education Act (NEA) (Law 9.394/1996), Article 23, XXIV http://www.planalto.gov.br/ccivil_03/Leis/L9394.htm

Resolution CNE 2/2001, 2
http://portal.mec.gov.br/cne/arquivos/pdf/CEB0201.pdf

Resolution CNE 4/2009 (including Article 6) http://portal.mec.gov.br/dmdocuments/rceb004_09.pdf

UNESCO Convention against Discrimination in Education (1960)
http://www.unesco.org/education/pdf/DISCRI_E.PDF

3

Canada

Greg M. Dickinson

When I attended elementary school in the 1950s in an upper-middle-class area of a mid-sized city in southwestern Ontario, Canada, the ground floor of my school was a classroom that was known as the "Opportunity Class." I have come to understand that whatever the children in that room were receiving, it was not opportunity, in neither an educational nor social sense. Those children were a segregated lot, both within and outside the school walls. Moreover, even when there was a measure of formal integration, for example, in trips to the YMCA to swim, they were still segregated by the abominable taunting and derision by the so-called normal students, behavior that went largely unchallenged by anyone in authority.

One of the boys in the Opportunity Class was my friend, Gordon, who also happened to live across the street from me. He was bright enough to play Monopoly® and beat me at it and to devise with me some pretty clever ways to get into trouble. Yet, Gordon had a severe speech impediment that his parents refused to address for religious reasons and, as a result, he spent his school years being treated as if he were what people with cognitive challenges have historically been called, an "idiot" or a "moron."[1] Many years later, when I was a professor at the law school, I happened across Gordon on campus. In his characteristic slurred speech, which I had long before learned to decipher, he told me he had been working as a pastry chef at the university for years. After a short chat, Gordon rode off on his motor scooter. I learned later from others that Gordon was indeed a talented chef.

In human rights law the word *opportunity* is used frequently. In special education law it is used constantly. Over the course of the half century since the days of the Opportunity Class, things have changed to the point where children with cognitive disabilities and other challenges that affect their ability to learn can reasonably expect that, even if understanding and social acceptance are not exactly what they would hope for, the law will offer a means of enforcing their entitlement to be recognized and valued as human beings and members of Canadian society equally deserving of concern, respect, and consideration.

Equality transcends access to the tangible world and has as much, perhaps more, to do with experiencing human dignity. Both should be the goal of special education. In Canada, the enactment of human rights codes, beginning in earnest in the 1960s, initially provided people with disabilities a measure of formal equality, or equal access. The development of more sophisticated human rights theories, including the notions of substantive equality and systemic discrimination, pushed policy makers to greater lengths in the attempt to go beyond equality of access and to reach for equality of condition. The arrival of the *Canadian Charter of Rights and Freedoms* in 1982 provided a legal vehicle for these more expansive equality theories to be examined and applied.

This chapter offers a glimpse at special education in Canada and some of the legal issues that help define it. I say "glimpse" because a chapter of this length cannot be all things to all people, especially in covering a topic as broad, deep, and rich as special education. Also confounding any kind of exhaustive examination is the simple fact of variation across the provinces of Canada. The chapter begins by looking at the constitutional and legal framework governing special education. For the sake of expediency the chapter discusses Ontario's legislation and special education scheme. Next, the chapter examines questions of identification, classification, and placement of students with special needs, emphasizing the process and the procedural fairness and natural justice requirements that are built into it or required by common law. Along with the role of the courts in decision making in special education through judicial review and appeals, the chapter considers the relatively recent use of alternative dispute resolution in special education matters. The chapter concludes by discussing three "emergent issues" in special education in Canada: special education for First Nations children, discrimination in disciplining children with disabilities, and constitutional claims of entitlement to government funds to pay for expensive therapeutic services for children with autism.

THE LEGAL CONTEXT

The Constitutional Framework

Canada is a confederation comprising ten provinces and three territories. The constitutional document governing the distribution of legislative authority between the federal and provincial/territorial governments is the *Constitution Act, 1867*, formerly the *British North America Act, 1867*. In education, section 93 of the *Act* reserves almost complete legislative competence to the provinces and territories.[2]

The only limitation on the plenary power of provinces over education is the proviso in section 93 that they may not legislate in derogation of denominational school rights that existed by law in 1867. Unlike in the United States, with some exceptions, there is no direct constitutionally sanctioned federal presence in education in Canada. Those exceptions relate to the federal government's overall legislative authority, set out in section 92 of the *Constitution Act, 1867*, over aboriginal peoples (and hence their education) and the military (and the education of the children of military personnel). However, Ottawa has been able legitimately to influence provincial educational policies via its legislative authority over related areas such as the national economy, research and development, human resource training, Canadian culture and official languages. The spending power of the federal government has also been used to provide considerable leverage in persuading provincial governments to take up federal educational initiatives.

The upshot of this constitutional arrangement is that thirteen different public education systems exist in Canada, one in each province and territory, each of which has enacted comprehensive education or school acts and subordinate regulations. Although there are obviously significant commonalities among these acts, they are, as a matter of law, distinct, and it cannot be said that any nationalizing legal force, akin to the American No Child Left Behind, exists. About all that can be said is that inasmuch as the provisions of the constitutionally embedded *Canadian Charter of Rights and Freedoms*[3] (*Charter*) apply to education and schooling, the rulings of the Supreme Court of Canada apply to each province and territory and thereby establish a semblance of centralization of educational policy. More discussion of the *Charter* and its influence on the rights of children with special needs occurs below.

Due to the constitutional distribution of powers, direct funding for public education in Canada, except in the case of First Nations schools, is provided at the provincial and local levels. In general, schools are funded by a combination of provincial grants and local school district revenue drawn from real property taxes. A trend toward centralization in educational governance has meant that in some provinces the provincial government has taken more or complete control of the funding process. In Ontario, for example, since reforms in 1997, school boards have been prohibited from raising additional tax revenue above a provincially set equalized mill rate. Similarly, provisions for special education funding vary across the provinces. In Ontario, the basic per pupil foundation grant is supplemented through special purpose grants, which include a Special Education Grant (SEG). The SEG, which provides enveloped funds for students who require special programs, services, or equipment, contains five components: the special education per pupil amount (SEPPA), the high needs amount, the special equipment amount, the special incidence portion, and the facilities amount. For 2009–2010, the SEPPA amounts were $755.47 for junior kindergarten to grade 3, $581.57 for grades 4 to 8, and $383.80 for grades 9 to 12.

Provincial Legislation Affecting Special Education[4]

The provincial acts with the greatest impact on the right to, provision of, and administrative process related to special education are the various provincial education and school acts. In general, the acts themselves establish broad purposes, rights, and responsibilities while regulations and provincial ministerial policy memoranda and guidelines flesh out the details of categorization, delivery modes, individual education plans, funding, identification, placement and review processes, appeals and dispute resolution.

Insofar as special education in the twenty-first century is very much defined in terms of human rights, it should not be surprising that provincial human rights codes prohibiting discrimination based on disability[5] potentially play a role in issues of access, placement, and funding as well as the treatment special needs students receive in school. A particular concern has been how disciplinary policies and practices can operate as systemic discrimination against special education students. This concern is developed in more detail under the heading Emergent Issues. While such human rights codes preclude discrimination against persons with disabilities, it must be noted that some recognize that disability often precludes any realistic chance of a person exercising a right in any meaningful way. Section 17 of Ontario's *Code* provides that "[a] right of a person under this Act is not infringed for the reason only that the person is incapable of performing or fulfilling the essential duties or requirements attending the exercise of the right because of disability." There is nonetheless a requirement that an attempt be made to reasonably accommodate the needs of a person with a disability up to the point of undue hardship on the individual responsible for the accommodation, taking into consideration cost, outside sources of funding, and health and safety requirements.[6]

Other provincial legislation aimed generally at the rights of persons with disabilities can also impact the rights and treatment of students with special needs. A prime example is the *Accessibility for Ontarians with Disabilities Act*,[7] which was enacted in 2005 but came into effect in 2010. The *Act*, which applies to every school board, college, and university in Ontario, requires public institutions to ensure that their policies, practices, and procedures are consistent with the core principles of the legislation, including independence, dignity, integration, and equality of opportunity. Along with a duty to communicate with persons with disabilities in a manner that takes into account their disabilities, the *Act* imposes the obligation to advise these individuals of temporary disruptions in services or access to facilities that they use.

Finally, it could also be said there is potential for child welfare legislation to affect students with special needs in school inasmuch as their particular exceptionalities may not only identify them as requiring special education services and programs but also identify them as "a child in need of protection." Ontario's *Child and Family Services Act*,[8] the provisions of which are common among the child welfare acts of virtually all the provinces, includes among its definitions of a child in need of protection as a child who has suffered emotional harm demonstrated by serious delayed development and there are reasonable grounds to believe that the harm is the result of the actions of, or the failure to act by, the child's parent. Also included under this *Act* are cases where a child has suffered or is at risk of suffering such emotional harm and the parents refuse to consent to services or treatment to prevent, remedy, or alleviate the harm. Similarly, a child is in need of protection where he or she "suffers from a mental, emotional or developmental condition that, if not remedied, could seriously impair the child's development," and his or her parent refuses to consent to treatment to remedy or alleviate the condition.[9] Under this *Act*, a person who deals with children in a professional capacity, including teachers and principals, has an ongoing legal obligation to report suspicions of such situations to a children's aid society.[10] Failure to report is punishable by a fine and/or imprisonment. In this respect, educators have a responsibility to their exceptional pupils that transcends educational services and programming.

The Canadian Charter of Rights and Freedoms

The *Canadian Charter of Rights and Freedoms* provides a potentially powerful legal vehicle for the parents of exceptional pupils to invoke to protect the educational rights of their children. Enacted in 1982 as part of Canada's "repatriated" constitution, the *Charter* applies to governmental action and actors, including school boards and their employees.[11] The strong equality rights embedded in the *Charter* have obvious application to special education. Section 15(1) states that "[e] very individual is equal before and under the law and has the right to the equal protection and equal benefit of the law without discrimination and, in particular, without discrimination based on . . . mental or physical disability." Claims of reverse discrimination by those not falling within the groups protected under section 15(1) are unlikely to succeed in light of section 15(2), which provides that subsection 1 does not preclude any law, program or activity aimed at ameliorating conditions of disadvantage.[12] In *Eaton v. Brant County Board of Education*,[13] the Supreme Court of Canada considered the application of section 15(1) in a case involving a dispute between parents and school authorities over whether a student with severe disabilities should be integrated within the regular classroom or educated in a special class. The details of this landmark case are discussed below.

Section 7 of the *Charter* also has been implicated in special education rights cases, although on fewer occasions than has section 15. Section 7 provides that "everyone has the right to life, liberty and security of the person and the right not to be deprived thereof except in accordance with the principles of fundamental justice." The concepts of liberty and security of the person are most apt to be raised in the context of special education. Segregating a child and limiting her chances to develop socially with her age peers could arguably interfere with a liberty interest. Security of the person has been interpreted by the Supreme Court of Canada to mean bodily integrity or physical safety. As such, it could have implications where a placement decision is unsafe for either a special needs child or others in the classroom. It has not been uncommon for the parents of so-called normal students to argue that the safety of their children was compromised by the integration of a special needs child, especially where the child's exceptionality was behavioral. Even teachers have mounted such claims about their own safety.[14] Such cases would seem more to involve issues of a board's obligation to accommodate the special needs of the child and whether accommodation posed undue hardship in the form of a threat to safety.

Section 7 also states that the state may deprive a person of liberty or security of the person only in accordance with the principles of fundamental justice. These principles, which the Supreme Court of Canada has said comprise both substantive and procedural elements, have been held to be similar to but not identical to the administrative law concept of natural justice.[15] Hence, the common law principles guaranteeing fair process, in general the *audi alteram partem* doctrine,[16] the doctrine of procedural fairness,[17] and the rule against bias are incorporated within section 7 and are applied to ensure that fair notice, disclosure, opportunity to respond orally, or at least in writing depending upon the stage of the proceedings, rights of appeal, and the right to have one's case decided by a fair and impartial adjudicator are all engaged in the protection of special education students' rights. It is likely unnecessary to resort to the *Charter* to access such procedural rights as they are required under Canadian administrative law and, in some provinces, by statutory codification of the rules of natural justice.[18]

International Law

Though not legally bound by such documents, Canada has signed a number of international declarations and covenants guaranteeing access to education and the rights of the disabled. Among them are the *Covenant on Economic, Social and Cultural Rights*, the *Convention on the Rights of the Child* and the *Declaration of the Rights of Disabled Persons*.

In a federal nation such as Canada, problems arise when provinces have legislative jurisdiction over matters about which the federal government has signed international law documents. In short, it is impossible for the federal government to order a province to comply with such a document or with a ruling of an international adjudication body.[19]

IDENTIFICATION, PLACEMENT, AND REVIEW

In Ontario, an elaborate legislative scheme governs identification, placement, and review of students with special needs. Accordingly, it is impossible to provide more than a bare outline of the even the most relevant of such provisions.[20] Also, there are obviously provincial variations. Ontario's is not precisely Alberta's scheme, and so on. Still, I am confident that the commonalities are sufficient among the various provincial systems that adopting one as a model will be useful and not terribly misleading. Moreover, since Ontario is Canada's most populous province, the use of its legislative scheme could be justified on that ground alone, while many, east, west, and north, might disagree.

First, it must be understood that the *Education Act* of Ontario places a statutory onus on the Minister of Education to ensure that all exceptional children in the province have available to them appropriate special education programs and services without fee and to provide for the parents of such children to appeal the appropriateness of the special education placement. In addition, the Minister must require school boards to have and implement procedures for early and ongoing identification of the learning abilities and needs of pupils, prescribe standards for such procedures, define exceptionalities of pupils, prescribe classes, groups or categories of exceptionality and require boards to use such definitions and prescriptions.[21]

Exceptionality

Under section 1 of the *Act*, an "exceptional pupil" is one whose behavioral, communicational, intellectual, physical or multiple exceptionalities are such that he or she is considered to need placement in a special education program by a school board committee established under the terms of the *Act*. Understandably, the generality of the definition can pose problems. In conformity with the statutory duty discussed above, the Minister provided additional definitions and categories of exceptionality.[22] For example, a behavioral exceptionality is defined as

> A learning disorder characterized by specific behavior problems over such a period of time, and to such a marked degree, and of such a nature, as to adversely affect educational performance, and that may be accompanied by one or more of the following:
> (a) an inability to maintain interpersonal relationships;
> (b) excessive fears or anxieties;
> (c) a tendency to compulsive reaction;
> (d) an inability to learn that cannot be traced to intellectual, sensory or other health factors, or any combination thereof.

Communication disorders include autism, deaf and hard of hearing, language and speech impairment, and learning disability; intellectual exceptionality is subdivided into giftedness, mild intellectual disability, and developmental disability; physical exceptionality, though specifically including blindness and low vision, broadly means "a condition of such severe physical limitation or deficiency as to require special assistance in learning situations to provide the opportunity for educational achievement equivalent to that of pupils without exceptionalities who are of the same age or developmental level"; and, multiple exceptionalities are defined as a "combination of learning or other disorders, impairments, or physical disabilities, that is of such nature as to require, for educational achievement, the services of one or more teachers holding qualifications in special education and the provision of support services appropriate for such disorders, impairments, or disabilities."

Identification

Identification of exceptional pupils usually occurs formally through the Identification, Placement, and Review Committee (IPRC) process established in accordance with the *Education Act* or informally through the school's agreeing to simply provide a student with an individual education plan, services, and programming without going through the statutory process. Such informal arrangements apply to students who are educated without the need for special education placements.[23] It has been suggested that bypassing the formal process may violate the intent of the *Act* and not be in the interests of students and parents who do not have the benefit of information collected regularly for the purpose of assessment and annual review.[24]

Each school board in Ontario must have at least one IPRC, one member of which must be a principal or a supervisory officer. The rest of the Committee members are normally teachers and special education specialists. It is possible to appoint members from outside the school board, although parental consent would be required for such members to access students' school records and school information because of limitations imposed by provincial privacy legislation.[25]

Students can be referred to an IPRC for identification by either their principals or their parents. Already identified students must have their cases reviewed by an IPRC at least once in the school year unless the parents provide written consent to dispense with the review. IPRC meetings are informal, but the Committee must abide by the principles of procedural fairness, which include providing parents with relevant information, allowing parents to attend meetings with a representative or advocate, allowing the student if sixteen or older to be present, allowing both to participate in discussions about the student, and allowing both to be present when the Committee makes its decision about identification and placement.[26]

Placement

A good deal of confusion surrounds the meaning of *placement* as the term is used in the *Act*. The matter is of some significance because, under the *Act*, parents may appeal placements but not special education services or programming. Special Education Tribunals have been of a mixed mind when deciding whether placement includes the services and programming to be provided in that placement. It seems somewhat counterintuitive to consider the two things in isolation. After all, the most meaningful part of students' special education experiences are arguably the curricula and services they receive, not the setting in which they are delivered. In any event, it is beyond the scope of this chapter to explore this issue further, although there is an array of tribunal and court decisions which have done so.[27]

Little is said in the *Education Act* to guide an IPRC in deciding a proper placement. As indicated above, the Minister is required to provide the means for parents to appeal the appropriateness of placements, leaving one to conclude that the IPRC is on its own in determining what is appropriate in individual cases. Disputes over IPRC placement decisions have usually involved a difference of opinion as to whether exceptional pupils would be better served by integrated or segregated placements. Most often, but not always, parents have argued for the former and school authorities for the latter. A cynic might predict a reversal in that trend as tighter budgets tempt boards to educate exceptional pupils in mainstream classrooms where, in some instances, the delivery of services and programming might be more cost efficient, especially with fewer special education aides on site.

Unlike the *Education for All Handicapped Children Act*,[28] on which Ontario's sweeping special education reforms (Bill 82) of 1980 were modeled, Ontario's legislation does not mandate integration, although in the wake of a landmark and controversial Supreme Court of Canada ruling in an integration case,[29] the province amended a regulation to place an onus on IPRCs to consider first whether regular classroom placements would meet students' needs and be consistent with parental wishes.[30]

Of Constitutional Presumptions, Parental Wishes, and the Child's Best Interests: Integrating Emily

Eaton v. Brant County Board of Education is not only the premier special education ruling in Canada, it is also one of the most important rulings by the Supreme Court of Canada on the meaning of the concept of equality in general. Emily Eaton was a young girl with cerebral palsy which had left her with severe developmental delay, no established system of communication, and very significant physical disabilities. Emily was placed in a regular class for kindergarten and grade 1; however, an IPRC subsequently determined that she should be placed in a segregated special education class. The Eatons appealed this placement decision, and the case eventually reached the provincial Special Education Tribunal.

Evidence was introduced indicating that Emily frequently disrupted the class by yelling loudly and often had to be removed to be escorted up and down the hall until she quieted down. At other times she slept in class. Safety concerns were also raised inasmuch as Emily attempted to place small items in her mouth, necessitating close monitoring by her educational aide. The Tribunal concluded that Emily's experience in a regular classroom setting failed to achieve the intended social inclusion objective and, in fact, had had the opposite result. Evidence showed that Emily had become isolated within the class. Despite the arguments of Emily's parents that she had a right to be in an inclusive setting under the equality rights provisions of section 15 of the *Charter*, the Tribunal ruled that it would be in Emily's best interests to be placed in a self-contained special education class with some opportunities for inclusion in a regular class setting.

After their application for judicial review of the Tribunal's decision was dismissed by the Divisional Court, Emily's parents appealed to the Ontario Court of Appeal. The Court of Appeal overturned the rulings of the lower court and the Tribunal, finding that Emily's right to an education without discrimination because of disability created a presumption that she was to be educated in an inclusive setting. The Court found that the *Education Act*'s failure to establish such a presumption was a denial of *Charter* equality rights. In what only could be described by strict constructionists as a classic act of judicial legislating, the Court of Appeal "read up" the *Education Act* to include a provision that, in the absence of evidence that an integrated placement was not in a student's best interests, and unless the parents' wishes were to the contrary, the student was to be placed in a regular classroom. Hence, the appeal order left in place a constitutional presumption of inclusion that only clear evidence of its not being in a child's best interests or a parental veto could displace.

This case was, to a large degree, about onus of proof. The onus, if the Court of Appeal decision were to stand, would fall squarely on the school board to prove that inclusion was not in the best interest of the student. Even then, the parents would still hold the trump card.

On further appeal, the Supreme Court of Canada disagreed adamantly with positions taken by the Court of Appeal. First, the Supreme Court held, section 15 of the *Charter* does not guarantee special education students a right to inclusion in a particular setting but rather to an education. Second, the Court rejected the Court of Appeal's notion of a constitutional presumption in favor of integration. Such a presumption, the Court reasoned, would interfere with the careful adjudication of cases based on the best interest of individual students, all of whom were different. Moreover, the Court did not think that parents should have the ability to trump a decision taken by a Special Education Tribunal on the basis of relevant evidence as to what was in the best interests of their child. The Court explained that parental views should be taken into consideration but not be determinative.

The Supreme Court admitted that equality rights cases involving persons with disabilities were difficult and distinguishable from discrimination cases based on other grounds, such as race or sex. The Court noted that the latter were characteristics in which there was no individual variation and which were entirely irrelevant to how the members of such groups should be treated by the state. The Court pointed out that the same could not be said in the case of disability, where wide variations can exist resulting in the need for careful investigation of the facts of each case and where true equality requires the recognition and accommodation of the very reason for the differential treatment. The Court acknowledged that this is referred to as the "difference dilemma"; in some cases, people simply need to be treated differentially due to their disabilities in order to provide them with chances for equal educational opportunities. Hence, the Court was of the opinion that segregation could, in one instance, violate equality and, in another, protect it.

On reflection, there is nothing radical about the philosophical approach of the Supreme Court of Canada in *Eaton*. The notion that it is sometimes necessary to provide differential treatment in recognition of the different characteristics or contexts of individuals is nothing more than a restatement of fundamental Aristotelian ethics. Vertical equity "consists in the appropriately unequal treatment of individuals who are unequal in relevant respects."[31] The trick, of course, is to recognize what are "relevant respects" and distinguish them from stereotypical assumptions, some so vile as to rationalize apartheid and other forms of racial segregation and persecution.

APPEALS AND ALTERNATIVE DISPUTE RESOLUTION

The Appeal Process

One of the principles of natural justice, or fundamental justice to use the *Charter*'s language, is that an individual subject to a ruling of a court or tribunal should have the ability to appeal that ruling to a higher judicial authority. The term *appeal* is used here generically as, in Canada, tribunal and court rulings can be subject to both judicial reviews and appeals. Judicial review is an administrative law concept that relies on the common law tradition of superior courts supervising the actions and decisions of inferior tribunals and courts.

Judicial review is typically undertaken where it is claimed that a tribunal or court exceeded its jurisdiction, failed to exercise its jurisdiction, acted illegally or in bad faith, showed actual bias (or heard a case in which where there was a reasonable perception of bias), made procedural errors such as violating the rules of natural justice or procedural fairness, or applied incorrect conclusions of law, or made patently unreasonable decisions that ignored or misapprehended the evidence. It is unusual for a judicial review court to consider the merits of a case and substitute its opinion for that of the inferior court or tribunal. In fact, considerable curial deference is shown to tribunals hearing cases in which they have expertise, such as special education tribunals.

The remedies most often given by courts on judicial review involve declarations of violations of certain rights or administrative law principles and the setting aside of tribunal decisions and/or orders. The cases are then routinely sent back to the tribunals, usually differently composed, to be reheard taking into consideration the findings of the reviewing courts. Appeals, on the other hand, are established by legislation and typically deal with errors of law made by lower courts or tribunals. In general, appeal courts can substitute their opinions on the merits of cases or order new trials of the matters at issue.

The appeal process in special education cases in Ontario is quite extensive and has both informal and formal stages. It should be noted that judicial review can always be sought for decisions of a statutory decision maker, subject to the inherent discretion of superior courts to hear the cases. However, Ontario's *Education Act* and regulations also provide for three appeals.

The decision of an IPRC relating to identification and placement can be appealed by a parent to a Special Education Appeal Board (SEAB) set up by the school board in question. The SEAB is a tripartite body composed of a member appointed by the school board, a member appointed by the parents, and a chair appointed usually by the agreement of the other two members. The board conducts its business at a consultative meeting rather than a hearing and passes on to the school board its nonbinding decision in the form of a recommendation which the board decides to accept or reject. Although not required to conduct a hearing, a school board has a common law obligation to comply with the rules of procedural fairness and extend an opportunity to the parties to make submissions orally or at least in writing.

Parents who disagree with the school board's decision may appeal it to a provincially appointed Special Education Tribunal (SET), which is the final appeal body in the statutory process. Only students who are adults, that is, over the age of eighteen years, may initiate appeals. Some have commented that it may offend *Charter* principles of equality not to allow so-called emancipated minors to appeal decisions in cases affecting them.[32] SETs are composed of panels of members selected from a roster of provincial appointees, mostly special education experts and parent advocates. A case is heard by a panel of three members, one of whom chairs the hearing.

Hearings are legally formal, and counsel is often present on behalf of parties. In Ontario, the *Statutory Powers Procedure Act* (*SPPA*)[33] and common law rules of natural justice and procedural fairness govern the Tribunal's process.[34] The *SPPA* provides minimum rules of procedure that cover the definition of parties; reasonable notice of hearing; information to be furnished to parties before the hearing; the order of proceeding at the hearing; the necessity that hearings be held in public except in cases of intimate personal matters which would likely include special education cases;[35] the right to counsel; the right to call, examine and cross-examine witnesses; admissibility of evidence; adjournment; maintenance of order; the need for written final decisions and orders; the need for written reasons for decisions if requested by a party; and the need for a written record of the proceedings. The Tribunal has developed Special Education Tribunal Rules of Procedure to reflect its statutory and common law due process responsibilities.[36]

Ontario's special education process has been criticized for being too complex, lengthy, prescriptive, legalistic and adversarial. Nadya Tymochenko argued against this legalism and in favor of a system that lends itself to more creative and less confrontational problem solving. She advocated for a system that relies more on mediated settlements:

> Mediated settlements are one way that parents might have a substantive and positive influence on the educational supports and programs being provided to their child. Further, mediation is not an adversarial process and the working relationship between the school board and the parents might be better preserved.[37]

Tymochenko noted that some school boards had implemented mediation training programs for administrators with a view to resolving difficult matters of contention between school boards and parents prior to their proceeding to a tribunal.

Alternative Dispute Resolution

Whether out of reaction to criticisms such as those leveled by Tymochenko or simply as part as the general movement in law toward alternative dispute resolution over the last decade, Ontario has recognized that there is an important role to be fulfilled by mediation in special education disputes. Mediation can occur at any stage of the process should both parties wish to participate in it. Significant benefits can accrue from mediating special education disputes, including reducing the alienation of parents and school officials as the result of an adversarial process and streamlining the process and shortening the time line to resolution of a special education matter. One of the great and unfortunate ironies in special education cases is that the circumstances of the subject child have often changed greatly by the time the matter has worked its way through the process, often rendering the legal disposition moot.[38] Moreover, even if a dispute remains unsettled after mediation, on the parties' consent some of the points of contention may be removed, making a subsequent hearing less complex and time consuming.

A Practice Direction of the Ontario Special Education Tribunal has provisions for mediation during a hearing. If at any point during a hearing the parties request mediation, the Tribunal chair may temporarily adjourn the proceedings. Unless the parties already had a mediator, the chair will appoint one. The Practice Direction provides that all discussions during mediation are confidential and cannot be disclosed to the Tribunal should a hearing resume. Nor can the mediator be compelled to appear as a witness at the hearing or at any other proceeding dealing with the same matter. The Tribunal receives only the results of the mediation.

If all matters are resolved, appeals are withdrawn. The Tribunal can issue a consent order reflecting the mediated agreement should the parties request one. If only some of the matters in dispute are resolved, the hearing will begin or resume, possibly with an agreed statement of facts. If none of the matters in dispute is resolved, the hearing will begin or resume, as the case may be.

In a special education resource guide, the Ontario Ministry of Education encourages parents to consider the benefits of mediation while offering helpful hints on how to approach and prepare for mediation.[39] Mediation holds great promise for reducing the cost and strain of a litigious process and serving the best needs of the child more quickly. Moreover, it is commonly accepted that a resolution arrived at by the agreement of two parties, whether mediated or not, is more apt to be palatable to each party than one imposed by a board of experts, or likely even worse, a court.

EMERGENT ISSUES

The title of this section suggests that the issues to be discussed have only recently come into view. They have not; some, if not all, have been known for some time, but their full implications have become more apparent given a changing educational policy, financial and legal landscape. There are doubtless other emergent issues in Canadian special education. These three were chosen because, in one respect or another, they strike at the essence of special education, especially the vulnerability of students with special needs and how impacted they are by government policies and actions or the lack thereof.

Special Education for First Nations Children

When special education is discussed it is often done in a way that considers students with special needs as a population distinguished only by the array of educationally related exceptionalities: learning disabilities, physical challenges, communicational disorders and the like. Often forgotten is that the constituency of students with special needs is also stratified by socioeconomic condition and race. A perfect example is the plight of First Nations students in Canada.

Little has been documented about the topic. Yet, the problems that First Nations children experience with educational attainment and retention as a result of their special conditions and needs are well known. The problems First Nations children have accessing appropriate special education is often exacerbated by the remoteness of the locations in which they live and the isolation of their communities from one another, both of which hinder attraction and retention of teaching staff as well as cooperative and efficient delivery of services. Moreover, one study in Quebec showed that 47 percent of the First Nations children enrolled in schools participating in it had been identified as having a condition or disorder that impacted on their ability to learn.[40] In general, it has been suggested that the incidence rate of exceptionalities calling for special education is "several times higher" among First Nations students than in the general population.[41]

Under the Constitution,[42] Canada's First Nations fall within the legislative jurisdiction of the federal government, which therefore is also responsible for the education of First Nations children. However, the *Indian Act*[43] is silent when it comes to affording a right to an appropriate education for any First Nations children, let alone those requiring special education.[44] In their groundbreaking comprehensive study of First Nations education policy in Canada, Paquette and Fallon point out that until very recently the delivery of special education to First Nations students has been sporadic and by dint of the good fortune of living in a community in which such programs were offered. Even then, the authors note, such programs fall far short of those offered in provincial schools. Students who did not reside in such communities were simply placed in regular classrooms with teachers who were untrained to deal with the learning problems which confronted them.[45] This situation is hardly a recipe for educational success and retention of either student or teacher.

Some signs of minimal "progress" have emerged within the last decade or so. Pilot projects undertaken by the First Nations Educational Council of Quebec and the First Nations Education Steering Committee in British Columbia have shown some promise, and the federal government's tutor escort program has provided funding for minimal training for would-be educational assistants in First Nations communities. Despite these initiatives, Paquette and Fallon deliver a pessimistic prediction: what they call "the tragic status quo in special education" will continue "for some time to come for at least two reasons."[46] First, they conclude there is no reason to believe that the substantial investment of policy effort and money required for appropriate special education for First Nations children is forthcoming. Although the federal government announced in 2004 it would be investing $101 million in special education for First Nations across Canada, Paquette and Smith extrapolated from their study of special education for First Nations students in Quebec that at least a quarter billion dollars would be required.[47] The announced intention of the government aside, it appears that only about $60 million have been provided.[48] Second, there is an inertia stemming from intergenerational culture and social capital available to support special education initiatives. The lack of special education for the parents and grandparents of today's students is a barrier to the immediate success of special educational programming initiatives. As Paquette and Fallon put it, "adults with learning disabilities that have been adequately addressed during their school careers have a much better chance of supporting their own children's learning and their motivation, than parents whose disabilities have simply been ignored and who have eventually failed or been pushed out of school."[49]

As with so many First Nations policy issues, the correct answer is elusive. Nevertheless, Paquette and Fallon offer what appears to be a sensible recommendation. While money is necessary, it is insufficient to guarantee success. This has been proven time and time again in educational policy, not only in the First Nations context. What is needed is what the authors call "functional aggregation," a scheme whereby individual First Nations cede decision-making power and resources to aggregate organizations comprising representatives of several First Nations. In this way, lack of capacity and diseconomies of scale could be overcome.

Discipline of Children with Special Needs

One of the most prominent themes in educational policy changes in Canada over the last decade has been a movement toward so-called zero-tolerance school disciplinary regimes. The *Safe Schools Act* (*SSA*)[50] enacted by the Ontario legislature in 2000 is a prime example. This *Act* replaced one section of the *Education Act* that up to then had provided principals and school boards with almost complete discretion over student suspensions and expulsions, with a detailed code of rules and procedures comprising some sixteen sections. Although not employing the phrase *zero tolerance*, the *Act* enumerated behaviors that would result in mandatory suspension or expulsion, depending on the particular behavior, leading to the inexorable conclusion that zero tolerance was the name of the game. Despite lip service having been paid to so-called mitigating factors, many were concerned about the legislation's seemingly cold indifference toward context. There were plenty of reasons to be concerned about the legislation's compliance with constitutional principles, but the one most relevant to the present discussion was that it discriminated against students with special needs, especially where the special needs resulted from a behavioral exceptionality.

A fundamental paradox was thus set up with special needs students caught at the centre: on the one hand, the *Education Act* required the Minister to ensure that the needs of exceptional students were accommodated so that they received an appropriate education;[51] on the other hand, concerns about school safety had cemented in place a set of rigid, decontextualized rules that penalized students for their behavior by removing them temporarily or permanently from school. It stands to reason that students with behavioral exceptionalities would have been the main clientele of the masters of the new regime. And they were.[52]

This did not sit well with many, including the parents of exceptional students who were getting suspended for the very behaviors which the *Act* elsewhere required to be accommodated through special education services and programming. Complaints were made to school administrators, policy makers, the media, and ultimately the Ontario Human Rights Commission, which, as part of a broader study of special education in the province, investigated whether the *SSA* discriminated against students on the grounds of race, ethnicity, and most important for present purposes, disability. The Commission produced a preliminary report[53] in 2002 in which it identified human rights issues in education. It followed up by inviting extensive feedback and representations from interested parties through written submissions and public hearings. In 2003, the Commission subsequently released its final report, entitled *The Opportunity to Succeed: Achieving Barrier-Free Education for Students with Disabilities*.[54]

The final report dealt with many issues, among them the impact of the *SSA* on exceptional pupils. The Commission noted that many participants in the consultation process had alleged that the *Act* had discriminatory effects on students with disabilities and that, in many cases, students were suspended or expelled without due consideration of their right to accommodation of their disability. Moreover, disability was not explicitly included in the mitigating circumstances set out in the legislation. The Commission heard from a legal clinic specializing in children's rights that there had been an increase in the number of reported suspensions and expulsions of students identified as exceptional by their boards. Often students were being expelled for the very behavior that made them exceptional.[55] Those consulted also told the Commission about "restrictive disciplinary practices taking place in some classrooms" and students with disabilities being subjected to forced isolation, often outside of the classroom, to control their behavior. Some participants commented on the harmful effects of being excluded, whether by suspensions, expulsions, or in-school isolations. Apart from the obvious effect on students' right to attend, such exclusions can harm their dignity and reduce their ability to enjoy the same benefits and privileges experienced by others. Moreover, the Commission heard that *SSA* provisions were being used more strictly against "children with disabilities from racialized communities."[56]

Before recommending policy actions, the Commission commented on the difficult task that school officials have in dealing with students whose disabilities caused uncontrollable and sometimes violent behavior. The Commission recognized that the balance between respecting the rights of persons with disabilities and ensuring safe school environments is a delicate one:

> where a student engages in behavior that impacts upon the well-being of others, it may be open to education providers to argue that to accommodate that student would cause undue hardship on the basis of health and safety issues, specifically, that the accommodation would pose a risk to public safety. However, the seriousness of the risk will be evaluated only *after* accommodation has been provided and only after appropriate precautions have been taken to reduce the risk. The onus of proof will be on the education provider to provide objective and direct evidence of this risk. . . . A mere statement, without supporting evidence, that the . . . risk is "too high" based on impressionistic views or stereotypes will not be sufficient.[57]

The Commission ended this part of its report by recommending that educators be required to use discretion in applying the *SSA*, assess whether appropriate accommodation has been given a student with a disability, and implement progressive disciplinary measures prior to suspending or expelling the student.[58]

A human rights complaint launched against the Ministry alleging the discriminatory impact of the *SSA* was eventually settled on the following terms, among others, whereby the Ministry agreed to

- continue a comprehensive review of the safe schools provisions of the *Education Act* while requesting amendments to the relevant regulations to include mitigating factors and
- require principals and school boards to consider mitigating facts prior to suspending or expelling any students. The mitigating factors are:

  a. whether racial or other harassment was a factor in the student's behaviour;
  b. whether the principles of progressive discipline have first been attempted;
  c. the impact of suspension or expulsion on the student's continued education;
  d. whether the imposition of suspension or expulsion would likely result in an aggravation or worsening of the student's behaviour or conduct;
  e. the age of the student;
  f. in the case of a student with a disability, whether the behaviour was a manifestation of the disability and whether appropriate accommodation, based on the principle of individualization, has first been provided; and
  g. the safety of other students.

- consider proposing legislative amendments requiring the application of progressive discipline, such as in-school detentions, peer mediation, restorative practice, referrals for consultation, and/or transfer, before use of suspension and expulsion;
- support the efforts of school boards that are prepared to collect data on suspensions and expulsions and their impact on *Code*-protected students through hiring an independent, expert and qualified researcher to work with school boards to develop best practices and data collection methods that are consistent with the Commission's *Guidelines for Collecting Data on Enumerated Grounds under the Code* and to ensure parent, student and community input into data collection best practices and to report back to the Ministry. Upon the completion of the research, the Ministry will re-examine its existing position on race-based data collection;
- request approval for development of a policy regarding alternative education programs for students who are expelled or on long-term suspensions (more than five school days);
- invest in resources for teachers and guidance counsellors to inform them of strategies for teaching racialized students;
- provide principals, vice-principals and trustees responsible for expulsion hearings/suspension appeals with training on antiracism, antidiscrimination, cross-cultural awareness and accommodating students with disabilities as well as training on how to apply discipline in a nondiscriminatory manner.[59]

In the wake of its own review of the *SSA* and the settlement with the Human Rights Commission, the government enacted amendments to the *Education Act*,[60] the most significant of which were restoring some discretion to principals, introducing the practice of progressive discipline, and increasing the number of contextual factors to be taken into account prior to giving a suspension or expulsion. If nothing else, Ontario's experience with the *Safe Schools Act* in the context of human rights is an instructive illustration of the process of policy formulation, implementation, critique, and reform.

Hard Choices: The Funding of Applied Behavioral Analysis (ABA)/ Intensive Behavioral Intervention (IBI) Therapy for Children with Autism

For social welfare governments in 2010 equity involves making fundamentally important choices about where to spend increasingly scarce resources. While governments have argued that these choices are a matter of legislative or executive discretion beyond the reach of judicial review, courts have held that that discretion must still conform to constitutional standards and hence be subject to judicial review.[61]

Hard cases make bad law, so the saying goes, and a series of cases in Canada dealing with challenges to governments' refusal to fund expensive therapy for children with autism proves the truth of the saying. ABA/IBI therapies came to the fore in the 1990s as a promising approach in effecting positive changes in the behaviour of children with autism. A number of cases resulted when provincial government ministries refused for various reasons to provide the $40,000 or so per child per annum required to obtain the therapy. The claimants, who were the parents of children with autism, met with defeat on several fronts. In Ontario, the Special Education Tribunal ruled in a series of cases that the therapy was not educational in nature and, hence, its provision was not the responsibility of a school board. It was neither a placement nor an educational service or program. In support of its decisions, the Tribunal drew a distinction between IBI, which was delivered by a trained therapist under the supervision of a clinical psychologist, and applied behavioral principles, which teachers learned during teacher training and used in their classroom practice.

In *Wynberg v. Ontario*,[62] the claimants tasted victory at the trial level when the Ontario Superior Court of Justice held that once the government undertook to provide the service of ABA/IBI for preschoolers it violated the *Charter* by arbitrarily terminating it for children age six and over, especially given the government's awareness that autistic children entering the school system were not having their special needs met.[63] The claimants had argued that "without ABA/IBI therapy, which they claimed was also a special education program or service, their children could not access education and receive equal treatment in the provision of educational services."[64] On scant evidence and in contradiction to the findings of the Special Education Tribunal, the court declared that the therapy was educational and that the Minister of Education had not considered the therapy as a possible educational strategy but had always treated it as psychological therapy or treatment. Hence, the court ruled that the government's refusal to fund the therapy was systemic discrimination on the basis of disability.[65] This euphoric victory was short-lived as the Court Appeal reversed, extending as MacKay says traditional judicial deference to legislative discretion in matters of funding priorities.[66]

The issue of whether ABA/IBI is a health or educational service remains undetermined by the Supreme Court of Canada. The Supreme Court dismissed an application for leave to appeal in *Wynberg*. Based on the Supreme Court's refusal to hear *Wynberg*, its judgment in *Auton v. British Columbia*, which showed deference to legislative discretion in the prioritization of health care spending, and the decisions of the Special Education Tribunal, there seems to be little reason for claimants to expect a favorable ruling.

The publicity surrounding *Wynberg* and related cases put considerable pressure on the Ontario government to respond to what seemed to be an injustice. In 2007, the Ministry of Education released *Policy/Program Memorandum No. 140* dealing with incorporating ABA methods into special education programming for students with autism spectrum disorders. Under the memorandum, "principals are required to ensure that ABA methods are incorporated into the IEPs of students with ASD, where appropriate." Although ABA/IBI therapy available to children with autism remains unfunded after the age of six, there is some solace in the recognition by the government that with greater cooperation the benefits of ABA can be realized at school through its introduction into the individual education plans of students with autism. However, the capacity to deliver such enhanced programs, and to pay for them, remains in question.

CONCLUSION

The rights of Canadian students with special needs have come a long way from the days of "opportunity classes" and classes for the "trainable retarded."[67] Special education reforms and human rights laws have made integration the norm. Although rejected by the Supreme Court of Canada as a constitutional presumption, integration is at least statutorily recognized as a primary consideration in placement decisions. Even so, the Supreme Court made it clear in *Eaton* that the vertical equity dimensions of disability rights cases require that individual cases be considered on their own facts to ensure that the determinative factor in special education placements is in the best interests of the child. Parental wishes, while they are to be considered, cannot trump what the evidence shows is best for their children.

Special education processes, especially those in Ontario, have become heavily layered, legalistic, and formal. The good news is that in a due process sense, the rights of children and parents are well protected by the statutory provision of procedural fairness and natural justice in addition to the role of the courts in judicial review and appeals of special education decisions made by school boards and tribunals. The not-so-good news is that the complexity and legalistic nature of the process have left it open to justifiable criticism for overreliance on labeling and adversarialism that alienates parties while consuming so much time that cases are often moot by the time they are legally resolved. There is growing acceptance of alternative dispute resolution as a way of reducing the adversarialism and drain on time and resources that accompany an overly legalistic system. There is now provision for mediation in the special education processes of Ontario and other provinces.

Three areas of special education which have attracted the attention of human rights advocates and the legal community are special education for First Nations students, discrimination against students with disabilities under strict discipline policies, and attempts by parents of children with autism to use the *Charter* to argue entitlement to government funding for expensive therapy. The status of each of the areas can be summed up, respectively, as promising but slow developing, addressed at least by the law and policy if not in practice, and dismal.

Some initiatives and government money are on the scene in First Nations special education although, as in most First Nations policy matters, money alone will not solve the problem and effective action can be expected to be woefully slow. Direct and systemic discrimination against students with disabilities as a result of Ontario's zero-tolerance-styled *Safe Schools Act* has been addressed by human rights complaints that resulted in a settlement with the government of Ontario. The settlement was accompanied by legislative and policy action emphasizing the contextual nature of disciplining student misconduct, especially in the case of students with behavioral disabilities when the very reason for their identification as an exceptional pupil is likely to be at the root of their conduct.

Litigation mounted by the parents of children with autism claiming a violation of *Charter* rights by governmental refusal to fund therapy, as either an educational or health service, has been unsuccessful at the appellate levels. While the Supreme Court of Canada has yet to rule in a case dealing with ABA/IBI as an alleged educational service, there appears little reason to expect a positive result for the claimants. Although the Ontario Ministry of Education has taken measures to introduce elements of ABA into special education programming, the ABA therapy provided by trained therapists under the direction of clinical psychologists remains unfunded after age six.

In Canada, education is clearly a welfare right. However, nowhere in the Constitution is such a right identified, except in the case of minority language instruction rights or denominational school rights. In the absence of arguing successfully that the *Charter's* guarantees of liberty and security of the person can be seen as providing a right to education, Canadians are reliant on provincial education legislation to provide it. As a statutory right, it is subject to shifting political and economic winds and the never-ending struggle over scarce government funds. In some provinces, such as Ontario, the only right explicitly provided to children at large is to attend school. In Ontario, the rights of special education students are broader than those of nonexceptional pupils inasmuch as the former have a statutory right to appropriate educational services. Nonexceptional pupils and their parents who are dissatisfied with the quality of the education delivered in their schools are left with attempting to bring civil actions against school authorities for educational malpractice, which for reasons essentially the same as those that have spelled failure in cases in the United States, are almost certain to be rejected by the courts.

NOTES

1. *See* Vera C. Pletsch, *Not Wanted in the Classroom* (London, ON: The Althouse Press, 1997) for a discussion of the history of the social and professional treatment of people with intellectual disabilities.

2. Parallel provisions were included in the constitutional acts accompanying the entrance of provinces into Confederation after 1867.

3. Part I of the *Constitution Act, 1982*, being Schedule B to the *Canada Act 1982* (U.K.), 1982, c. 11.

4. Due to the sheer volume of provincial legislation dealing with special education and the limited scope of this chapter, Ontario's will be used throughout as exemplary. While variations exist, the broad strokes referred to are largely similar. Ontario's legislation is the *Education Act*, R.S.O. 1990, c. E. 2.

5. *See, e.g.*, Ontario's *Human Rights Code*, R.S.O. 1990, c. H. 19 provides the following in section 1: "Every person has the right to equal treatment with respect to services, goods and facilities, without discrimination because of . . . disability."

6. *Ibid.*, section 17(2). The Supreme Court of Canada considered reasonable accommodation to the point of undue hardship and established some interpretive parameters in *British Columbia Public Service Employee Relations Commission v. British Columbia Government and Service Employees' Union*, [1999] 3 S.C.R. 3 (S.C.C.) and *British Columbia (Superintendent of Motor Vehicles) v. British Columbia (Council of Human Rights)*, [1999] 3 S.C.R. 868.

7. S.O. 2005, c. 11.

8. R.S.O. 1990, c. C. 11.

9. Section 37.

10. Section 72.

11. Section 32.

12. There are similar provisions in the *Human Rights Code* of Ontario protecting special programs from reverse discrimination claims. See *supra* note 5, section 14.

13. *Eaton v. Brant (County) Board of Education*, [1997] 1 S.C.R. 241 (S.C.C.).

14. I have heard it suggested that the *Occupational Health and Safety Act*, R.S.O. 1990, C. O. 1, section 43(3), would permit a teacher to stop work where he or she believed an exceptional pupil posed a physical threat.

15. *See Reference re Section 94(2) of the Motor Vehicle Act*, [1985] 2 S.C.R. 486 (S.C.C.).

16. Literally meaning "hear both sides," this doctrine is aimed at ensuring a fair opportunity to make one's case.

17. In *Nicholson v. Haldimand-Norfolk (Regional Municipality) Cmmrs. of Police*, [1979] 1 S.C.R. 311, the Supreme Court of Canada held that a statutory decision maker whose decisions impact a person's rights and interests is under a duty to provide procedural fairness, which includes the right to notice that one's

rights and interests are being dealt with and the right to make at least written submissions.

18. *See, e.g.,* the *Statutory Powers Procedure Act,* R.S.O. 1990, c. S. 22.

19. *See, e.g., Waldman v. Canada* (2000), 7 IHRR 368 (Inter-Am. C.H.R.), (1999), United Nations Human Rights Committee, available online at http://www.unhchr.ch/tbs/doc.nsf/0/b3bfc541589cc30f802568690052e5d6?Opendocument.

20. To support my case, I will simply relate a situation I experienced in a graduate education law class I was teaching just after the enactment of major special education reforms in Ontario that continue to be the foundation of the current system. One of my students had been seconded by his board to the Ministry of Education to work on the implementation of the new legislation. He asked me whether he could demonstrate to the class how the process of identification, placement, review and appeals worked by showing them a flowchart he had created for the Ministry. I agreed. At the next class, after requesting class members to put some tables together, he unrolled a flowchart that he had created (accurately and completely I should say) on a roll of brown butcher's paper. The chart extended from the front of the room to the second last row of seats!

21. *See* the *Education Act supra* note 4, section 8(3).

22. Ontario Ministry of Education, *Special Education Handbook* (Toronto: Author, 1981), revised and updated by Ontario Ministry of Education, *Standards for School Boards' Special Education Plans* (Toronto: Author, 2000).

23. Brenda Bowlby, Catherine Peters, and Martha MacKinnon, *An Educator's Guide to Special Education Law,* 2nd ed. (Toronto: Canada Law Book, 2010), p. 55.

24. *Ibid.*

25. *Ibid.,* pp. 77–78.

26. *Ibid.,* p. 85.

27. *Ibid.,* pp. 57–66. The authors discuss the issue and cases in more detail.

28. Pub. L. No. 94-142, 20 U.S.C. section 1401 *et seq.*

29. *Eaton v. Brant County supra* note 13. This case is discussed in detail in a later section.

30. O. Reg. 181/98, section 17. A major bone of contention in *Eaton* was whether parents' wishes trumped the decision of a Special Education Tribunal made in consideration of the child's best interests.

31. A. J. Culyer, "The Promise of a Reformed NHS: An Economist's Angle" (1991) 302 *Br. Med. J.* 1253 at 1254.

32. *Supra* note 23, pp. 158–159.

33. *Supra* note 18.

34. *Supra* note 23, p. 164.

35. Student information is confidential under both the *Education Act* and generic provincial privacy legislation.

36. The rules are available at http://www.oset-tedo.ca/eng/process.html#rules.

37. Nadya Tymochenko, "Special Education in Ontario—Is It Workable?" (2002) 12 *Educ. & L. J.* 213, pp. 238–239.

38. For example, in *Eaton,* by the time the parents won at the Court of Appeal level they had already moved Emily to a Roman Catholic school that agreed to place her in an integrated class.

39. *See* Ontario Ministry of Education, *Special Education: A Guide for Educators* (Toronto: Author, 2001) available at http://www.edu.gov.on.ca/eng/general/elemsec/speced/guide.html, quoted in Bowlby, Peters, and MacKinnon, *supra* note 23, p. 135.

40. Jerald Paquette and Gerald Fallon, *First Nations Education Policy in Canada* (Toronto: University of Toronto Press, in press) at 229. The authors point to the high incidence of fetal alcohol syndrome as a particularly serious barrier to effective teaching and learning in First Nations schools.

41. *Ibid.*

42. *Constitution Act, 1867* (U.K.), 30 & 31 Vict., c. 3.

43. *Indian Act*, R.S.C. 1985, c. I-5.

44. Paquette and Fallon *supra* note 40, p. 228.

45. *Ibid.*, pp. 228–229.

46. *Ibid.*, p. 230.

47. *Ibid.*, p. 231.

48. Personal communication with Jerald Paquette, 13 September 2010. The failure of the government to provide the full amount may have been based on its skepticism that First Nations communities were well organized enough, including appropriate infrastructure, to make effective use of the funds.

49. Paquette and Fallon *supra* note 40, p. 230.

50. S.O. 2000, c. 12, section 3.

51. *Education Act*, R.S.O. 1990, c. E.2, section 8(3).

52. Anomalous and confusing situations can arise out of the tension between special education and safe school provisions. For example, In *Bonnah (Litigation Guardian of) v. Ottawa-Carleton District School Board* (2003), 64 O.R. (3d) 454 (Ont. C.A.), a principal had attempted to invoke safe school provisions in the *Education Act* and regulations to effect a transfer of a special needs student who acted aggressively and arguably posed a threat to other students. The eleven-year-old had developmental disabilities and functioned at the level of a kindergarten student. An IPRC review recommended that the student be removed from his grade 2 class and returned to a school which catered to students with similar disabilities. The parents immediately appealed, thus freezing any change in his placement. Citing safety concerns, the principal attempted to affect the transfer. The principal relied on his authority under section 265(1)(m) of the *Education Act*, which allows principals to refuse to admit to the school or classroom a person whose presence is deemed detrimental to the physical or mental well-being of the pupils. He also justified his action under Regulation 474/00, which had been made as part of the 2000 *Safe Schools Act* reforms and which states that a person is not permitted to remain on school premises if, in the principal's judgment, his or her presence is detrimental to the safety or well-being of a person on the premises. The Court of Appeal acknowledged that the principal had such statutory authority but that its use could be judicially reviewed if no genuine safety concerns existed. In the present case, because the board could not alter the student's placement during the stay pending appeal, a Hobson's choice was set up as indicated by the court:

> The most the Board could do . . . was offer an alternative placement to Zachary's parents where, in the Board's view, the safety concerns did not arise. Zachary's parents would

then have to decide whether to send Zachary to that other school pending the outcome of their appeal. If they declined to do so, Zachary would remain out of school. (p. 466)

For a comment on this case, see Greg M. Dickinson, "Court of Appeal Rejects Use of 'Safe Schools' Provisions to Transfer Exceptional Pupil" (2004) 13 *Ed. & L. J.* 455.

53. Ontario Human Rights Commission, *Education and Disability: Human Rights Issues in Ontario's Education System* (2002). Available online at www.ohrc.on.ca.

54. Ontario Human Rights Commission, *The Opportunity to Succeed: Achieving Barrier-Free Education for Students with Disabilities* (2003). Available online at www.ohrc.on.ca.

55. *Ibid.*, p. 22.

56. *Ibid.*, p. 23.

57. *Ibid.*, p. 24, quoting Ontario Human Rights Commission, *Policy and Guidelines on Disability and the Duty to Accommodate* (March 2001), available online at www.ohrc.on.ca. Emphasis in original.

58. *Ibid.*

59. Ontario Human Rights Commission, *Human Rights Settlement Reached with Ministry on Safe Schools.* Available online at www.ohrc.on.ca.

60. *See An Act to Amend the Education Act in Respect of Behaviour, Discipline and Safety*, S.O. 2007, c. 14 and O. Reg. 472/07, Suspension and Expulsion of Pupils. This regulation adds eight "other factors" to the already existing mitigating factors that principals must take into account if they would mitigate the seriousness of the conduct for which students may be suspended (section 3).

61. *See* William Smith and William Foster, "Equality in the Schoolhouse: Has the Charter Made a Difference?" In Michael Manley-Casimir and Kirsten Manley-Casimir, *The Courts, the Charter, and the Schools*, 14–38 (Toronto: University of Toronto Press, 2009) p. 25, referring to *Eldridge v. British Columbia (Attorney General)*, [1997] 3 S.C.R. 624 (S.C.C.) and *Concerned Parents for Children with Learning Disabilities Inc. v. Saskatchewan (Minister of Education)* (1998) 170 Sask. R. 200 (Q.B.).

62. *Wynberg v. Ontario* [2006] O.J. No. 2732 (Ont. C.A.).

63. Wayne MacKay, "The Lighthouse of Equality: A Guide to Inclusive Schooling" in Manley-Casimir and Manley-Casimir *supra* note 61, p. 50.

64. Brenda Bowlby and Rachel Arbour, "Special Education and the *Charter*: The Effect of the Equality Provisions and *Charter* Litigation on Educational Policy and Practice in Ontario" in Manley-Casimir and Manley-Casimir, p. 82.

65. *Ibid.*

66. *Supra* note 63.

67. *See* Pletsch's discussion of "labels and the law" in *Not Wanted in the Classroom supra* note 1, pp. 9–33.

4

China

Ran Zhang

In China, the Second National Survey of Persons with Disabilities reveals that as of 2006, 2,460,000 children from ages six and fourteen had one or more disabilities. Of these children, about 63 percent were formally enrolled in school settings that were either inclusive or restrictive.[1] The Second National Survey of Persons with Disabilities also reports the illiteracy rate for the population of individuals with disabilities aged fifteen or above was 43 percent. Undoubtedly, the total elimination of illiteracy among individuals with disabilities largely depends on special education beginning early in life. Education is a widely recognized human right, and individuals cannot be deprived of this right because of disabilities. Therefore, focusing on the legal rights of students with disabilities is crucial both for social development as well as for individual freedom and flourishing.

This chapter begins with a brief overview of the sources of special education law in China. This overview sketches out a general picture of the relevant parts of the legal system and highlights a few most important principles of special education law in China. The chapter next analyzes major issues concerning the rights of students with disabilities, including identification and assessment, placement, curriculum and instruction, student discipline, dispute resolution, as well as the cost and funding of special education. The chapter concludes with a discussion of emerging issues and an assessment of special education law in China.

SOURCES OF SPECIAL EDUCATION LAW

The legal system in China relies heavily on code law. Accordingly, the sources of special education law in China include the Constitution, the Law on the Protection of Persons with Disabilities, various educational statutes, the Regulation on the Education of Persons with Disabilities, the Convention of the Rights of Persons with Disabilities, and various local and provincial statutes.

Of the sources of law, the Constitution has supreme authority. Article 45 of the 1982 Constitution stipulates, "the state and society help make arrangements for the work, livelihood and education of the blind, deaf, mute and other handicapped citizens." Article 46 defines education as a right and duty for Chinese citizens. Since these provisions are listed under the chapter of "Fundamental Rights and Duties of Citizens," it can be argued that persons with disabilities have a fundamental constitutional right to education in China. On the other hand, although the Constitution is at the top of the hierarchy of the sources of law, judges and legal scholars usually believe that the Chinese constitution cannot be directly cited in court opinions.[2] In fact, few cases in China have been decided based solely on the Constitution.[3] Thus, the specification of the rights of students with disabilities must rely on legal sources that come from lower levels than the Constitution.

The Law on the Protection of Persons with Disabilities, which was first enacted in 1990 and revised in 2008, is the overarching statute in the field of disability law. The 2008 version of the Law explicitly declares that persons with disabilities have equal rights to education.[4] The Law also pronounces the guiding principle of special education in China:

> Education for persons with disabilities shall be developed in terms of both the expansion of access and upgrading of the levels, with more emphasis on the former. Compulsory education shall be guaranteed, and priority shall be given to the development of vocational education. Efforts shall be made to carry out preschool education and gradually develop education at and above the upper secondary level.[5]

Clearly, this provision emphasizes access to special education, especially during the compulsory education stage which, in China, covers elementary and lower secondary education. This section also highlights the role of vocational and technical training in special education. Besides this guiding principle, the Law on the Protection of Persons with Disabilities addresses the placement responsibilities of educational institutions,[6] lifelong education of persons with disabilities,[7] special education teacher preparation,[8] as well as the development of Braille, sign language, special education curriculum, and auxiliary teaching aids.[9]

Consistent with the Law on the Protection of Persons with Disabilities, a series of statutes, including the Compulsory Education Law of 2006,[10] the Vocational Education Law of 1996,[11] and the Higher Education Law of 1998[12] include special education provisions within their purview. More details of such provisions can be found in the Regulation on the Education of Persons with Disabilities of 1994, which was issued by the State Council in accordance with the Law on the Protection of Persons with Disabilities and relevant educational statutes.

The Regulation on the Education of Persons with Disabilities is an administrative regulation that deals specifically with special education. Pursuant to this Regulation, educational agencies at county levels or above are in charge of special education in their regions with other relevant agencies, usually those pertaining to health and civil affairs, fulfilling their respective duties.[13] The Regulation also addresses an array of issues relevant to special education, including identification, assessment, curriculum and instruction, cost and expenditure, and teacher training, most of which are discussed in greater detail in the next section of this chapter.

Besides these authoritative sources of special education law in the higher stratum of the legal hierarchy, state and provincial/municipal educational agencies in addition to local legislatures make rules relevant to students with disabilities. The Ministry of Education issues administrative rules to address specific issues of special education. Most notably, the implementation of inclusive education in regular schools[14] and the operation of special education schools[15] are both governed by such rules. Local administrative rules may further spell out implementation details or provide more protection to students with disabilities beyond state requirements. For instance, the Ministry of Education asks "capable township central schools" and "schools with a relatively larger number of disabled students" to set up a special education consulting room (*fudaoshi*) "step by step."[16] Since the target schools are vaguely defined, they do not seem to have an immediate duty to act. In comparison, the Education Commission of Shanghai Municipality explicitly requires officials in regular schools "with more than ten disabled students enrolled" to open a special education consulting room and to hire one full-time teacher in charge of the room.[17]

Besides various domestic sources of law discussed above, China signed the Convention of the Rights of Persons with Disabilities in 2007[18] and ratified it in 2008.[19] However, in general, international conventions do not automatically become a source of law for disputes in China; they must first be incorporated into domestic law. Indeed, a significant driving force for the 2009 revision of the Law on the Protection of Persons with Disabilities was to align it with the Convention of the Rights of Persons with Disabilities.[20]

THE RIGHTS OF STUDENTS WITH DISABILITIES

Identification and Assessment

The Law on the Protection of Persons with Disabilities of 2008 defines a person with a disability as "one who has abnormalities or loss of a certain organ or function, psychologically, physiologically, or in anatomical structure and has lost wholly or in part the ability to perform an activity in the way considered normal."[21] Thus, this definition limits persons with disabilities to those with physical or mental impairment while including those with "visual, hearing, speech, physical, intellectual, or psychiatric" disability or a combination of these conditions. Following this enumeration, the law includes the catchall phrase "other disabilities."[22]

Early identification of children with disabilities is the responsibility of health care providers, educators in preschools, and families. Health care providers and educators in preschools are supposed to provide parents or guardians of children with disabilities with "consultation and guidance on the early identification, rehabilitation, and education."[23] In Hebei Province, for example, early disability identification must be integrated into the regular physical checkups of children.[24]

For children with disabilities who have reached school age, educational and health care agencies at the county level should offer consulting on schooling options (*jiuxue zixun*), assessing their disabilities and offering placement opinions.[25] It is not clear from the wording of the law whether these local agencies are required to take positive action to reach all disabled children in their region.

Before students with disabilities can be placed in regular schools, the type and severity of their disabilities needs to be evaluated.[26] Students with visual or hearing disabilities are evaluated by personnel in hospitals, rehabilitation centers for children with disabilities, or special education professionals employed in special education schools for the blind or the deaf. The evaluation of children with intellectual disabilities follows a different procedure. Students are first recommended by their parents or teachers and then screened, with participation from parents and teachers, by an evaluation group composed of medical and educational professionals. If screening occurs at the township level, the results of the evaluation must be approved by a county-level evaluation team in order to ensure their accuracy.[27] Additionally, the law mandates that the evaluations of children with intellectual disabilities, especially those with mild intellectual disabilities which are difficult to judge, must be completed more cautiously and are subject to periodic reevaluations.

The law is silent as to whether parental consent must be obtained before evaluation or whether parents of children with disabilities have a right to request reevaluations or independent evaluations. Since such rights are not generally available in educational law in China, presumably parents of children with disabilities lack entitlements. As such, dissatisfied parents would have to negotiate with local educational agencies or schools on a case-by-case basis.

Placement

Placing students with disabilities in inclusive settings is a growing trend in special education in China. The Compulsory Education Law of 1986, the first educational statute enacted in the People's Republic of China, asked local governments to establish "special education schools (or classes) for blind, deaf and mute, and retarded children or adolescents."[28] The law did not mention general education for students with disabilities at all. A 1989 state policy, approved by the State Council, *suibanjiudu*, established attending regular classes as a practice of inclusive education as one of the ways of providing education to students with visual or intellectual disabilities.[29]

The 1990 Law on the Protection of Persons with Disabilities provided that depending on the nature and severity of the disabilities of children, "ordinary or special educational methods" (*jiaoyu fangshi*) shall be used.[30] The Law also outlined the principle that general elementary or lower secondary schools, those in the compulsory stage, must admit students with disabilities who are capable of adapting themselves to study in such schools.[31] This was the first time that a statute mandated that regular schools open their doors to students with disabilities. In 1994, the Ministry of Education issued an administrative rule specifically on *suibanjiudu*, promoting and directing the placement of students with disabilities in regular classrooms.[32] This document signaled a new direction in the development of special education in China. In the same year, 1994, the Ministry of Education issued the Regulation on the Education of Persons with Disabilities, which set out three major modes of special education provision for disabled students of compulsory education age:

1. *Suibanjiudu*, or attending regular classes within general education schools;
2. Attending special education classes within general education schools, child welfare institutions, or other organizations;
3. Attending special education schools.[33]

As a result, the placement of students with disabilities in China has a combination structure, with *suibanjiudu*, special education classes, and special education schools as three possibilities. In 2008, among the 417,440 students with disabilities receiving compulsory education, 62 percent attended regular classes, 37 percent were enrolled in special education schools, and only 1 percent were placed in special education classes within general or vocational education schools.[34]

Usually, students with visual disabilities, hearing disabilities, mild, and sometimes moderate, intellectual disabilities, or other kinds of disabilities attend regular classes in general education schools once they have passed the assessment.[35] Students with severe disabilities or who are unable to cope with regular classroom atmospheres and routines are educated in special education classes or schools. According to the Compulsory Education Law of 2006, "local governments at the county level or above shall, where necessary, set up special schools or classes for school-age children who have visual, hearing, and intellectual disabilities."[36] The enrollment, instruction, and management of special education schools are governed by the Regulation on Special Education Schools of 1998, an administrative rule issued by the Ministry of Education.

According to the law, special education classes are institutional arrangements wherein the small numbers of students with severe disabilities does not justify establishing special education schools or when local educational agencies lack the resources to open such schools. These classes are more like miniature special education schools that, although situated in larger inclusive environments, offer students face-to-face interaction that occurs primarily in restrictive settings.

In 2008, there were 1,640 special education schools and 684 special education classes within general or vocational schools in the compulsory education stage nationwide.[37] Both special education schools and special education classes are required to have "facilities appropriate for the study, rehabilitation, and living of students with disabilities."[38]

General education schools also have begun to have a duty, albeit an unclearly defined one, to provide accommodation and assistance to students with disabilities. The Law on the Protection of Persons with Disabilities of 1990 seemed to suggest that placement in inclusive settings depends on whether students can handle study in mainstream classes on their own. The Regulation on the Education of Persons with Disabilities of 1994 began to require mainstream schools, subject to local situations, to "provide convenience and conditions on study and life" to students already admitted.[39] Given its dependence on local resources and conditions, this is only a soft duty; it also only targets students with disabilities who have already been admitted to general education schools. In contrast, the Compulsory Education Law of 2006[40] and the revised Law on Protection of Persons with Disabilities of 2008[41] require mainstream schools or institutions to admit students with disabilities who are otherwise qualified and are capable of receiving ordinary education *and* to offer "convenience and assistance" to their study; there are no longer any strings attached.

To date, there has not yet been sufficient clarification on what constitutes the "convenience or assistance" that school officials must provide for students with disabilities. Admittedly, the 2008 Law on the Protection of Persons with Disabilities already mandated that "newly-built, renovated or expanded buildings" meet accessibility requirements[42] and that accommodation be provided to students who are blind in entrance examinations to upper-level schools.[43] It is not clear whether accommodation should be made available to students with other kinds of disabilities or in other kinds of testing, such as on final examinations. As noted, an educational consulting room (*fudaoshi*), which is equipped with special education aids as well as full- or part-time counselors, is encouraged or required to be present, depending on local rules or policies. Yet, it is unlikely that, given the combination structure of student placement and the frequent consideration of local conditions, that schools or local educational agencies are required to provide all related aids, services, or assistance necessary for students with disabilities to benefit from inclusive educational settings.

Curriculum and Instruction

Students who are placed in inclusive settings usually follow the same curricula and use the same textbooks as their peers (with the exception of the blind, who use Braille textbooks), but specific learning content or requirements can be adjusted.[44] Individualized education plans (IEPs) should be made and included in the special records for students with disabilities.[45] In Shanghai, each student shall also receive individualized training of no less than thirty minutes during each school day.[46]

For students who are placed in restricted settings, the state educational agency has designed a special curriculum to be followed by special education schools. Textbooks used in special education schools usually have to be reviewed by an educational agency at the state or provincial level.[47] Compared to mainstream schools, special education schools are supposed to place greater emphasis on physical education, art education, and vocational education in addition to therapy or rehabilitation.[48] Instruction is generally conducted on the basis of student grouping, and individualized instruction may be provided in schools where there are necessary conditions.[49] Therefore, special education schools do not have to make IEPs for each student.

Regardless of their placements, the evaluation of learning for students with disabilities should employ multiple criteria. The test-based evaluation method for regular students should not automatically be extended to students with disabilities. Although formative assessments are emphasized,[50] students with disabilities usually do not repeat grades.[51] If students cannot meet their learning requirements by graduation, they can be issued certificates of completing compulsory education.[52] It appears that when it comes to learning evaluations, special education law in China places more emphasis on different standards for students with disabilities than it does on accommodations.

Student Discipline

Under the Education Law of 1995, school officials have the authority to discipline students.[53] Still, compared to the general student population, those with disabilities enjoy slightly more substantive protection but are not entitled to special procedural safeguards.

Teachers are generally prohibited from using corporal punishment on students, discriminating against students, or insulting their human dignity, regardless of whether they are teaching children who are disabled.[54] Teachers in special education schools are particularly warned to be sensitive of students' self-esteem and self-respect and not to make sarcastic remarks.[55]

In China, expulsion of students is generally prohibited during the compulsory stage.[56] Students who commit serious wrongful acts may be given a warning (*jinggao*), a severe warning (*yanzhong jinggao*), or documentation of violation (*jiguo*) as disciplinary action.[57] If students behave well afterward, the disciplinary acts of warning or severe warning can be withdrawn from their records. Although not deemed as disciplinary actions, if students attending mainstream classes are found no longer fit to study in inclusive settings, they can be transferred into special education schools or classes.[58]

Suspension and time-out must be used parsimoniously with disabled students. Unless special reasons exist, students with disabilities in regular classes shall be not suspended or punished by means of given time-outs.[59] While it is possible that this rule was designed to prevent the abuse of these measures by classroom teachers, its text does not specify what qualifies as "a special reason."

Students with disabilities do not receive procedural protections in the disciplinary process. Moreover, unlike in the United States, students are not entitled to manifestation determinations as to whether their misbehaviors are related to their disabilities. Presumably, while some teachers consider whether the misbehavior is a result of students' disabilities, others may not do so. Indeed, currently no national educational law in China affords due process rights to elementary and secondary students with disabilities. In recent years, some local educational agencies or schools have begun to recognize students' due process rights and provide those faced with disciplinary actions with the rights to notice and hearings.[60] Students with disabilities within the jurisdictions of these agencies can certainly claim their due process rights accordingly.

Dispute Resolution

Special education laws mainly mention two kinds of disputes. The first kind of dispute arises when officials at general elementary or lower secondary schools refuse to accept students with disabilities who can handle regular classroom life or when educators in high schools, vocational schools, or higher educational institutions deny access to those who meet the state-established physical eligibility standards.[61] The second kind of dispute occurs when teachers insult or apply corporal punishment to students with disabilities.[62]

For the first kind of dispute, students with disabilities and their parents can report incidents to the educational agencies in charge of the schools. Agency officials may order educators in the schools to rectify the situations and, when violations are of a severe nature, render disciplinary actions against "the persons in charge or others directly responsible."[63] If agency officials refuse to interfere, students and their parents can file claims for administrative review on nonfeasance against the agencies.[64] However, students with disabilities and their parents lack private causes of action against school officials.[65] This means that placement disputes can only be resolved via administrative channels with the remedy being limited to changes of placements. Parents are not usually reimbursed for the tuition or other costs incurred during the period when they are denied access to the school.

For the second kind of dispute, teachers or other school personnel who insult, apply corporal punishment to, or use physical violence on students with disabilities may incur administrative, criminal, or civil liabilities because these acts are prohibited by law in China. Within administrative channels, teachers may be disciplined or even fired.[66] If acts are so severe that they constitute crimes, teachers can be penalized under the criminal code.[67] If acts result in student injuries, tort liability applies and teachers are responsible for the damages.[68] Students and their parents certainly have causes of action concerning the civil liability. In addition, if acts take place in the course of teachers' fulfillment of their job-related duties, students can directly seek monetary damages from the schools,[69] which can pursue reimbursement from the teachers.[70]

Persons with disabilities can seek help from the China Disabled Persons' Federation (CDPF), a nongovernment organization that is backed by the state. CDPF and its local branches are supposed to safeguard the lawful rights and interests of persons with disabilities and have the right to ask relevant agencies to conduct investigations or take other appropriate actions. The agencies must pursue such investigations or actions and offer replies.[71] Given this, CDPF and its local branches may become actors in the dispute resolution process, thereby affording students with disabilities additional leverage.

Cost and Funding Issues

The new Compulsory Education Law of 2006 abolishes the levy of the miscellaneous fee (*zafei*),[72] so that students do not have to pay the direct cost of compulsory education. This general rule can be applied automatically to students with disabilities. In addition, under the Law on the Protection of Persons with Disabilities of 2008, students with disabilities who are receiving compulsory education receive free textbooks and subsidies of their boarding costs,[73] which is only enjoyed by those from economically disadvantaged families under the Compulsory Education Law.[74] The Compulsory Education Law also makes it a general principle that the State Council and the local governments at the county level and above "guarantee" the receiving of compulsory education by school-aged children and adolescents with disabilities.[75] The law singles out and emphasizes the education of students with disabilities.

For noncompulsory education, students with disabilities may receive financial aid according to relevant state regulations or policies.[76] At vocational schools or vocational training institutions, students with disabilities may enjoy partial or total tuition waivers.[77] If such students are economically disadvantaged, they may also have total or partial waivers of other fees.[78]

The legal arrangements discussed above only deal with the direct cost of education, such as tuition and school fees, and part of the costs that students would usually pay in attending school, such as textbooks or boarding costs. The laws do not account for the special expenses necessary for students with disabilities to benefit from attending school. The wording of the laws does not make it clear as to whether parents of students with disabilities have to pay out of their pockets for the cost of disability assessments, psychological consulting, and the various therapies students receive after enrollment. It seems that educational institutions in China are beginning to have a more clearly defined duty to provide "convenience and assistance" to students with disabilities, but what constitutes "convenience and assistance" is yet to be defined.

The Law on the Protection of Persons with Disabilities of 2008 does require local governments to provide poor students with disabilities with "relief and subsidy according to regulations for the basic medical care, rehabilitation services, and installment and replacement of necessary assistive devices" and to offer "nursing subsidies, where appropriate, for persons with disabilities who cannot take care of themselves in everyday life."[79] Even so, since these are part of general social security programs it is possible that they do not meet all the needs of students with disabilities. The support or relief they provide is usually far from sufficient to cover the costs for students with disabilities to attend school.

Funding special education is primarily a responsibility of local governments, as the state government provides funds to support special education in the relatively less developed middle and western regions of China as well as students with disabilities from economically disadvantaged families.[80] Still, the relevant laws have created measures to ensure the funding of special education. First, special education expenditures must be "ensured" by all levels of governments and are supposed to "increase gradually" as overall educational spending increases.[81] Second, if necessary, governments at the county levels or higher can establish special education funds in addition to designating set proportions of general compulsory education funding for special education.[82] Third, during the compulsory education stage, the standard for operating expenses, excluding teachers' salaries, per student in special education schools or classes must be set higher than those in general education schools.[83] Fourth, educational agencies of all levels are supposed to increase the expenditures related to having students with disabilities educated in mainstream classrooms.[84] Along with these direct funding measures, special education teachers receive special allowances in China.[85]

EMERGING ISSUES

As discussed earlier, elementary and lower secondary schools cannot deny access to students with disabilities who can adapt to school life while other educational institutions must admit children who are otherwise qualified and meet state-established physical eligibility standards. In recent years, students with disabilities who are denied access to schools have begun to claim their rights as discrimination on the basis of disabilities has become a persistent topic in public discourse. This public concern has also led the state to revise its physical eligibility standards, allowing individuals with disabilities greater access to educational institutions.

In 1995, in the first such case ever filed in China, a student with infant paralysis challenged officials of a specialized upper secondary school, alleging that they denied his application for admission even though he scored higher than the admission minimum but had had infant paralysis. After the student filed suit, school officials changed their position and granted him admission, leading him to withdraw the case.[86] Even though this case did not result in an judicial order justifying the rights of the student, it was fairly well publicized, sending a signal to other individuals with disabilities that the status quo can be questioned and that their fate can be different from that which is prescribed.

The Ministry of Education in 2003 changed its physical eligibility standards for college students, opening the door of higher education to a wider range of individuals with disabilities. Under the earlier standards issued in 1985, general higher education institutions could not admit students whose two arms or two legs could not function, whose sum of corrective visual acuity of two eyes is below 1.0, the equivalent to 20/20, or whose hearing in each ear falls below two meters.[87] Since these standards were legal mandates that colleges and universities had to abide by, the discrimination against students with disabilities was de jure. The new 2003 standards removed the above-mentioned restrictions and also left more latitude to higher education institutions. The standards became an "advisory guideline," under which colleges and universities could design their own physical eligibility standards for different areas of studies.[88] Based on these new standards, general higher education institutions are still allowed to deny admission to students with high blood pressure, asthma, chronic kidney disease, or malignant tumors. Students can be excluded from higher education for the simple reason that they suffer from such conditions. At the same time, though, the 2003 standards clearly warn that general higher education institutions cannot deny access to individuals with physical disabilities who meet other admission requirements and can handle their chosen programs of study. This can become a direct source of law for relevant students claiming their rights.

Among those fighting for equal opportunity in admission processes, a strong voice comes from those who are Hepatitis B virus (HBV) carriers. Similar to the situation of HIV-positive people who do not show symptoms of AIDS, HBV carriers do not show symptoms of Hepatitis B disease. Based on a 2006 national survey, this group of individuals was estimated at 93 million in China.[89] Under the 2003 standards, university and college officials can refuse to admit HBV carriers into educational programs for early childhood education, flight or navigation technology, food processing, or food science. In practice, many medical schools and research institutes also closed the door to these students.[90] However, HBV is rarely contagious in normal interpersonal interaction.[91] Feeling deprived of equal educational opportunity, HBV carriers started to use legal weapons to challenge the discriminatory admission practices and policies. They created an Internet forum to share information and provide mutual support,[92] engaged in performance art just outside China's two most prestigious universities to express their anger and helplessness as second-class citizens,[93] and, most important, gained sympathy and support from journalists, intellectuals, and the first generation of human rights lawyers in China.[94] These activist HBV carriers have initiated a social movement against discrimination.

In February 2010, the Ministry of Human Resources and Social Security, the Ministry of Education, and the Ministry of Health jointly issued a more forceful policy to prevent discrimination against HBV carriers.[95] According to this new policy, except with prior approval from the Ministry of Health, no educational institution can subject their applicants to HBV tests. Supposedly, without HBV testing, educational institutions would have no way to identify and thus discriminate against HBV carriers.

Although the controversy regarding HBV carriers so far has been basically settled, the issue itself still poses an important theoretical question. Undoubtedly, what has happened is a social movement against discrimination. Yet, questions remain as to what kind of discrimination may be present. Many advocates in this movement ground their claims on the principle of equal educational opportunity, which still does not answer the question as to what kind of discrimination is occurring. As discussed earlier, the definition of disability in China includes mental and physical impairments. In order to qualify as individuals with disabilities, persons need "fully or partially lose the ability to perform an activity in the way considered normal."[96] Even so, since HBV carriers do not lose any function, strictly speaking, they do not qualify as individuals with disabilities such that the principle against discrimination due to disability[97] does not necessarily apply to them. In attempting to resolve this legal "gap," the disability definition should be expanded to include the situation where persons are regarded as having a disability. Although HBV carriers do not have problems performing activities, many people in the society believed that they are deficient or disabled. While persons regarded as having disabilities do not need to have the rights to special education or related services, when it comes to equal protection, they should enjoy the special protections associated with disabilities.

CONCLUSION

This chapter has discussed major issues and new developments concerning the rights of students with disabilities in China. Overall, China maintains a dual system of special education, with a majority of students subject to inclusive education while others are placed in restrictive settings. Still, mainstreaming is the trend. While more legal and policy documents design or regulate the substantive aspects of special education, procedural safeguards for students with disabilities are largely lacking. In addition to all these issues, the following few questions deserve special attention in conceptualizing special education law of China as a whole.

First, although Chinese citizens have both a fundamental constitutional right to education[98] and the education of children with disabilities in the compulsory education stage is supposed to be "guaranteed,"[99] the provision of special education is by no means available at all costs. According to the laws, the government's responsibilities to provide special education and relevant services are often associated with terms such as "where/if necessary" or "when local conditions exist." In practice, this means that if local governments do not believe needs exist or they lack sufficient resources, they can choose not to follow the law. Although street-level bureaucrats are always engaged in coping behaviors,[100] with so much officially recognized leeway the protection of students with disabilities in China is at risk of being watered down. Many legal provisions on special education also sound like encouragement rather than mandates.[101] Therefore, students with disabilities hardly have a full entitlement to education in China.

Second, it is unclear whether and to what extent private schools must follow the laws discussed in this chapter. While the state encourages the establishment of private schools serving children with disabilities,[102] it is unclear what happens if their parents insist on sending their children to regular private schools. It is as yet unresolved as to the extent to which these schools must provide convenience and assistance to students with disabilities. Also, it is unsettled whether private school can charge students special fees. All of these questions remain in need of clarification.

Third, both the Compulsory Law and the Law on the Protection of Persons with Disabilities have been revised since 2005 in addition to China's having ratified the Convention of the Rights of Persons with Disabilities in 2008. Even so, the Regulation on the Education of Persons with Disabilities, the administrative regulation specifically addressing special education and outlining the entire special education system, was issued as early as 1994. In light of the recent changes in the upper levels of legal sources, the Regulation on the Education of Persons with Disabilities, the most relevant source of special education law, is about to undergo further revisions.

NOTES

1. National Bureau of Statistics of China, 2006 年第二次全国残疾人抽样调查主要数据公报 [Report of the 2006 Second National Survey of Disability], no. 2 (2007).

2. Supreme People's Court, 关于在刑事判决中不宜援引宪法作论罪科刑的依

据的批复 [A Reply on the Inappropriateness in Citing the Constitution in Criminal Decisions] (1955) *and* 关于人民法院制作法律文书如何引用法律规范性文件的批复 [A Reply on How People's Courts Cite Laws in Issuing Their Legal Documents] (1986).

3. For a discussion on this issue, *see* Heidi Ross and Ran Zhang, *Guest Editors' Introduction: The Limits and Possibilities of Responsive Justice*, CHINESE EDUC. & SOC'Y, vol. 39, iss. 4, 3–10 (2006).

4. Art. 21. Compared with the 1990 version, the current version added the word *equal*.

5. Art. 22.

6. Art. 25–26.

7. Art. 27.

8. Art. 28.

9. Art. 29.

10. Art. 6, 19, 31, 43, 57.

11. Art. 7, 15, 32.

12. Art. 9.

13. Art. 5.

14. Commission of Education, 关于开展残疾儿童少年随班就读工作的试行办法 [Trial Methods of Inclusive Education] (1994).

15. Ministry of Education, 特殊教育学校暂行规程 [Trials Rules on Special Education Schools] (1998).

16. Trial Methods of Inclusive Education, art. 19 (1994). The room is equipped with teaching and learning aids, rehabilitation equipment, books and materials. It serves as a resource center, providing support and assistance to the delivery of special education within regular schools.

17. Education Commission of Shanghai, 关于加强随班就读工作管理若干意见 [Several Opinions on Strengthening Inclusive Education Regulation in Shanghai], sec. 3, art. 5 (2006).

18. On March 30, 2007.

19. On August 1, 2008.

20. 关于残疾人保障法修改总体框架的方案及其说明（征求意见稿）[Plan of Revising the Law on the Protection with Disabilities and Its Explanations: A Draft Soliciting Feedbacks] (2005).

21. Art. 2.

22. *Ibid.*

23. Regulation on the Education of Persons with Disabilities, art. 12 (1994).

24. Provincial Government of Hebei, 河北省残疾人教育实施办法 [Implementation Methods for the Education of Persons with Disabilities], art. 8 (2001).

25. Regulation on the Education of Persons with Disabilities, art. 16 (1994).

26. Trial Methods of Inclusive Education, art. 5 (1994).

27. However, in poor countrysides where screening cannot be properly done, students suspected of mild intellectual disabilities can temporarily attend general education classes without evaluation.

28. Art. 9.

29. 关于发展特殊教育的若干意见 [Several Opinions on Developing Special Education], art. 6, 7 (1989).

30. Art. 19.
31. Art. 22.
32. Trial Methods of Inclusive Education (1994).
33. Art. 17. This Regulation also stipulates that for those school-age students, who because of their health condition cannot attend a school, local governments shall make an effort, if possible, to provide other forms of compulsory education to them. This does not sound like a legal mandate which local governments have to follow immediately. It is largely up to local governments' voluntary action.
34. Computed based on the data in Basic Statistics of Special Education of 2008, published by the Ministry of Education on December 24, 2009. http://www.moe.gov.cn/edoas/website18/29/info1261648301467429.htm (last visited July 18, 2010).
35. Trial Methods of Inclusive Education, art. 4, 5 (1994).
36. Art. 19.
37. Computed based on data in Basic Statistics of Special Education 2008 (2009).
38. Compulsory Education Law, art. 19 (2006).
39. Art. 47.
40. Art. 19.
41. Art. 25.
42. Art. 53.
43. Art. 54.
44. Regulation on the Education of Persons with Disabilities, art. 21 (1994); Trial Methods on Inclusive Education, art. 14 (1994).
45. Trial Methods on Inclusive Education, art. 15, 16, 19, 31 (1994).
46. Several Opinions on Strengthening Inclusive Education Regulation in Shanghai, sec. 3, art. 3 (2006).
47. Regulation on Special Education Schools, art. 19 (1998); Regulation on the Education of Persons with Disabilities, art. 20 (1994).
48. Regulation on Special Education Schools, art. 26–28 (1998).
49. Regulations on the Education of Persons with Disabilities, art. 19 (1994).
50. Regulation on Special Education Schools, art. 31 (1998); Trial Methods on Inclusive Education, art. 17 (1994).
51. Trial Methods on Inclusive Education, art. 34 (1994); Regulation on Special Education Schools, art. 13 (1998). But students with intellectual disabilities may repeat a grade in elementary education.
52. Trial Methods on Inclusive Education, art. 34 (1994); Regulation on Special Education Schools, art. 13 (1998).
53. Art. 28.
54. Compulsory Education Law, art. 29 (2006); Minor Protection Law, art. 21 (2006); Teacher Law, art. 37 (1993).
55. Regulation on Special Education Schools, art. 23 (1998).
56. Compulsory Education Law, art. 27, 57 (2006); Minor Protection Law, art. 18 (2006); Regulation on Special Education Schools, art. 15 (1998).
57. Commission of Education, 小学管理规程 [Standards on Elementary School Governance], art. 15 (1996); Regulation on Special Education Schools, art. 15 (1998).

58. Regulation on Special Education Schools, art. 12 (1998).

59. Trial Methods of Inclusive Education, art. 32 (1994).

60. *See, e.g.*, Bureau of Education of Qingdao City, 青岛市中小学处分暂行规定 [Trial Rule on Disciplinary Action in Elementary and Secondary School, Qingdao City], art. 12, 13 (2002).

61. Compulsory Education Law, art. 19, 57 (2006); Law on the Protection of Persons with Disabilities, art. 25 (2008).

62. Teacher Law, art. 37 (1993); Compulsory Education Law, art. 55 (2006); Regulation on the Education of Persons with Disabilities, art. 50 (1994).

63. Compulsory Education Law, art. 57 (2006).

64. 行政复议法 [Administrative Review Law], art. 6 § 9 (1999). An administrative litigation may also be filed against the agency if school attendance is recognized as a form of "personal or property rights" by the specific court. 行政诉讼法 [Administrative Litigation Law], art. 11 § 5 (1989).

65. Even though Article 60 of the Law on the Protection of Persons with Disabilities (2008) stipulates that aggrieved persons with disabilities can file a lawsuit, Article 63 of the same statute restricts the resolution of disputes over students' placement to the administrative chancel. In comparison, Article 64, the very next provision that deals with employment, clearly affords employees or job candidates a right to sue. Given this legal configuration, it is very likely that Article 63 is believed to supersede Article 60. Students with disabilities then do not have a private cause of action in placement disputes.

66. Regulation on the Education of Persons with Disabilities, art. 50 (1994); Teacher Law, art. 37 (1993).

67. Teacher Law, art. 37 (1993).

68. General Principles of Civil Law, art. 119 (1986). The damages are usually limited to compensation. Punitive damages are rarely granted.

69. Ministry of Education, 学生伤害事故处理办法 [Rules in Dealing with Student Injury Accidents], art. 9 (2002).

70. *Ibid.*, art. 27.

71. Law on the Protection of Persons with Disabilities, art. 8, 59 (2006).

72. Compulsory Education Law, art. 2 (2006); *compared with* 义务教育法实施细则 [Detailed Implementation Guideline on the Compulsory Education Law], art. 17 (1992).

73. Art. 21.

74. Art. 44.

75. Art. 6.

76. Law on the Protection of Persons with Disabilities, art. 21 (2008).

77. Vocational Education Law, art. 32 (1996).

78. Regulation on the Education of Persons with Disabilities, art. 28 (1994).

79. Art. 48.

80. 残疾人教育工作"十一五"实施方案 [Implementation Plan for the 11th Five-year Program on the Education of Persons with Disabilities (2006–2010)] (2007).

See also Regulation on the Education of Persons of Disabilities, art. 44 (1994); Law on the Protection of Persons with Disabilities, art. 21, 24 (2008); Compulsory Education Law, art. 42–47 (2006).

81. Regulation on the Education of Persons of Disabilities, art. 44 (1994).

82. *Ibid.*

83. Compulsory Education Law, art. 43 (2006).

84. Trial Methods of Inclusive Education, art. 28 (1994).

85. Law on the Protection of Persons with Disabilities, art. 28 (2008); Compulsory Education Law, art. 31 (2006).

86. *Wang Wei v. Pingdingshan Finance and Commerce School* (1997). The background and relevant legal documents can be found at Zhang Dakui, 全国首例残疾中学生状告报考学校侵犯受教育权案始末 [A Complete Account of the First Admission Lawsuit Filed by a Student with Disability against the School], 法律与生活 [Law and Life], iss. 2, 34–35 (1998).

87. Ministry of Education & Ministry of Health, 普通高等学校招生体检标准 [Standards for the Physical Examination of Entrants into General Higher Education Institutions] (1985).

88. Ministry of Education, Ministry of Health, & CDPF, 关于印发《普通高等学校招生体检工作指导意见》的通知 [A Notice on the Dissemination of the Advisory Guideline on Physical Examination in College Admission into General Higher Education Institutions] (2003).

89. Ministry of Health, 卫生部发布会介绍免疫规划和乙肝、疟疾防治工作 [Press Conference Release], April 21, 2008. http://www.gov.cn/xwfb/2008-04/21/content_950425.htm (last visited July 19, 2010).

90. Yirenping Center, 中国高等教育乙肝歧视状况调查 [A Survey of Discrimination against HBV Carriers in Chinese Higher Education] (2008).

91. It spreads mainly through pregnancy, blood, and sex.

92. http://bbs.hbvhbv.com/. The forum is entitled 肝胆相照, meaning "sincere treatment of each other." 肝胆相照 is a Chinese adage, and the first Chinese character is the word for *liver*.

93. Liu Zening & Li Shasha, 大学生名校门前抗议歧视乙肝 [Protest against Discrimination of Hepatitis B Patients in front of the Gate of a Famous University], 新京报 [The New Beijing News], April 11, 2009.

94. *See, e.g.*, Wen Quan, 20 名专家学者呼吁高考招录消除歧视 [Twenty Experts Call for the Elimination of Discrimination in College Admission], 法制日报 [Legal Daily], July 24, 2009.

95. 关于进一步规范入学和就业体检项目维护乙肝表面抗原携带者入学和就业权利的通知 [A Notice on Further Regulating the Use of HBV Testing in Admission or Recruitment Processes] (2010).

96. Law on the Protection of Persons with Disabilities, art. 2 (2008).

97. *Ibid.*, art. 3, 21.

98. Constitution, art. 46 (1982).

99. Law on the Protection of Persons with Disabilities, art. 22 (2008).

100. R. Weatherley & M. Lipsky, *Street-Level Bureaucrats and Institutional Innovation: Implementing Special-Education Reform*, 27 HARVARD EDUCATIONAL REVIEW 171 (1977).

101. Helen McCabe, *The Beginning of Inclusion in the People's Republic of China*, 28 RESEARCH & PRACTICE FOR PERSONS WITH SEVERE DISABILITIES 16 (2003).

102. Law on the Protection of Persons with Disabilities, art. 24 (2008); Regulation on the Education of Persons with Disabilities, art. 45 (1994).

5

The Legal Rights of Students with Disabilities in England

Special Needs, Special Rights?

Neville Harris

In a sense, a discussion focused on the "rights of students with disabilities" seems inconsistent with both the prevalent discourse of inclusiveness surrounding education and children's policy in England[1] as well as the idea of universal entitlement. International convention obligations which the United Kingdom (UK) has accepted reflect universalism in seeking to guarantee a right to education to all, as in the requirement under the European Convention on Human Rights that "no-one shall be denied the right to education"[2] and the declaration in the Universal Declaration on Human Rights that "everyone has the right to education."[3] Nevertheless, international law also acknowledges the necessity for protecting some people against less advantageous treatment through provisions providing for equal enjoyment of rights regardless of personal characteristics such as disability;[4] it also recognizes the need for special assistance for individuals with disabilities,[5] as discussed by Byrne and Lundy in this volume.

In England, domestic law singles out students with disabilities in order to afford specific protections and to ensure that special arrangements that are necessary for their education are set in place.[6] This is important, for one of the benchmarks against which the effectiveness of the state arrangements for education may be judged should be the extent to which they advance the interests of children and young people with significantly reduced capacity in realising educational goals and expectations.

The advancement of the interests of such students in England occurs via two separate although partly interrelated legislative schemes. One seeks to provide protection against discrimination on the ground of disability in relation to education: the Disability Discrimination Act 1995, as amended by the Special Educational Needs and Disability Act 2001, and in due course to be replaced by the Equality Act 2010.[7] The other scheme, in part IV of the Education Act 1996, applies to children with "special educational needs" (SEN), a statutory term which focuses on children who have a reduced learning capacity rather than a disability per se, as discussed in this chapter. This latter scheme aims to ensure that the needs of such children are identified and appropriately responded to, whether through standard educational provisions of the kind made for students in general or provisions that are special in the sense of being more specifically tailored to meet the identified educational needs. This scheme also aims to enable such children and especially their parents to influence the arrangements made for their education. The rights arising from these provisions are in addition to those enjoyed by students in general on matters such as standards of provision or religious or cultural preferences.[8]

The law of SEN has become particularly important in England for an array of reasons. First, quite a high proportion of children are classed as having SEN: one child in five, 20.9 percent as at January 2010,[9] according to official figures. This compares with a much smaller estimated proportion of children classed as having a disability, at between 3 percent and 5.4 percent of the school population as a whole, depending on which method of calculation is used.[10] A comparison of the two sets of figures illustrates that some children may have SEN due to "learning difficulties" but would not be classed as disabled under the 1995 Act.

The law of SEN is also important because of the way in which rights are a dominant feature of the legal framework. They include various procedural rights, including rights of appeal, that go significantly beyond those found in other areas of education, as discussed below. The potential for disputes in this field is particularly high as the policy and resource constraints on local authorities limit these agencies' ability to grant the wishes that parents have specific rights to express under the legislation, one of whose underlying aims is to involve them as partners with professionals in ensuring that the needs of their children are met.

A third reason for the importance of this area of the law is that it reflects a number of key policy goals whose realization can be highly problematic. Perhaps the most significant of these is "inclusion." This involves maximising the placement of children with SEN in mainstream settings rather than educating them separately and in isolation from students who do not have SEN. Given the pressures on them to meet the other policy objectives that the central government has pursued in recent decades, notably those of raising overall standards and operating in competition with other schools on the basis of educational outcomes, specifically examination success, school officials have been "caught in a tension between the inclusion agenda and the education reform agenda."[11] Another tension arises from the idea that there should be specified in fairly precise and legally binding terms by local authorities details of the education that must be provided to children, thereby affording guarantees to some students that are unavailable to others.

This is linked to the fourth reason why this field has become so important, namely that meeting the obligations owed in respect of individual students with SEN involves greater average expense than that incurred on other children. For example, it was reported in 2007 that the total number of children with SEN whose needs had to be met by a placement outside their local authority area, often at a residential school, was £11,000 and the average annual cost per student was £57,000.[12] By contrast, the average spend, including capital costs, per pupil in schools in England in 2007–08 was £5,620.[13]

The law of education in the UK is regionalized.[14] Northern Ireland and Scotland each have their own education legislation, and Wales has increasing legislative autonomy.[15] As such, this chapter concentrates on England, whose 8,100,000 students[16] represent approximately 80 percent of the total UK school population.[17]

THE EVOLVING LEGAL FRAMEWORK

The origins of the present law of special education in England can be found in the Education Act 1981. The Act gave effect to many of the recommendations of the Warnock Committee, whose report, published in 1978,[18] was groundbreaking in its attempt to break from the notion that students whose educational progress was hindered by disablement should be categorized exclusively with reference to various impairments and that they should be segregated from other groups of children. It sought, instead, an inclusive approach which involved integrated provision for children identified as having "special educational needs" due to difficulty in learning alongside other children wherever possible.[19] Warnock also placed great emphasis on parental participation and involvement in decisions concerning the education of children, reinforced by a framework of rights, including appellate rights. Also advanced was the idea of maintaining a written record of the needs of children and the provision required to meet them, known as a "statement."

The dominant features of the 1981 Act continue in the present law. Indeed, it retains the pivotal classification of children as having SEN if they have a "learning difficulty which calls for special educational provision to be made for [them]," being a provision that is additional to or different from that made for the generality of children of the same age in the area.[20]

The report and Act initiated a huge cultural shift in the field of education and continues to dominate the policy discourse. They are said to have been successful in "proliferating, if not spawning, an industry of special educational needs which remains,"[21] a comment which reflects the fact that considerable professional and financial resources are tied into this area of provision.

By the 1990s concerns emerged that the goals of Warnock were not fully being realized. For example, the views of parents were not being given sufficient weight in the assessment of their children.[22] Local authorities, of which there are currently 150 in England, differed in some cases quite widely in their approach to some of their key responsibilities, such as in the rates at which students were identified as needing a statement.[23] The flexibility in the notion of "special educational needs" that had been regarded as advantageous at the outset was found in practice to generate uncertainty: a report indicated that school staff were "working without a practical definition of special educational needs" and that local authorities were finding it very difficult to budget for provision for children with statements, because there was "no firm basis on which to assess how many pupils will require extra help."[24]

Between 1987 and 1991 there was a more than 10 percent increase in the proportion of children with statements. Although the proportion of school students with statements was still only approximately 2 percent, a House of Commons Committee called for a reduction.[25] The increase was causing strains on local authority budgets and a risk that if the trend continued, "resources will be spread over a larger number of pupils than was envisaged in the Warnock report."[26] A contributory factor in the increase was almost certainly the emergence and growth of consumerism in education, a facet of which was significant parental demands concerning provision.[27] Appeals were increasing in number, and many ended up in the in-tray of the Secretary of State.[28] The influence of "benign professionalism" and the idea of equity in this field were beginning to be weakened by "choice, competition and parental self-interest."[29]

In 1992 an official report recommended improvements to the system.[30] The report identified a need for national guidance to clarify the basis on which the judgments that faced local authorities such as whether there should be a statement should have been made. The report also called for parents of students who required statements to be given a right to state a preference for schools to be specified as the placements of their children and to appeal if denied it. Further, the report recommended that the processes of assessment and the making of statements should be speeded up through the introduction of prescribed time limits for their completion.

The Education Act 1993 gave effect to these recommendations. The national guidance took the form of a *Code of Practice,* which local authorities and schools were required to take into account in carrying out their functions.[31] Provision was made in the Act for setting maximum time limits for the completion of assessments and making of statements.[32] Parents acquired a right to express preferences for schools to be specified in the statements of their children with local authorities placed under the duty to adhere to parental choices unless, for instance, they were incompatible with the efficient use of resources. An attempt was made to reduce the numbers of statements made by local authorities by imposing a threshold of necessity. Previously, local authorities were to make statements when in their "opinion" the assessment of children suggested that one should be made; thenceforth under the 1993 Act the question would be whether it was "necessary" to determine the special educational provision to be made for children. In reality, this new test did not achieve its objective and the numbers of statements continued to rise. The 1993 Act also tightened up the inclusion duty by applying it to all such children and not as previously only those with statements.

Finally, and particularly importantly, the 1993 Act introduced an independent appeal tribunal to determine, in a more timely fashion, appeals against a range of specific SEN decisions made by local authorities which was wider than under the previous system.[33] The tribunal, known as the Special Educational Needs Tribunal (SENT), was established in 1994. It was the first and remained the only appellate body in the field of education in England that was required to have a panel with a legally qualified chairperson for each hearing. Moreover, appeals against the decisions of SENT could be made to the High Court on a point of law. Although the courts had already become involved in SEN challenges through the process of judicial review[34] in landmark cases which held that a need for speech therapy was covered by the legislation on SEN[35] and clarifying the requirements of the contents of statements,[36] the establishment of a direct appeal route led to a significant development of case law in this field, which today far exceeds that covering any other field of education.[37] Despite later reforms, the above features have continued, although, as discussed below, the tribunal has been restructured. Diverse education statutes were consolidated into a single Act, the Education Act 1996, and the SEN provisions were placed in part IV of the Act, where they remain.

From 1997, when the new Labour Government by Tony Blair was elected, there was a considerable investment of capital resources in education, combined with an emphasis on raising educational standards, significantly improving levels of pupil attainment, reinforced by national targets, and a more coordinated approach to services provision. Arrangements concerning SEN and disability were to be firmly integrated into general educational policy and social provision for disabled people more generally.[38]

The government preferred "direct support" for children with SEN rather than expending resources on "bureaucratic procedures," such as making statements. The government argued that there were strong educational, social, and moral grounds for children with SEN to be educated in mainstream schools.[39] The government also wanted to explore the use of mediation rather than the appeal system for resolving disputes.[40] The government thus established a clear agenda for ensuring that children with SEN were identified early, increasing the inclusion rate and reducing the numbers of statements.[41]

Following a period of consultation, the government set out a three-year programme of reform,[42] parts of which required changes to the legislation, others to the Code of Practice. Most of the changes were implemented in 2002, under part 1 of the Special Educational Needs and Disability Act 2001 and a new *Special Educational Needs Code of Practice* (2001).[43] Apart from a small number of relatively minor subsequent changes, these still comprise the current framework. In addition to offering detailed guidance on all aspects of the SEN regime, the *Code* sets out the fundamental principles underpinning it:

- Children with SEN should have their needs met;
- The SEN of children will normally be met in mainstream schools or settings;
- The views of children should be sought and taken into account;[44]
- Parents have a vital role to play in supporting the education of their children;[45]
- Children with SEN should be offered full access to a broad, balanced, and relevant education, including appropriate curricula for the foundation stage and the National Curriculum.[46]

The 2001 Act made very important changes to the law. First, the duty to educate children with SEN in mainstream schools was strengthened[47] by establishing a legal presumption that all students without statements should be educated in mainstream schools and limiting the circumstances in which those with statements may not be educated in such settings.[48] Second, new duties were placed on local authorities to ensure that advice and information were made available to parents of children with SEN in their area and that arrangements for the resolution of disagreements between parents and schools and/or local authorities were available.[49] Third, schools were placed under a duty to inform parents of children without statements of special educational provisions made at the schools of their children.[50] Fourth, the Act introduced clear procedures, incorporating parental involvement, for the amendment of existing statements.[51] Fifth, stricter obligations were placed on local authorities to comply with orders made by the tribunal,[52] whose name and role were extended. The SENT became the Special Educational Needs and Disability Tribunal (SENDisT), reflecting its widened jurisdiction that now included complaints of disability discrimination against schools and local authorities.[53]

Despite these improvements there remain significant difficulties with the field of SEN. Recently, a government-commissioned inquiry led by Sir Brian Lamb[54] resulted in a set of recommendations designed to improve parental involvement and confidence in the SEN system. The Lamb report is discussed in the emerging issues section of this chapter.

As mentioned above, the disability discrimination duties are set out in separate legislation, part 4 of the Disability Discrimination Act (DDA) 1995, as amended. The rights of students with disabilities under this framework are based on the recommendations of the Disability Rights Task Force that was established in 1997 to review the DDA and make suggestions for reform. Its report[55] recommended that in order to fill an "unacceptable" gap in the DDA's protection of school students it should be given a right not to be unfairly discriminated against by school officials or local authorities and that it should cover all aspects of school life, including decisions on school admission.[56] The Report also proposed that there should, in effect, be a duty to make "reasonable adjustments" to policies, practices, and procedures which placed students with disabilities "at a substantial disadvantage to others,"[57] although not the making of physical alterations to buildings. School officials might, for example, have to timetable classes with a wheelchair-bound child in a ground-floor room if a building did not have an elevator. However, the Task Force acknowledged that a "defence" was required because in some situations differential treatment of a disabled student might be justified, such as where a physical disability precluded certain practical work or where students' severe behavioral problems necessitated their segregation. The report also recommended that access to education for students with disabilities should be strengthened by placing a duty on school officials and local authorities to plan strategically towards the realization of this goal.[58]

It is clear that the Task Force's recommendations were pragmatic and realistic rather than purely idealistic. For example, the needs of children for auxiliary aids and services could be dealt with via the current SEN framework rather than through additional DDA duties.[59] Establishing a duty to make physical alterations to school premises in response to the needs of individual children was considered less effective towards improving the position of students with disabilities collectively than a strategic general duty to publish plans to improve physical access to facilities and work towards increased accessibility.[60] The Task Force was also seemingly conscious of local budgetary constraints, but nevertheless proposed that schools should be prepared to expend small amounts to effect minor physical alterations to premises. With regard to redress, it was proposed that rather than the standard process of complaint to the county court, there should be a right to bring a complaint under the DDA to the SENT as it then was, which was a less formal body and one in which legal representation was less important.[61]

The government accepted all of the above recommendations.[62] The recommendations were included in the 2001 Act and were expected to have a "considerable impact" on schools and local authorities.[63] The DDA 1995, which will be replaced by the Equality Act 2010 when the latter is brought into force, although the law's protection in this field will be mostly unaltered,[64] outlaws discrimination against school students either. The DDA forbids students from being treated less favorably than other children who are not similarly disabled[65] where such treatment is unjustified or by a failure to take reasonable steps to prevent their being substantially disadvantaged compared to peers[66] to the detriment of the person(s) concerned. These duties apply in the context of admission to school, including the terms of admission; the education or associated services provided; or exclusion, whether temporary or permanent.[67] Complaints lay to the SENDisT, but as discussed below, on 3 November 2008 its jurisdiction was subsumed within the new First-Tier Tribunal, which is also responsible for SEN appeals. A further appeal became possible on a point of law to the Upper Tribunal (Administrative Appeals Chamber), but no longer to the High Court.[68]

The DDA 1995 also requires local authorities to prepare accessibility strategies and plans such as on improving the physical environment in schools and enhancing the participation of students with disabilities in curriculum as well as to review and, where appropriate, revise them.[69] A new disability Code of Practice covering schools was also issued,[70] separate from the SEN *Code of Practice*, which was referred to above. One of the matters the disability *Code* addresses is the relationship between the DDA and the Education Act 1996. The *Code* states that the former is intended to "dovetail" with the latter and that "[t]o the extent that disabled children rely on special educational provision to have their needs met, equal opportunities for disabled children are dependent on the quality of the provision made through the SEN framework."[71]

Unfortunately, it has been found that the relationship between the DDA 1995 and the SEN framework has not worked well, largely due to schools' misunderstanding and lack of awareness of their duties under the former. When it conducted an investigation into SEN in 2006 the House of Commons Education and Skills Committee learned that there was "increasing confusion between SEN and disability" and "a great deal of work still to do to pull together the disability and SEN agendas and legislation."[72] The idea of a coordinated response both nationally and locally to the needs of students with disabilities was also promoted via the government's *Every Child Matters* strategy. This strategy emphasised a partnership approach to services for children, with, for example, better coordination between different public and voluntary agencies, integrated planning, and joint commissioning of services.[73]

KEY FEATURES OF THE LEGAL/ADMINISTRATIVE FRAMEWORK AND ITS OPERATION: FUNDING, IDENTIFICATION, AND ASSESSMENT

Leaving aside special schools, namely those exclusively serving pupils with SEN, schools receive funding allocations based on a formula which is weighted to take account of the numbers of enrolled students with SEN. The funding allocation forms part of the delegated budget provided to schools by the local authority that retains amounts needed to meet costs involved in, for example, providing central support services and advice to schools and to fund the educational provision that is identified in the statements of SEN which schools cannot provide from their own delegated budgets. This is still the basic position, although the delegation of an increased amount of funding has been encouraged in recent years but has proved controversial, with assertions that some children are not being assessed or issued with statements because extra funding to meet the needs of such students is being delegated to schools.[74] A House of Commons Committee reported that while delegated funding gave school officials the flexibility to intervene early to meet needs, its disadvantage was that "the money is not ring-fenced and it is difficult to know whether it is being spent on SEN."[75]

A range of duties are owed to children identified as having SEN. Their extent in individual cases depends on the level of support that students need and how much progress they can make with support provided by the school alone. The basic duties include the duty on the local authority to arrange for parents to be provided with advice and information relating to the needs of their children and the duty to publicize its advice and information services.[76] School governing bodies must use their "best endeavours" to make sure that children with SEN receive the special educational provision they need.[77] The duties increase once children undergo formal assessments with a view to the making of statements.

It was noted above that children with SEN are those who have a "learning difficulty" calling for special educational provisions to be made for them.[78] The definition of learning difficulty is that of having a "significantly greater difficulty in learning than the majority of children of that age" or having a "disability which either prevents or hinders him from making use of educational facilities of a kind generally provided for children of his age. . . ."[79] Children must not merely be those whose capacities to learn are reduced; they must also as a result of that difficulty require "special educational provision," which, as noted above, is provision of a kind that is not provided to the generality of students in the area. That these rather broad definitions have survived unaltered should not be taken to imply that they have been unproblematic. For example, the law, reflecting a flexible approach, does not prescribe which conditions or disablements are covered. Juridical analysis regarding conditions such as dyslexia[80] and a need for speech therapy,[81] both of which were held to be covered, and giftedness[82] and cultural needs,[83] which were held not to be SEN, has been important.

The definition of "special educational provision" has received perhaps the most judicial attention. Legal disputes centered on this definition are not surprising given its potential implications for local authority expenditure. When it is set out in a child's statement such provision is mandatory and must be funded, whereas *non*educational provision is discretionary. Unfortunately, the courts have found the dividing line between the two forms of provision somewhat fuzzy. For instance, in a case concerning a boy aged twelve who could not walk, sit up, or stand and was totally reliant on adults for all of his mobility needs and for dressing, washing, toileting, and feeding, the question whether his needs for physiotherapy, occupational therapy, and speech therapy were educational needs requiring special educational provision was held by the Court of Appeal to be a matter for the local authority or the tribunal to determine. Parliament had deliberately chosen to leave certain matters to professionals' interpretation. Sedley LJ wrote that while there were some areas of provision that would be clearly either educational or noneducational, there was a "potentially large intermediate area of provision" which was capable of ranking as either and in respect of which the relevant bodies were expected "to exercise a case-by-case judgment which no prescriptive legislation could ever hope to anticipate."[84]

The categories of SEN used by the Department for Education for the compilation of statistics are fairly broad. The largest categories, by primary type of need, in January 2009 were, in descending order, "severe learning difficulty"; "moderate learning difficulty"; Autistic Spectrum Disorder; behavioral, emotional, and social difficulties (BESD); and "profound and multiple learning difficulty."[85] Yet, there were significant variations between boys and girls.[86] The statistics help to give a broad picture of the kinds of conditions that are most likely to affect children with SEN, but as with the broad notion of SEN itself they present a rather generalized picture which can lead to oversimplification of students' problems.

As a House of Commons Committee put it, "Children exist on a broad continuum of needs and learning styles but do not fit into neat categories of different sorts of children."[87] These broad official categories of SEN also emphasize the distinction between the legal concepts of SEN and disability. Although some of the SEN categories are specifically related to a physical or mental disability, notably those of "hearing impairment" and "visual impairment," most are not. In the DDA 1995,[88] disability is defined as a physical or mental "impairment," including one arising from a mental illness, whether a clinically recognized mental illness or not, which has a "substantial and long-term adverse effect" such as one that lasts, or is likely to persist, for at least twelve months, on the person's "ability to carry out normal day to day activities."

Activities include both mental elements such as the exercise of memory or the ability to "concentrate, learn or understand" as well as physical aspects such as manual dexterity or physical coordination. Although there is an obvious overlap between some of the categories of SEN and disability, the differences in the statutory constructions of the two concepts[89] reflect the different principal purposes of the respective Acts—namely, to meet educational needs through appropriate provision and to prevent inferior treatment relative to other people on account of a person's physical and/or mental disablement. Since there is a duty under the DDA 1995 to make "reasonable adjustments," as noted, provision made by school officials could be directed at both meeting SEN and preventing disadvantages for the purposes of the 1995 Act in some cases.[90]

A significant disability such as deafness, blindness or severe autism will usually have been identified before children enter formal education. In the case of other children, parental concern and/or the fact that pupils are not making satisfactory progress should precipitate identification. Under the 1996 Act, school governing bodies also have a duty to make teachers aware of the importance of identifying and providing for students with SEN.[91] The SEN *Code of Practice* places a good deal of emphasis on the monitoring of progress by teachers and the importance of early identification of needs. Not all teachers are experts in diagnosing diverse forms of SEN. If pupils were struggling or appeared to have problems, teachers would probably be expected, as part of their ordinary professional duties and in accordance with the *Code*, to refer them to the school's Special Educational Needs Coordinator (SENCO) or a senior member of school staff.[92]

The process of intervention is referred to in the *Code* as "School Action." The strategies to enable children to progress would be recorded within Individual Education Plan (IEPs), to be reviewed at least twice a year. IEPs have no specific legal status, and decisions over them carry no appeal rights. Children who make little or no progress over prolonged periods and who have chronic behavioral or communication problems may need the support of external services; such arrangements, to be included in IEPs, are classified as "School Action Plus."[93]

If school officials consider that children have "demonstrated significant cause for concern," they would be expected to refer pupils to local authorities.[94] Moreover, negligent failure by educational professionals to do so could be actionable in tort.[95] When students are referred to them, authorities have to decide whether a formal assessment is needed with a view to determining the special educational provision that is required; in other words, whether a statement of SEN is needed. Local authorities have a separate duty to identify children who may need statements.[96] Formal assessments requested by parents or governing bodies may not be made where previous statutory assessments occurred within the previous six months.[97]

Consistent with the principle of parental participation in assessments, local authorities have a duty to serve parents with notice of proposed statutory assessments of their children. This arises where authorities consider that children have or probably have SEN and it is "necessary for the authority to determine the special educational provision which any learning difficulty [the child] has may call for."[98] Notice must provide parents with information on the assessment procedure, the name of the authority's officer from whom further information can be obtained, and their right to make representations and to submit written evidence.[99]

At the end of this consultation process, and at any rate within six weeks from the request, authorities have to decide whether to carry out assessments and then give written notice of their decision. Parents who want their children to be assessed often feel a profound sense of disappointment when the authority refuses to do so. Research has shown that parental confidence in such decisions tends to be undermined by inconsistent explanations given for them by different officers and by inconsistent messages from different professionals on whether an assessment would be appropriate.[100] Although decisions regarding assessments may have very important bearings on the future education and its outcomes for children, the argument that such an action might affect the enjoyment of the right to education for the purposes of the European Convention on Human Rights may be difficult to sustain given the amount of flexibility given to individual states' organization and governance of public education.[101] However, there is a right of appeal to the First-Tier Tribunal over a decision not to comply with a request for an assessment.

The conduct of assessments is regulated.[102] The idea is that assessments will be multiprofessional in which medical, educational, social and psychological expertise, as appropriate, is brought to bear. Assessments normally have to be carried out within ten weeks from decisions to assess.[103] Parents have a right to attend any examinations of their children and to submit any information.[104] In addition to the professional advice to be sought when carrying out assessments, authorities must seek advice from the parents.[105]

Despite the emphasis placed on parental rights, there is an element of compulsion: parents may be fined if the child is of compulsory school age and does not attend the examination.[106] Although the legislation does not specifically require the views of children to be taken into account, the SEN *Code of Practice* directs local authorities to seek to obtain those views and record them as part of the assessment process. If children are unable to contribute, their views should be sought via appropriate agents, be it parents, class teachers, educational psychologists, or other adults who know the child involved.[107]

DECISIONS CONCERNING PLACEMENT AND OTHER ASPECTS OF EDUCATION: INCLUSION, CHOICE, AND FUNDING

There is an important interplay between three key policy principles and their corresponding legislative provisions: first, an inclusion principle, that students with SEN should generally be educated in mainstream settings alongside pupils without such needs; second, a partnership principle, that since parents may be assumed to know their children best and be considered to have legitimate moral claims to influence the educational environments in which their children will be educated, they should have some input into the arrangements to be made for the children, including a degree of choice over their placements; and third, a formalization principle, that for children whose needs require formal assessments there should be formal records of their needs and the provision to meet them to ensure certainty and to guarantee the rights of children to appropriate provision.

As noted earlier, the first of these principles was reinforced under the 2001 Act. Children with SEN for whom no statements are maintained must be educated in mainstream, as opposed to special, schools. There is also a statutory presumption that children for whom there is a statement will be educated in mainstream schools. This presumption can only be rebutted on the grounds that such placements would not be compatible with the wishes of the parents or with the provision of efficient education for other children.[108] Prior to the 2001 Act there was a similar exception to this inclusion duty, but it applied to all children with SEN, regardless of whether they had statements.

Attempts to invoke the European Convention on Human Rights to support parental preferences concerning inclusion, on the ground that the Convention requires that respect must be paid to the right of parents to have their children taught in accordance with their philosophical convictions,[109] have not been successful.[110] However, parents continue to have a right to elect to educate their children at independent, or private, schools at their own expense, although relatively few do so; the requirement for education in a mainstream setting gives way to this parental right when exercised.[111]

Despite the strengthening of the inclusion duty via the 2001 Act, the proportion of children with SEN being educated in mainstream schools has been falling. As of January 2009, when 221,671 students were the subject of statements, 55.6 percent were educated in mainstream primary or secondary schools, 3 percent fewer than in 2006 and over 5 percent fewer than in 2000; 37.5 percent were placed in maintained special schools and 3.9 percent were placed in independent or nonmaintained special schools.[112]

Although inclusion is widely supported in principle, its success in practice may be dependent on schools being properly supported by both central and local policies and by support services, funding, and well-trained staff, which cannot be guaranteed; and in any event some parents worry that their children will not cope well emotionally or educationally in mainstream settings.[113] An Audit Commission report commented that "[d]isproportionately high levels of non-attendance and exclusion among children with SEN suggest that some are having a poor time" and called for local and national action to ensure that schools have the skills necessary to make inclusion successful.[114] In response to this and other criticisms, the government brought forward in 2004 plans for a new Inclusion Development Programme.[115]

The making of statements provides opportunities for parents to exercise a degree of choice. Statements are made by local authorities and must have the prescribed contents,[116] set out in separate parts: a child's personal details (part 1), details of the child's SEN (part 2), the special educational provision to be made for the child (part 3), the name or the type of school at which the child should be placed (part 4), any noneducational needs the child has (part 5), and any noneducational provisions which the local authorities propose to make for the child (part 6). In addition, the professional advice secured as part of the assessment process (above) must be appended.

The legal effect of statements, once made, is that local authorities must ensure that the specified educational provisions are made for the children; the authorities may arrange for any specific noneducational provisions to be made for the children; and schools named as the placements for children have a statutory duty to admit them.[117] As noted, therefore, authorities must fund the special educational provisions which they specified.

Local authorities sometimes resist a high level of specificity regarding the educational provision described in statements in order to avoid commitments to particular levels of resource provisions which may be difficult to adjust later without going through the formal process of statement amendment.[118] If the placements of children are in independent schools named in statements, local authorities must also pay the relevant costs associated with them, such as school fees. The fact that the fundamental issue in decisions on statements is the question of funding and costs is reinforced by the SEN *Code*'s advice that the decisions of local authorities whether to make statements should hinge on whether any educational provisions children need could be met by schools from their own resources, with or without support from outside professionals.[119] If answered in the affirmative, statements should not be needed.[120] Yet, in general, local authorities have a significant degree of discretion over the making of statements.

The first stage in making statements involves the issuing of draft statements following assessments. Local authorities must send parents a copy of proposed statements along with notice explaining their rights in connection with it.[121] The parents' principal rights, governed by Schedule 27 to the 1996 Act, are: (i) to express a preference (and to give reasons for it) for local authority maintained schools to be named in the statement; (ii) to make representations to the authority about the content of the statement; (iii) to meet with one of the local authority's officers to discuss the statement and possibly a subsequent meeting to address further concerns;[122] and (iv) to appeal against the contents of the statement.[123]

The schools selected by parents must be included in part 4 of statements unless either of two statutory grounds applies. The first is that a school is unsuitable for a child, having regard to the child's age, ability or aptitude or SEN. The second is that the child's attendance at the school would be incompatible with the efficient use of resources or the efficient education of other children alongside whom the child would be educated.[124] Parents attach a high premium to securing their choice of schools, but local authorities frequently rely on these grounds of exception, and especially the inefficient use of resources, where parental wishes would give rise to significant additional expense. The critical questions have been how the extra costs of placements sought by parent should be assessed, such as, for example, whether the cost of transporting the child to the school should be considered relevant[125] and the point at which the cost of preferred placements should outweigh their educational advantages.[126]

Many other disputes over statements have concerned the division between their specified educational and noneducational provisions.[127] Due to the fact that they only must fund educational provisions, local authorities may often be keen to classify arrangements as noneducational. Many of the recent disputes around this issue have concerned the needs of children for a "24 hour curriculum" or "waking day" curricula,[128] in which activities outside of school settings are considered as part of the response to their educational needs: are they necessarily a form of "educational" provision, so that local authorities have a duty to fund residential placements in order that all their SEN can be met?[129] Similar issues and equivalent processes arise in connection with proposed amendments to statements. Statements have to be reviewed annually, and amendments can be proposed. Where statements are already in operation and specify named school placements, parents also have a right to request that different schools be named.[130]

Some of the best specialist provisions for children with disabilities are in the private sector. The law permits such provision to be arranged by local authorities, and clearly if such schools offer the only environment that can truly meet the needs of children, then authorities would have no alternative but to fund the placements. As noted, since the parental right under Schedule 27 to express a preference for school placement is restricted to local authority funded schools, it excludes independent schools. Parents who want independent schools named as placements may seek support from the general duty on local authorities under Section 9 of the Education Act 1996 to "have regard to the general principle . . . that pupils are to be educated in accordance with the wishes of their parents, so far as that is compatible with the provision of efficient instruction and the avoidance of unreasonable public expenditure."

The parental right arising out of this duty is thus subject to similar conditionality to that affecting the Schedule 27 preference right. Although Section 9 decisions often require a similar balancing exercise involving weighing up the extra costs of provision against its educational benefits,[131] the courts have indicated that "parental preference will not prevail over unreasonable public expenditure."[132] It seems fairly clear that the right under Section 9 is weaker than that under Schedule 27 in terms of facilitating parental choice of SEN provision,[133] even though it may be more difficult for a local authority to show that expenditure would involve an inefficient use of resources under Schedule 27 than to show that expenditure would be unreasonable (under Section 9).[134]

The range of rights held by parents concerning statements aside, the technicality of the law and the procedures undoubtedly presents barriers to their enjoyment. Parents may well need guidance. In meeting their duty to ensure that parents of children with SEN receive advice and information, local authorities are expected to make arrangements for "parent partnership services" (PPS)[135] and must provide parents with contact details of the local PPS when sending draft statements.[136] Minimum standards that PPSs are expected to meet in carrying out their role have been specified, emphasizing the provision of accurate and "neutral" information on parents' rights and the relevant law and procedures.[137] Although PPS support for parents is important, the quality of these services varies due in part to differences in their personnel and budget levels.[138]

As indicated, parents have various rights in connection with assessments and the making of statements. However, many parents lack confidence in exercising them and in the system itself. The inspection and standards watchdog Ofsted reported in 2006 that formal assessment was overly complex and gave insufficient account to children's views and that while statements were helpful in identifying needs and recording information that was useful when students moved school or settings, the process was "overly cumbersome and bureaucratic."[139] Recent research found that parental experience of the assessment process was stressful, and some parents lacked confidence in engaging with professionals in order to, for example, question the contents of statements, which they often found difficult to understand.[140] The Lamb Inquiry recommended enhanced support for parental involvement in these processes, improved local authority communication with parents and better training for staff.[141] Lamb's essential message is that "it is not the current system that is at fault but rather the failure to comply with both the spirit and the letter of the framework."[142]

Dispute Resolution

As noted, there is a well-established independent appeals process dating back to 1994 for SEN disputes and now involving appeals to the First-Tier Tribunal (FTT) (Health, Education and Social Care Chamber). The Tribunal continues to be comprised of a legally qualified member, now a "tribunal judge," and two other members with appropriate expertise in SEN/disability. The reforms, under the Tribunals, Courts, and Enforcement Act 2007, also established the Upper Tribunal as the second-tier appeal body. SEN and disability cases are dealt with by this tribunal's Administrative Appeals Chamber. No other kinds of educational dispute brought by parents or children in England have a second-tier appeal route.

Most legal challenges in SEN/disability cases ultimately take the form of an appeal to the FTT. However, in a small number of cases, namely those concerning the legality of decisions or actions by schools or local authorities which are not covered by the statutory grounds of appeal[143] or where the legality of broader policies is in question, legal challenges involve application for judicial review. This was the pre-1994 route for all SEN cases where judicial rulings were sought. It now has only a residual role.[144]

The FTT operates under procedural rules which cover matters from entitlement to oral hearings, the right to bring witnesses and make use of representatives, and interlocutory matters concerned with the lodging of appeals, the replies of local authorities and so on.[145] The Tribunal is, in effect, under a duty to try to minimise the level of formality in the hearing. The post-2001 procedures have incorporated a "case management" element designed to assist in the expeditious and efficient resolution of the appeal, including early settlement. The average duration of appeal from registration to disposal is long and has lengthened since the early years of the Tribunal, as the number of appeals has increased: it was 6.4 months in 2008–09 and 5.8 months in 2007–08.[146] Yet, only about one-third of cases proceed to hearings; the majority are settled or withdrawn at an earlier stage, although a large number are settled at the eleventh hour.

Only parents have the right of appeal, or complaint, in disability cases, not the children themselves.[147] This can be problematic where children are in the care of local authorities as a "looked after" child, since a local authority which is the potential respondent to an appeal is also, in law, the child's "parent." The UN Committee on the Rights of the Child, which has made reference to this problem, has recommended that children with SEN should have an independent right of appeal throughout the UK.[148]

The number of appeals registered grew each year between 1994–95 and 2002–03, at which point they peaked at just over 3,500. Since then the number has fluctuated but has remained over 3,000 each year.[149] The number of disability discrimination cases has been much smaller, less than 150 per annum and only 100 in 2008–09.[150] Still, this is not perhaps surprising, as disagreements over SEN would be expected to arise more frequently than concerns about disability discrimination per se. Note that the rules of procedure permit discrimination complaints to be pursued in combination with an SEN appeal, in the same proceedings.

Since its inception, the Tribunal has earned a good reputation for being generally fair and unbiased. It is on the whole trusted by parents and their legal and other advisers.[151] The recent Penfold survey found a general perception among parents that Tribunal hearings had been "a good experience," offering "a professional environment without animosity," although some reported that the hearings were overly formal and courtlike.[152] Local authorities, on the other hand, are less satisfied with the tribunals. In Riddell et al.'s survey it was discovered that 43 percent of English authorities regarded tribunals as unsatisfactory or highly unsatisfactory and officers perceived that "the tribunal's approach favoured parents," especially parents who were "articulate and able to afford legal backing."[153] There is other evidence that it is middle-class parents who are best able to cope with and make effective use of the tribunal process[154] while those from low socio-economic backgrounds are at a disadvantage.[155] Lamb reported that many parents thought that bringing appeals was "too difficult and complex" and were unable to fight their cases without legal help, prompting a recommendation that support should be available as "exceptional funding" under the legal aid scheme in particularly complex cases.[156] Legal representation was used at the hearing by 22 percent of parents in 2007–08, falling to 18 percent in 2008–09,[157] but most of those who used it would have had to pay for it.

The success rate for appeals at the tribunal certainly offers parents encouragement to follow this route: in 2008–09 the proportion of appeals upheld in relation to the three categories of case with the most appeals was as follows:

- refusal to assess: 66 percent were upheld
- statement contents excluding named school placement: 94 percent upheld
- statement contents including named school placement: 92 percent upheld

Even in appeals solely concerning school placement, where resource issues often dominate, 61 percent of appeals succeeded.[158]

There is a general policy push in the UK towards alternative dispute resolution, including the use of mediation.[159] Mediation was playing a role in SEN disputes by the late 1990s, but there was a concern that the process was insufficiently independent of the parties to the dispute.[160] Often it was undertaken by parent partnership services. The government acknowledged the problem while accepting the recommendation that mediation would only have a chance of succeeding if its availability became mandatory.[161]

The 2001 Act requires local authorities to "make arrangements with a view to avoiding or resolving disagreements between authorities and parents' about the exercise of their functions concerning SEN and to ensure that independent persons were appointed for this work."[162] It is clear that mediation is what is anticipated.[163] Different mediation provision arrangements are made by local authorities, with many buying in services from established mediation organizations either individually or in regional groups.[164] Legal representation in mediations is discouraged, but parties may have lawyers present with them as advisers.[165]

Local authorities are under a duty to make the dispute resolution arrangements known to parents in general and to inform them individually when notifying them of the decision about their children.[166] Despite these duties and the fact that opting for mediation does not interfere with the right of appeal since the two processes can run concurrently, mediation has not been greatly used.[167] Indeed, in a survey in which fifty-five local authorities provided information the average number of actual SEN mediations in 2007–08 was just over one per authority.[168] The researchers uncovered a number of reasons for the paucity of mediations, in particular parents' lack of awareness or proper understanding of mediation; their lack of trust in the process; their overriding desire to have the Tribunal decide their case; and the influence of advisers and representatives' negative views of mediation.[169] The Tribunal, on the other hand, is attractive for being able to make definitive rulings in cases in which informal negotiations have not resolved disputes. Negotiations, in fact, play an important role in this field and are another reason why the more formal process of mediation tends not to be used.

At the same time, there have been some problems with the implementation of Tribunal decisions. Although there are time limits for taking steps ordered by tribunals, such as giving notice of assessments or making statements,[170] some authorities delay or avoid implementation. In such a case, parents would have to apply for judicial review to compel authorities to act or seek redress via complaints of "maladministration" to the independent Local Government Ombudsman (LGO).[171]

The LGO is a statutory body set up to deal with complaints against local authorities, although it cannot entertain school-based complaints relating to matters covered by a right of appeal.[172] If maladministration has occurred and has resulted in an injustice to the complainant, an LGO can make a number of recommendations for remedies by authorities, ranging from apologies through to the taking of specific remedial actions or the payment of compensation, including compensation for inconvenience. While the LGO cannot issue binding rulings, its recommendations are almost always adhered to by the parties.

In 2008–09 there were 232 complaints about SEN lodged with the LGO in England.[173] Recently, the LGO's jurisdiction was extended to include complaints about the actions of head teachers and governing bodies of schools; initially this has occurred only on a pilot basis in selected areas.[174] The LGO route is probably not one that most advisers would recommend for SEN disputes not only because it will probably take longer to reach a conclusion but also since the focus of investigations will be on processes and administration rather than the educational and legal merits of disputes.[175]

EMERGING ISSUES

Following a change of government to the current Conservative-Liberal Democrat Alliance administration in May 2010, it remains to be seen how far the previous administration's SEN policy agenda will be adopted. Particularly important is the question of how far the new administration takes up the previous government's commitment to act on key issues highlighted by the Lamb inquiry, outlined earlier.

The Labour Government's implementation plan in response to Lamb included improvements to training for staff undertaking SEN work; better information and advice for parents; improvements to parent partnership services; better quality statements of SEN; and a new right of appeal against a refusal to amend a statement.[176] The last of these was introduced in the final days of the last Parliament.[177] Further, the extension of the LGO jurisdiction to include school-based complaints was also a response to Lamb. The Labour Government also expressed support for the idea that students should be given an independent right of appeal in SEN cases and to complain in disability cases, but only established a working group on those matters.[178] Moreover, the Labour Government proposed to relaunch the legal aid "exceptional funding" scheme for SEN cases.[179]

The confidence of parents in general, not merely those with children with SEN, was also to be improved via new statutory "parent guarantees." The guarantees (there were also "pupil guarantees") were to be set out in a document issued by the Secretary of State. These guarantees related to the realisation of specified "ambitions" concerned with, for example, exercising choice and having parents engaged in the learning and development of their children, with information and support to facilitate these opportunities. Even so, it is not clear that the guarantees would have been easily enforceable, if at all, and their purpose seems on reflection to be somewhat political. In any event, they did not have opposition support and were dropped in the runup to the general election.

One of the major concerns arises out of the policy, followed by both the current government and its predecessor, of encouraging officials in local authority maintained schools to change status to "academies." Academies are officially classed as independent schools but are in large part funded by the state, although they may also receive some private/corporate sponsorship. Academies, which operate under a funding agreement with the Department for Education, must provide education for students with "different abilities" who are drawn from their local area.[180] This effectively means that it would not be possible for a funding agreement to be made with a school that selects by ability,[181] which should in theory ensure access for students with SEN. As Wolfe explains, though, academies are not subject to the range of statutory duties concerning SEN unless their funding agreements expressly put them under any such obligations.[182] Academies would not thus be covered by the SEN *Code* unless agreements imposed that obligation on them. Moreover, even if local authorities agreed to name academies in statements of SEN they would be under no statutory obligation to admit children.[183] The latter difficulty has to some extent been overcome via a new model agreement, but as Wolfe concludes, the legal position of a child with SEN will vary from one academy to the next and overall they would have "weaker entitlements" than children in local authority schools.[184]

There have been concerns that academies may be turning away some children with SEN.[185] Not all of the funding agreements currently in operation expressly prohibit such actions,[186] although if children are disabled, the Disability Discrimination Act 1995 would afford some protection. An Academies Bill designed to facilitate and increase the takeup of academy status is currently being debated in Parliament, and assurances are being sought that as the government's policy of expanding the number of academies from the current 203 proceeds, the rights of children with SEN will be adequately protected.[187] This is also a concern in respect of the government's current policy of encouraging and facilitating parents and others to establish "free" schools.

Another issue that has emerged concerns the position of students who reach the end of their period of compulsory schooling, at age sixteen. If pupils remain in schools, then statements of SEN that is in force will continue to have effect. However, if instead children attend postschool education such as a college of further education, the obligation of local authorities under the statement of SEN would not be expected to continue. This remains the case despite the fact that local authorities are under a new general duty to ensure that there is sufficient education and training provision for those over compulsory school age to meet their reasonable needs having regard, inter alia, to "any learning difficulties" they may have.[188]

A similar new duty applies in respect of young people aged sixteen to eighteen who are in youth detention.[189] One of the key issues that has arisen is whether local authorities can simply treat statements as being no longer in force if sixteen-plus students leave school or whether authorities must initiate formal procedures for ceasing to maintain the statements, in which case the parents have various rights, including a statutory right of appeal.[190] The Court of Appeal has recently explained that statements do not automatically cease in every case when students leave school, so that formal cessation procedures would need to be applied in some cases.[191] This, then, affords parents and students additional safeguards in cases where pupils enter a postschool provision on a temporary or trial basis.

CONCLUSION

The legal framework governing SEN is a dominant one in the field of education in England, with enormous practical implications for education professionals and local authorities. At the same time, disability discrimination law provides some baseline guarantees of equality of treatment through opportunities for redress and positive obligations on education providers to address causes of disadvantage. Yet, when it conducted an investigation in 2006, the House of Commons Education and Skills Select Committee found that there was "increasing confusion between SEN and disability" and "a great deal of work still to do to pull together the disability and SEN agendas and legislation."[192] The position has not materially improved over the period since then.

The SEN field is one in which the rights which are enjoyed are "special" in terms of affording far greater guarantees of participation and redress compared with those available to the families of non-SEN children. The exercise of these rights has a marked effect on relationships between parents and local authorities, raising parental expectations and introducing tensions as local authorities are forced to balance individual entitlements with collective needs. The educational arrangements that the law requires to be put in place for students with SEN may sometimes meet needs without satisfying parental wants or preferences. For the most part, the most potent rights in this field offer procedural guarantees rather than substantive entitlements, although it could be argued that the former hold the key to the realization of the latter, as the experience of the appeal process bears testament. Yet, it is clear that for many parents the experience of exercising these rights has not been a positive, "empowering" one.

Increasingly, one of the keys to reducing tensions in the relationship between parents and schools or local authorities is considered to be the provision of assistance to parents to know and understand how and why decisions are made and how the procedures operate, including those for resolving disagreements. It is hoped that that would be conducive to the ongoing partnership approach that is regarded as a better way of determining children's educational futures than an adversarial one.

What seems to have been neglected is the hugely bureaucratic and complex legal and administrative framework itself. As noted, for example, the Lamb inquiry took the view that the system was fine; it simply did not operate in the way that was intended. Still, structural reform may also be needed if the law's core objective of seeking to ensure that the needs of every child with SEN are identified and appropriately provided for is to be more fully realized.

In this regard, what has also to be properly understood is the contribution that the rights of parents and, although less dominant, those of their children, make to the realization of that objective. The rights may be regarded as fulfilling some kind of wider objective of reallocating or rebalancing power between citizens and bureaucracies, which is consistent with the calls for parents to be given more "confidence" in using them and engaging in the relevant processes. Still, they have been regarded as essential to the effectiveness of the educational system as a whole in delivering the best outcomes for children with disabilities and/or SEN. However, the problem is that the realization of this goal remains highly dependent on the capacity of individual parents to utilize their rights effectively and in the best interests of the children, which is variable. This reinforces the need for a greater focus on the rights of children for, as Fortin argues, there is "an obvious need to consider the disabled child as a person in his or her own right, rather than accepting the parent's view of where and how the child should be educated."[193]

NOTES

1. Notably under the *Every Child Matters* policy initiative; see below.

2. European Convention for the Protection of Human Rights and Fundamental Freedoms (ECHR) (1950), Article 2 of the First Protocol.

3. UN Declaration on Human Rights (1948), Article 26.

4. See Article 14 of the ECHR.

5. For example, the UK is a signatory to the UN Convention on the Rights of the Child, which imposes an obligation "to ensure that the disabled child has effective access to and receives education, training, health care services [etc] . . . in a manner conducive to the child's achieving the fullest possible social integration and individual development . . .": Article 23.1 and 23.2. Note that the UK is yet to ratify the UN Convention on the Rights of Persons with Disabilities (2006).

6. The term *student* is being used here for the sake of conformity with other chapters even though in the UK *pupil* is more commonly used.

7. See below.

8. See L. Lundy, "Family Values in the Classroom? Reconciling Parental Wishes and Children's Rights in State Schools" (2005) *International Journal of Law, Policy and the Family*, 19, 346; and N. Harris, *Education, Law and Diversity* (Hart, 2007).

9. Department for Education, *Schools, Pupils and their Characteristics, January 2010 (Provisional)*, Statistical Release SFR 09/2010 (London: DfE, 2010), tables 7a and 7b.

10. A. Mooney, C. Owen and J. Statham, *Disabled Children: Numbers, Characteristics and Local Service Provision*, Research Report No. DCSF-RR042 (DCSF, 2008), p. 8. This is broadly consistent with an earlier figure given in P. Daniel and J. Ivatts, *Children and Social Policy* (Macmillan, 1998), pp. 40–41.

11. N. Frederickson and T. Cline, *Special Educational Needs, Inclusion and Diversity* (Open University Press, 2009), p. 27.

12. Audit Commission, *Out of Authority Placements for Special Educational Needs* (Audit Commission, 2007), p. 14.

13. Department for Children Schools and Families statistics, published at http://www.dcsf.gov.uk/rsgateway/DB/TIM/m002012/NSRStatsJuneGDP140809.pdf (accessed 21 June 2010).

14. For a children's-rights-based comparison of the law across the four UK jurisdictions, see N. Harris, "Playing Catch-up in the Schoolyard? Children and Young People's 'Voice' and Education Rights in the United Kingdom" (2009) *International Journal of Law, Policy and the Family*, 23(3), 331–366.

15. Government of Wales Act 2006, Schedule 5, as amended by the National Assembly for Wales (Legislative Competence) (Conversion of Framework) Order 2007 (SI 2007/910) and the Education and Skills Act 2008, Section 149. For example, the National Assembly for Wales now has the power to amend the Education Act 1996 to make separate legislative arrangements for Wales. This happened in 2009 when the Assembly introduced the Education (Wales) Measure 2009 (2009 Section 5) which, inter alia, gave effect to a policy adopted in Wales of conferring on children independent appeal rights in connection with various SEN decisions taken by local authorities and empowered the Welsh Minister to make

regulations giving children a right to exercise this right with the help of a "case friend." Similar changes were made to the Disability Discrimination Act 1995 in relation to Wales.

16. Department for Education, *Schools, Pupils and their Characteristics, January 2010 (Provisional)*, Statistical Release SFR 09/2010 (London: DfE, 2010), table 2a.

17. Scotland's total for 2009 is 700,000: Scottish government website http://www.scotland.gov.uk/Topics/Statistics/Browse/School-Education/TrendPupilNumbers (accessed 15 June 2010). The total for Wales is 466,000, as at 2008–09: taken from the Welsh Assembly government's StatsWales website: http://www.statswales.wales.gov.uk/TableViewer/tableView.aspx?ReportId=7538 (accessed 15 June 2010). The number in Northern Ireland, in 2009–10, is 323,000: Department of Education (Northern Ireland) website: http://www.deni.gov.uk/enrolment_time_series_updated0910.xls (accessed 15 June 2010).

18. H. M. Warnock (chair), *Special Educational Needs. Report of the Enquiry into the Education of Handicapped Children and Young People* (HMSO, 1978).

19. Warnock herself has changed her view on this issue, due to problems with inclusion in practice: M. Warnock, *Special Educational Needs: A New Look* (Philosophy Society of Great Britain, 2005).

20. Education Act 1996, Section 312(1), (2) and (4).

21. J. Swain, S. French and C. Cameron (with J. Adams), *Controversial Issues in a Disabling Society* (Open University Press, 2003), p. 126.

22. House of Commons Education, Science and Arts Committee, Session 1986–87, *Third Report, Special Educational Needs: Implementation of the Education Act 1981, Vol. 1.* HC201-1 (HMSO, 1987), para. 16.

23. Audit Commission and Her Majesty's Inspectorate, *Getting in on the Act. Provision for Pupils with Special Educational Needs: The National Picture* (HMSO, 1992).

24. Ibid., paras. 15 and 17.

25. House of Commons Education, Science and Arts Committee, Session 1992–93, *Meeting Special Educational Needs: Statements of Needs and Provision*, HC 287-I (London: HMSO, 1993), para. 32.

26. Ibid., para. 35.

27. N. Harris, *Law and Education: Regulation, Consumerism and the Education System* (Sweet and Maxwell, 1993).

28. The numbers of appeals reaching the Secretary of State more than trebled between 1984 and 1991: N. Harris, *Special Educational Needs and Access to Justice* (Bristol: Jordans, 1997), p. 19.

29. L. Florian and D. Pullin, "Defining Difference. A Comparative Perspective on Legal and Policy Issues in Education Reform and Special Educational Needs," in M. J. McLaughlin and M. Rouse (eds.), *Special Education and School Reform in the United States and Britain* (London: Routledge, 2000), 11–37, at p. 26.

30. Audit Commission and Her Majesty's Inspectorate, note 23 above.

31. Department for Education, *Code of Practice on the Identification and Assessment of Special Educational Needs* (London: DfE, 1994).

32. They were set out in the Education (Special Educational Needs) Regulations 1994 (SI 1994/1047), made under powers in the 1993 Act.

33. Department for Education, *Special Educational Needs: Access to the System—A Consultation Paper* (London: DfE, 1992).

34. This in essence refers to the public law jurisdiction of the courts in which the legality of executive action can be judged against various standards of rationality and procedural fairness: see H. W. R. Wade and C. F. Forsyth, *Administrative Law* (9th edn) (Oxford University Press, 2004). Wade and Forsyth (Ibid., p. 33) explain that "when hearing an appeal the court is concerned with the merits of a decision . . . When subjecting some act or order to judicial review, the court is concerned with its legality: is it within the limits of the powers granted? . . . 'lawful or unlawful'?"

35. *R v. Lancashire Court Council ex parte CM* [1989] 2 F.L.R. 279.

36. *R v. Secretary of State for Education and Science ex parte E (A Minor)* [1992] 1 F.L.R. 377.

37. It should be noted that the *Education Law Reports* series was also established in the UK in 1994, the year in which this appellate route to the High Court opened up. The courts have made it clear that the appeal route rather than judicial review should be pursued in cases where one or more of the relevant grounds of appeal apply: see *R v. Special Educational Needs Tribunal ex parte F* [1996] ELR 213, per Popplewell J at 217A.

38. Department for Education and Employment, *Excellence in Schools* Cm3681 (London: The Stationery Office, 1999), pp. 33–34.

39. Ibid., p. 34.

40. This is discussed later in this chapter.

41. Department for Education and Employment (DfEE), *Excellence for All Children: Meeting Special Educational Needs* Cm 3785 (DfEE, 1997).

42. DfEE, *Special Educational Needs: A Programme for Action* (London: DfEE, 1998).

43. Department for Education and Skills (DfES) (2001).

44. This principle forms the basis to an entire section of the *Code* (part 3, headed "Pupil participation").

45. Part 2 of the *Code* covers "Working in Partnership with Parents."

46. SEN *Code of Practice*, note 43 above, para. 1.5.

47. In addition to being consistent with government policy, as noted above, this was recommended by the Disability Rights Task Force, *From Exclusion to Inclusion. Final Report* (DRTF, 1999), p. 24.

48. Education Act 1996, Sections 316 and 316A, inserted by the 2001 Act, Section 1.

49. Education Act 1996, Sections 332A and 332B, inserted by Sections 2 and 3 of the 2001 Act. The reference to mediation is in the *Code of Practice*, clarifying the kind of "arrangements" that were contemplated.

50. Education Act 1996, Section 317A, inserted by the 2001 Act Section 7.

51. Education Act 1996, Schedule 27, as amended by the 2001 Act Section 10, Schedule 1.

52. Education Act 1996, Section 336A, inserted by Section 4 of the 2001 Act.

53. Disability Discrimination Act 1995 Sections 28A–28Q, inserted by the 2001 Act Sections 11–25.

54. Sir B. Lamb, *Lamb Inquiry, Special Educational Needs and Parental Confidence* (DCSF, 2009). See also Idem, *Report to the Secretary of State on the Lamb Inquiry Review of SEN and Disability Information* (DCSF, 2009) and Capita, *Children's Plan One-Year-On SEN Commitments: Information for Parents of Children and Young People with SEN and Disabilities, Final Report* (DCSF, 2009).

55. Disability Rights Task Force, *From Exclusion to Inclusion. Final Report* (DRTF, 1999).

56. Ibid., p. 27.

57. Ibid., p. 24.

58. Ibid.

59. An example of such an auxiliary service was held to be a provision for cleaning and changing a paraplegic student who suffered from faecal incontinence: see *K v. Special Educational Needs and Disability Tribunal and Governing Body of a Grammar School* [2006] EWHC Admin 622. When this case reached the Court of Appeal the court avoided this issue but held that even if the service provided did amount to part of the education or associated services (covered by Section 28A of the 1995 Act) the school had a defence of justification based on the fact that cleaning and changing the child were, in the circumstances, dangerous due to the need to lift the child and the requirement for additional changing facilities: *K v. The School and the Special Educational Needs and Disability Tribunal* [2007] ELR 234.

60. Note 55 above, p. 31.

61. Ibid., pp. 31–32.

62. See DfEE, *Towards Inclusion—Civil Rights for Disabled People. Government Response to the Disability Rights Task Force* (DfEE, 2001), paras. 2.16–2.13, http://www.dcsf.gov.uk/consultations/downloadableDocs/60_3.pdf (accessed 18 June 2010).

63. T. Linden, "Disability Discrimination in Education: the New Law" (2002) 3(2) *Education Law Journal*, 82–88, at p. 88.

64. This Act represents a major overhaul of antidiscrimination law, including disability discrimination law, under the previous government. The relevant provisions require a ministerial order to bring them into effect (at the time of writing this has not yet occurred).

65. There has been a question as to whether the test for determining whether a school's actions towards a disabled misbehaving child whose misbehaviour is the result of his or her mental disability should be whether school staff would have treated a child who misbehaves but whose behaviour is *not* related to a disability the same way. In *M School v. CC, PC and Another* [2004] ELR 89 the court held that the comparator should be a child who is neither disabled nor badly behaved. The child was therefore not unlawfully discriminated against on account of his or her disability.

66. But there is no duty to provide "auxiliary aids or services" in that regard: DDA 1995, s.28C(2)(b). See *Bedfordshire County Council v. Dixon-Wilkinson* [2009] E.L.R. 361.

67. DDA 1995, Sections 28A–28C. It is a defence to be unaware of the person's disability: Section 28B(3).

68. See below. Decisions of the Upper Tribunal and High Court form a body of precedent for the First-Tier Tribunal and contain important guidance on the law.

69. DDA 1995, Sections 28D and 28E.

70. Disability Rights Commission, *Disability Discrimination Act 1995, Part 4, Code of Practice for Schools* (London: The Stationery Office, 2002). The DDA 1995, Section 53A, empowers the making of codes offering practical guidance on how to avoid discrimination. A person will not be liable for failure to comply with a provision in the code (Section 53A[8]), but a tribunal or court must take any provision of

the code it considers relevant when deciding on a case before it (Section 53[8A]). The Disability Rights Commission, in whose name the code was published, has been replaced by the Equality and Human Rights Commission under the Equality Act 2006. See also DfES, *Promoting Disability Equality in Schools* (DfES, 2006).

71. Disability Rights Commission, note 70 above, para. 3.13.

72. House of Commons Education and Skills Committee, *Special Educational Needs, Third Report of Session 2005–06* Vol 1. HC 478-1 (The Stationery Office, 2006), paras. 35 and 111.

73. See also DfES, *Government Response to the Education and Skills Committee Report on Special Educational Needs (October 2006)* Cm 6940 (The Stationery Office, 2006).

74. Independent Panel for Special Educationa Advice, *Briefing Note: Challenging Local Authority Schemes for the Delegation of Special Needs Responsibilities to Schools* (IPSEA, 2007), at http://www.ipsea.org.uk/AssetLibrary/News/Briefing%20Challenging%20SEN%20Delegation.pdf (access 29 June 2010).

75. House of Commons Education and Skills Committee, note 72 above, para. 234.

76. Education Act 1996 Act, Section 332A, added by the 2001 Act Section 2. This advice and information is provided by Parent Partnership Services, hired by but meant to be at arm's length from, the local authority: see below.

77. Education Act 317(1)(a) and (2). If the local authority has informed the school that the student has SEN the school's governing body must ensure that the child's SEN are made known to all those staff who are likely to teach him or her: Ibid., Section 317(1)(b).

78. Education Act 1996, Section 312.

79. Ibid., Section 312(2).

80. *R v. Hampshire Education Authority ex parte J* (1985) 84 LGR 547.

81. *R v. Lancashire CC ex p CM (A Minor)* [1989] 2 FLR 279 (CA).

82. *S v. Special Educational Needs and Disability Tribunal and Oxfordshire County Council* [2005] ELR 443.

83. *G v. London Borough of Barnet and the SENT* [1998] ELR 480 (child's Jewish religion and culture could not be classed giving rise to SEN for the purposes of Part IV of the 1996 Act). In *A v. SENDIST and the London Borough of Barnet* [2004] ELR 293 the court nevertheless acknowledged that if a child had specific cultural needs they should be taken into account if they were relevant to his or her SEN or the provision to meet them.

84. *London Borough of Bromley v. Special Educational Needs Tribunal* [1999] ELR 260 at 295G–296A. See also *City of Bradford Metropolitan Council v. A* [1997] ELR 417, in which provision for a nurse for a pupil who suffered from unpredictable epileptic fits and had a range of other problems including visual impairment and cerebral palsy was held to be noneducational provision.

85. Department for Children, Schools and Families, *Special Educational Needs in England, January 2009* (DCSF, 2009), table 9, http://www.dcsf.gov.uk/rsgateway/DB/SFR/s000852/SFR14_2009.pdf (accessed 21 June 2010). These figures only include children with statements and those without them but receiving extra help via "School Action Plus": see below.

86. Girls' primary need was most likely to be moderate learning difficulty, while for boys it was autism among those with statements and BESD among those

helped via School Action Plus: Department for Children, Schools and Families, *Children with Special Educational Needs 2009: An Analysis* (DCSF, 2009), p. 11.

87. House of Commons Education and Skills Committee, note 72 above, para. 34.

88. Schedule 1, as amended by the Disability Discrimination Act 2005.

89. See further A. Blair and A. Lawson, "Disability Discrimination Reforms in Education—Could Do Better?" *Child and Family Law Quarterly* (2003), 15(1), 41–55.

90. In *Governing Body of X School v. SP and Special Educational Needs and Disability Tribunal* [2008] ELR 243; for example, the court upheld a tribunal's conclusion that a student who was excluded from school due to misbehaviour that arose from her attention deficit hyperactivity disorder (ADHD) was discriminated against unlawfully because the school had not made sufficient efforts to effect reasonable adjustments by contacting the child's consultant or an educational psychologist for advice on managing her condition. See also *Governing Body of Olchfa Comprehenisve School v. IE and EE* [2006] ELR 503, which also concerned a child with ADHD.

91. Education Act 1996, Section 317(1)(c).

92. SEN Code of Practice, op cit, section 5. The school has a duty to designate a member of staff at the school as a SENCO "having responsibility for co-ordinating the provision for pupils with special educational needs": Education Act 1996, Section 317(3A). The experience and qualifications needed for such a role are prescribed: Ibid., Section 317(3B) and the Education (Special Educational Needs Co-ordinators) (England) Regulations 2008 (SI 2008/2945), as amended.

93. SEN *Code of Practice*, op cit, paras. 5:56–5:60 and 6:62–6:69.

94. Ibid., paras. 5:62 and 6:71.

95. *X (Minors) v. Bedfordshire County Council; M (A Minor) and Another v. Newham London Borough Council and Others; E (A Minor) v. Dorset County Council; Christmas v. Hampshire County Council; Keating v. Bromley London Borough Council* [1995] 2 AC 633, as applied in *Phelps v. London Borough of Hillingdon* [2000] 3 WLR 776 (HL). See also *Liennard v. Slough Borough Council* [2002] ELR 527.

96. Education Act 1996, Section 321.

97. Ibid., Sections 328, 329 and 329A.

98. Ibid., Sections 323(1) and (2).

99. Ibid., Section 323(1).

100. C. Penfold, N. Cleghorn, R. Tennant, I. Palmer and J. Read, *Parental Confidence in the Special Educational Needs Assessment, Statementing and Tribunal System. Qualitative Study*, Research Report DCSF-RR117 (DCSF, 2009), p. 34.

101. In *H v. Kent County Council and the Special Educational Needs Tribunal* [2000] ELR 660, where the tribunal upheld a decision by a local authority not to conduct a statutory assessment in respect of a ten-year-old girl, it was held that there was no breach of the ECHR, Article 2 of the First Protocol, since the consequence was not deprivation of the child's right to education: "What is at issue is the machinery by which educational needs are assessed and subsequently met" (per Grigson J at para. 58).

102. Education Act 1996, Schedule 26 and the Education (Special Educational Needs) (England) (Consolidation) Regulations 2001 (SI 2001/3455).

103. Ibid.

104. Education Act 1996, Schedule 26, para. 4.

105. Education (Special Educational Needs) (England) (Consolidation) Regulations 2001 (SI 2001/3455), reg. 7.

106. Education Act 1996, Schedule 26, para. 5.

107. SEN *Code of Practice*, op cit, para. 7:85.

108. Education Act 1996, Sections 316(1) and (2), as inserted by the 2001 Act, Section 1.

109. Article 2 of the First Protocol, which also refers to religious convictions of parents.

110. *Simpson v. United Kingdom* (1989) 64 DR 188; *PD and LD v. United Kingdom* (1989) 62 D.R. 292; *Graeme v. United Kingdom* (1990) 64 D.R. 158; *Klerks v. Netherlands* (1995) 82 D.R. 41; *Cohen v. United Kingdom* (1996) 21 E.H.R.R. CD 104; *H v. Kent County Council and the Special Educational Needs Tribunal* [2000] ELR 660; *T v. SENT and Wiltshire County Council* [2002] ELR 704, QBD.

111. See Education Act 1996, Section 316A inserted by the 2001 Act Section 1.

112. Department for Children, Schools and Families, SFR 14/2009 *Special Educational Needs in England, January 2009* (DCSF, 2009); Idem, SFR 20/2007, *Special Educational Needs in England: January 2007* (DCSF, 2007); DfES, SFR 24/2005 *Special Educational Needs in England: January 2005* (DfES, 2005).

113. J. Fortin, *Children's Rights and the Developing Law* (3rd edn) (Cambridge University Press, 2009), pp. 451–456.

114. Audit Commission, *Special Educational Needs—A Mainstream Issue* (Audit Commission, 2002), p. 24.

115. Department for Education and Skills, *Removing Barriers to Achievement. The Government's Strategy for SEN* (DfES, 2004).

116. See the Education (Special Educational Needs) (England) (Consolidation) Regulations 2001 (SI 2001/3455), Schedule 2.

117. Education Act 1996, Section 324(5).

118. Disputes finding their way into the courts over this issue are manifold. In general the courts have been reasonably sympathetic to local authority arguments that a degree of flexibility may be needed in the way that the arrangements for the child are set out in the statement, enabling provision to be adjusted in line with the child's changing needs. But parents prefer the more solid guarantees offered by clearly specified levels of provision, such as a set number of hours of specialist support per week. See *R v. Secretary of State for Education ex p. E* [1992] 1 FLR 377, where the court stated that the specified provision must address the needs specified in the statement. The SEN *Code of Practice* indicates that the provision should "normally be quantified (e.g., in terms of hours of provision, staffing arrangements) although there will be cases where some flexibility should be retained in order to meet the changing special educational needs of the child concerned . . ." But flexibility was accepted as necessary in *R v. Cumbria County Council ex p. P* [1995] 337, which concerned the provision of speech therapy, and in *L v. Clarke and Somerset CC* [1998] ELR 129, although Laws J felt that a statement should not leave a doubt as to the provision that is needed and that, as a result, the specification of a particular number of hours of special provision may be needed. But in *S v. City and Council of Swansea* [2000] ELR 315, Sullivan J

warned against using a need for flexibility as "as an excuse for lack of specificity" and avoiding the detail where it could "reasonably be provided" (at 328E). In *E v. London Borough of Newham and SENT* [2003] ELR 286, the Court of Appeal held that ultimately the degree of flexibility that was tolerable was a matter for the Tribunal, taking account of all relevant factors. See also *J v. Devon County Council and Strowger* [2001] EWHV Admin 958 and *E v. Rotherham Metropolitan Borough Council* [2002] ELR 266.

119. If such professional support is provided the child would be educated under "School Action Plus." If not, then it would be "School Action" that is required.

120. SEN *Code of Practice*, op cit, para. 8:2.

121. Education Act 1996, Schedule 27.

122. Ibid., paras. 2–4.

123. Education Act 1996, Section 326.

124. Ibid., Schedule 27, para. 3.

125. *B v. Harrow London Borough Council (No.2)* [2000] ELR 1; *Essex County Council v. The Special Educational Needs and Disability Tribunal and S* [2006] ELR 452; and *R (M) v. Sutton Borough Council* [2008] ELR 123.

126. In *Surrey County Council v. P and P* [1997] ELR 516, where the student suffered from a range of sight problems and there was a dispute between the authority and the parents over the placement. The parents' choice would cost the local authority £8,000–£10,000 per annum more than the authority's preferred school. Kay J said (at 523C): "If the situation was that one alternative would result in significant additional expenditure, then provided both schools were appropriate for the child's special educational needs, the local authority would be entitled to justify sending the child to a school other than that of the parents' choice." In the event, the Tribunal concluded that the boy's needs could not be properly met at the school chosen by the local authority. In *R (D) v. Davies and Surrey County Council* [2002] ELR 416 the court held that as the local authority's choice of school was regarded as suitable its lower cost (£20,000 less than the mother's choice) was entitled to sway the matter. In *R (Wiltshire County Council) v. YM and SENDIST* [2006] ELR 56 Jackson J (at para. 20) commented, in a case where the cost differential between the parties' respective preferred placements was nearly £58,000 per annum, that the authority's statutory duty (1996 Act Section 324[4]), if naming a school in the statement, to specify a placement that was appropriate for the child did "not permit inappropriate educational provision to be made simply on the grounds of cost."

127. In *W v. Leeds City Council and the Special Educational Needs and Disability Tribunal* [205] ELR 459, the court regarded as justified a tribunal's view that arrangements specified in a statement for the constant supervision of an autistic child outside school hours did amount to educational provision. See also *London Borough of Bromley v. Special Educational Needs Tribunal* [1999] ELR 260.

128. The latter phrase may be preferable to the former. In *R (Wiltshire County Council) v. YM and SENDIST* [2006] ELR 56 Jackson J commented (at para. 18) that "the phrase '24 hour curriculum' is not a helpful one . . . No child literally requires a 24-hour curriculum."

129. In *R (Tottman) v. Hertfordshire County Council* [2003] ELR 763, the mother of an autistic child who had complex learning difficulties disagreed with

the local authority over the contents of his statement. She wanted the child to be placed at a residential school which offered a waking-day curriculum. The tribunal rejected the argument that the child needed a programme of special education throughout the waking day. The court found that the tribunal had approached the matter rationally. In *R (H) v. West Sussex County Council and Davis* [2006] ELR 471 the tribunal had rejected the mother's appeal against the local authority's refusal to specify a placement at a residential school offering a waking-day curriculum for a child with ADHD. The cost differential as between that placement and a placement at its special school was £110,000 per annum. The court upheld the Tribunal's decision. In *The Learning Trust v. MP and the Special Educational Needs and Disability Tribunal* [2007] ELR 658 the court held that arrangements in respect of a child's social needs do not need to be provided for unless and insofar as they are also educational needs. See also *R (TS) v. Bowen and Solihull Metropolitan Borough Council* [2009] ELR 148.

130. Education Act 1996, Schedule 27, para. 8.

131. See, for example, *Oxfordshire County Council v. GB and others* [2002] ELR 8; and *Wardle-Heron v. London Borough of Newham and the Special Educational Needs Tribunal* [2004] ELR 68.

132. *S v. London Borough of Hackney and the Special Educational Needs Tribunal* [2002] ELR 45, per Collins J at para. 40.

133. See *C v. Buckinghamshire County Council and the Special Educational Needs Tribunal* [1999] ELR 179; and *S and S v. Bracknell Forest Borough Council and the Special Educational Needs Tribunal* [1999] ELR 51.

134. This is because at issue under Schedule 27 is the negation of a mandatory duty: *Ealing LBC v. SENDIST* [2008] ELR 183 (per Plender J at paras. 14 and 15). The court held that the Tribunal had been wrong to assume that because the cost difference in this Section 9 case was £4,000 it did not amount to unreasonable public expenditure.

135. See Education Act 1996 Section 332A and the SEN *Code of Practice*, op cit, part 2.

136. Education (Special Educational Needs) (England) (Consolidation) Regulations 2001 (SI 2001/3455), reg. 14 and Schedule 1 Part A.

137. SEN *Code of Practice*, op cit, para. 2:21.

138. R. Rogers et al., *Evaluation of the Special Educational Needs Parent Partnership Services in England RR719* (DfES, 2006); N. Harris and E. Smith, "Resolving Disputes about Special Educational Needs and Provision in England" *Education Law Journal* (2009), 10(2), 113–132.

139. Ofsted, *Inclusion: Does It matter Where Pupils are Taught?* (Ofsted, 2006), paras. 58 and 59.

140. Penfold et al., note 100 above, chapter 4.

141. Sir B. Lamb, note 54 above.

142. Ibid., p. 6.

143. The statutory grounds are in various sections of the Education Act 1996. An appeal can be brought where the local authority decides: (i) not to make a statement (Section 325); (ii) to make, amend or not to amend a statement (Section 326; the appeal may, for example, be against the description of the assessment of SEN or the specified provision [including the school to be named or the fact that no school

is specified]); (iii) not to comply with a request by a parent of a child for whom a statement is maintained that the child be further assessed (Section 328); (iv) not to comply with a request by a parent of a child for whom there is no statement, that the child's needs be formally assessed (Section 329); (v) not to comply with a request by the head teacher that the needs of the child (whether in a statement or not) be formally assessed (Section 329A); (vi) not to comply with a request for the naming of a different school in a statement of special educational needs (Schedule 27, para. 8); and (vii) to cease to maintain a statement (Schedule 27, para. 11). Note in relation to ground (vii) that the local authority may not cease to maintain a statement until the determination of the appeal (Schedule 27, para. 11[5]). When Section 2 of the Children, Schools and Families Act 2010 comes into effect there will be a further ground of appeal: where the local authority has decided, following a review of a statement of SEN, that the statement should not be amended.

144. "[T]he present law is that if there is a statutory right of appeal it is to be exercised and, save in exceptional circumstances, judicial review will not be granted where the statutory right of appeal exists and has not been exercised": *R v. Special Educational Needs Tribunal ex parte F* [1996] ELR 213, per Popplewell J at 217.

145. The First-Tier Tribunal (Health, Education and Social Care Chamber Rules) 2008 (SI 2008/2699) and the Health and Social Care Chamber, *Practice Direction, Health and Social Care Chamber, Special Educational Needs or Disability Discrimination in Schools Cases* (2008).

146. Tribunals Service, *SENDisT Annual Report, 2008–09* (Tribunals Service, 2009), p. 2.

147. *S v. Special Educational Needs Tribunal and the City of Westminster* [1996] ELR 228; *S and C v. Special Educational Needs Tribunal* [1997] ELR 242.

148. Committee on the Rights of the Child, *Concluding Observations: United Kingdom of Great Britain and Northern Ireland*, CRC/C/GBR/CO/4 (Centre for Human Rights, 2008), para. 67. For a detailed discussion of this issue, including the position of "looked after children" and the independent right of appeal which has been introduced in Wales, see N. Harris, "Playing Catch-up in the Schoolyard? Children and Young People's 'Voice' and Education Rights in the United Kingdom" (2009) *International Journal of Law, Policy and the Family*, 23(3), 331–366.

149. Statistics taken from the annual reports published online at www.tribunals.gov.uk and http://www.tribunals.gov.uk/Tribunals/Documents/Publications/JudicialStatisticsPublication.pdf (accessed 28 June 2010).

150. Tribunals Service, Tribunals Service, SENDisT, *Annual Report, 2008–09*, p. 10. http://www.sendist.gov.uk/Documents/FormsGuidance/AnnualReports/AnnualReport_08_2009.pdf (accessed 28 June 2010).

151. For an early study, see N. Harris, note 28 above. In research by Genn et al. on the experience of minority ethnic groups using different tribunals, it was found that in the SENDisT being from such a background had a neutral impact on the outcome of cases. Other cross-ethnicity factors, such as language, literacy, culture, education, confidence and verbal fluency, influenced how well appellants were able to present their case: H. Genn, B. Lever, and L. Gray, with N. Balmer, *Tribunals for Diverse Users* (London: Department for Constitutional Affairs, 2006).

152. Penfold et al., note 100 above, p. 52.

153. S. Riddell, N. Harris, E. Smith and E. Weedon, "Dispute Resolution in Additional and Special Educational Needs: Local Authority Perspectives" *Journal of Social Policy* (2010), 25(1), 55–71, at p. 68.

154. N. Harris, note 28 above; J. Evans, *Getting It Right: LEAs and the Special Educational Needs Tribunal* (NFER, 1998); Idem, "The Impact of the Special Educational Needs Tribunal on Local Educational Authorities' Policy and Planning for Special Educational Needs" *Support for Learning: British Journal of Learning Support* (1999), 14, 2, 74–80.

155. House of Commons Education and Skills Committee, note 72 above, para. 220.

156. Sir B. Lamb, note 54 above, paras. 5.80–5.82.

157. Tribunals Service, *SENDisT Annual Report, 2008–09* (Tribunals Service, 2009), p. 9.

158. Ibid., p. 5. These figures include appeals which were partly upheld; in other words, the parents achieved at least part of what they were aiming for.

159. See e.g., Department for Constitutional Affairs, *Transforming Public Services: Complaints, Redress and Tribunals* (The Stationery Office, 2004).

160. J. Hall, *Resolving Disputes between Parents, Schools and LEAs: Some Examples of Best Practice* (DfEE, 1999).

161. Department for Education and Employment, *Meeting Special Educational Needs: A Programme of Action* (London: DfEE, 1998), ch. 1 paras. 8 and 11.

162. Education Act 1996, Section 332B(1), (3).

163. SEN *Code of Practice*, op cit, paras. 2.26–2.30.

164. Generally mediations are funded on a case-inclusive basis under service level agreement, meaning that the local authority covers administrative costs and pays up front for a certain number of mediations.

165. See Department for Education and Skills, *SEN Toolkit* (DfES, 2002).

166. Education Act 1996, Section 332B(5); and the Education (Special Educational Needs) (Consolidation) Regulations 2001 (SI 2001/3455), regs. 12 and 17.

167. S. Riddell, N. Harris, E. Smith and E. Weedon, "Dispute Resolution in Additional and Special Educational Needs: Local Authority Perspectives" *Journal of Social Policy* (2010), 25(1), 55–71.

168. N. Harris and S. Riddell, "Is Mediation in Need of Promotion?" *Tribunals* (2010) Spring, 13–16.

169. Ibid.

170. Education Act 1996, Section 336A; Education (Special Educational Needs) (Consolidation) Regulations 2001 (SI 2001/3455), reg. 25. For example, any statement that is ordered must be made within five weeks beginning on the day following the Tribunal's order.

171. The LGO's jurisdiction is governed by the Local Government Act 1974.

172. Apprenticeships, Skills, Children and Learning Act 2009, Section 206(3).

173. Local Government Ombudsman, *Annual Report 2008–09*, annex of "detailed statistics": http://www.lgo.org.uk/publications/annual-report/ (accessed 28 June 2010). In a small number of the most significant cases and ones where the local authority disagrees with the LGO's proposed settlement the LGO will publish a report on the case, anonymising the complainant; but only three such reports were issued in SEN cases in 2008–09.

174. Apprenticeships, Skills, Children and Learning Act 2009, part 10, chap. 2.

175. See, e.g., a recent report on London Borough of Barnet (Case 07A14912), at http://www.lgo.org.uk/complaint-outcomes/education/education-archive-2010-11/london-borough-barnet-07a14912/ (accessed 28 June 2010). Part of the complaint, which was upheld and led to an award of compensation totaling £2,500, concerned the local authority's delay in responding to a request to assess a girl's SEN.

176. DCSF, *Improving Parental Confidence in the Special Educational Needs System: An Implementation Plan* (DCSF, 2010).

177. Under the Children, Schools and Families Act 2010, Section 2.

178. DCSF, *Improving Parental Confidence in the Special Educational Needs System: An Implementation Plan* (DCSF, 2010), para. 4.25.

179. Ibid., para. 4.27.

180. Education Act 1996, Section 482.

181. D. Wolfe, "Academies and Special Educational Needs—A Health Warning" *Education Law Journal* (2007), 8(3), 170–176, at p. 171.

182. Ibid., at p. 172.

183. Ibid.

184. Ibid., p. 176.

185. House of Commons Education and Skills Committee, note 72 above, para. 200.

186. F. Miller, "Will Academies Meet Special Needs?" *Education Guardian*, 22 June 2010, 1–2.

187. See, for example, the comments of Lord Low that academies did not have the same duty as other schools under Section 317 of the 1996 Act to use their "best endeavors" to meet the needs of children with SEN, and the Bill did not clarify whether the SEN *Code of Practice* would need to be followed by academies: Hansard, House of Lords, Second Reading Debate, 7 June 2010, clauses 513–514.

188. Education Act 1996, Section 15ZA, inserted by the Apprenticeships, Skills, Children and Learning Act 2009, Section 41.

189. Education Act 1996, Section 18A, inserted by the Apprenticeships, Skills, Children and Learning Act 2009, Section 48 (in force from 1 September 2010). A further duty, not yet in force, would ensure that some form of special educational provision is made for a child with a statement of SEN if they are detained in youth accommodation: Education Act 1996, Section 562C, inserted by the 2009 Act, Section 50. The statement would continue, but the local authority's duty to ensure that the specified special educational provision made for the child is replaced by a duty on the host authority (i.e., the authority for the area in which the child is detained) to use its "best endeavours" to provide it or something approximating it or other provision if considered more appropriate.

190. See Education Act 1996, Schedule 27, paras. 9 and 11. The ground for bringing the statement to an end is that the authority is of the opinion that "it is not longer necessary to maintain it": para. 11(1).

191. *R (Hill) v. Bedfordshire County Council* [2008] ELR 660, per Lawrence Collins LJ at para. 108. It would automatically cease where the statement had "cease[d] to have any point," such as where child moves to postschool provision and the parents, local authority and college are all in agreement about that transfer. The local authority would need formally to decide to cease to maintain the statement if there was a continuing belief that the child might need and be given special educational

provision later. A related question has been whether if the student starts postschool education after an appeal to the First-Tier Tribunal has already been lodged but *before* it has been decided the appeal can be struck out for lack of jurisdiction. Recently the Upper Tribunal held that in the latter case the appeal should not be struck out. In one case, the tribunal could still impose an obligation on the local authority for provision that included schooling (*KC v. London Borough of Newham* [2010] UKUT 96 [AAC]) and in another there was still scope for argument over whether a statement should continue for a girl, aged nineteen, who had Down's Syndrome (*AW v. Essex County Council* [2010] UKUT 74 [AAC]).

192. House of Commons Education and Skills Committee, note 72 above, paras. 35 and 111.

193. J. Fortin, *Children's Rights and the Developing Law* (3rd edn) (Cambridge University Press, 2009), p. 457.

6

Malaysia

Fatt Hee Tie

The educational rights of students with disabilities in Malaysia are governed by three legal sources: the Federal Constitution,[1] the Education Act 1996,[2] and the 1997 School Regulations (Special Education).[3] In addition, international agreements such as the Dakar Framework for Action[4] and its specific references to issues of marginalization and exclusion of students with disabilities impact the educational rights of children with special educational needs in Malaysia.

Malaysia subscribes to the universal principle of education for all, recognizing that education is a basic human right. In so doing, Malaysia's position reflects that of Article 24 of the Convention on the Rights of Persons with Disabilities,[5] which advocates inclusive education for all children with special needs. In supporting the international effort aimed at inclusive education, Malaysia has played a more active role to encourage the concept and practice of inclusive education in schools.

Schools in Malaysia have been transformed gradually to meet the learning needs of children with disabilities, having adopted UNESCO's tripartite policy and justifications for inclusion education, namely: (a) educational justification where inclusive education strives to educate all children; accordingly, Malaysian schools are required to develop ways of teaching that accommodate individual differences in order to benefit all children; (b) social justification where inclusive schools are able to change attitudes towards diversity by educating all children together, forming the foundation for a just and nondiscriminatory society; and (c) economic justification, as it is less costly to establish and maintain schools to educate all children together as opposed to setting up a complex system of different types of schools specializing to serve the needs of various groups of students.[6]

The legal system in Malaysia did not formally provide educational opportunities for children with disabilities in 1957 when the country gained its independence from Great Britain.[7] In fact, previously, it was only during the latter part of the nineteenth century that schools in Malaysia began to address the educational needs of students with disabilities by creating special schools and classes for children with physical disabilities. However, most parents were reluctant to send their children with disabilities to these special schools due to the fear of embarrassment and having their young ill treated in school. The common type of children with disabilities that these special schools served were those with learning disabilities; orthopedic, visual and hearing impairments; and cerebral palsy. In the twentieth century, Malaysian educational leaders, lawmakers, and other self-advocacy groups acknowledged the need to meet the growing educational needs of students with disabilities.

There has been a gradual increase in the provision of facilities and schools for Malaysian students with disabilities. One example of what Malaysia provides is education for children with learning disabilities. In 2000, there were only 7,919 students with learning disabilities registered in these schools. Yet, by 2006, the number had increased to 20,814, along with a similar increase in the number of special schools and teachers.[8] To this end, primary and secondary schools have been selected to provide integrated special education programs for students with disabilities to participate and integrate into the local community.

In reviewing the status of special education in Malaysia, this chapter is divided into three main sections. The first part presents an overview of the constitutional sources of special education law. The second section examines the rights of students with disabilities, discussing the landmark case on special education that shaped legal developments on the legal rights of students with disabilities in Malaysia. The final part analyzes emerging issues in special education for Malaysian students with specific disabilities.

SOURCES OF SPECIAL EDUCATION LAW

The Federal Constitution, the supreme law in Malaysia, provides the framework governing the entire legal system. Students with disabilities have the same basic constitutional right to education as other children. Article 12 (1) of the Federal Constitution expressed the right in respect of education as "without prejudice to the generality of Article 8, there shall be no discrimination against any citizen on the grounds only of religion, race, descent or place of birth—(a) in the administration of any educational institution maintained by a public authority, and, in particular, the admission of pupils or students or the payment of fees. . . ."

At the same time, the Education Act 1996 expressed that the primary purpose of education in Malaysia was to enable all citizens to have a command of the knowledge, skills, and values that are needed in a highly competitive and globalised world. The mission of the education system strives to help students to realize their full potential as individuals. The National Education Policy, which is based on the National Philosophy of Education, seeks to develop the potential of all students in a holistic and integrated manner. The philosophy of education sets out that education is the right of all children. Thus, it is mandatory for educational opportunities to be extended to children with disabilities in Malaysia who are entitled to similar opportunities to receive quality education as their peers and to be equipped with the basic literacy skills as well as appropriate knowledge needed to live and work in the near future. Educational exclusion denies children with disabilities qualifications allowing for future survival. The law is concerned that with only limited access to quality education that is detached from mainstream settings, it is likely that children will drop out of a school system that is deemed irrelevant when the practice of isolation separates and marginalizes students with disabilities.

The Education Act 1996 contains provisions delineating the power and function of the Minister of Education. Under the law, the Minister of Education shall provide special education in special schools at the primary and secondary level (s. 40) as well as set up and maintain these special schools (s. 34). Special schools are defined as those providing special education as prescribed by regulations promulgated under section 41 (s. 2). The Act further defines special education as education focusing on the special educational needs of pupils (s. 2).

Pursuant to the terms of the 1996 Act, the power of the Minister of Education is extensive and wide ranging. The Minister has the power to prescribe the duration of primary and secondary education that is suitable to the needs of pupils in special education settings; the curriculum on special education; the categories of pupils requiring special education and the appropriate methods for educating those in each category of special schools (s. 41). Even so, the duration of primary and secondary special education shall not be less than the minimum duration for the nonspecial primary and secondary school (s. 41[2]). Moreover, the curriculum shall comply with the requirements of the National Curriculum as far as it is reasonably practicable (s. 41[3]).

The School Regulations (Special Education) 1997 defined pupils with special needs as those with visual, hearing, or learning disabilities (s. 2). It also defined a special education program as one of the following: a program in a special school for pupils with visual or hearing difficulties; an integrated program in an ordinary school for pupils with visual, hearing, or learning difficulties; or (c) an inclusive education program for pupils with special needs who are able to attend a normal class with pupils who are not disabled. The Ministry of Education further defined pupils with learning disabilities as: children with Down Syndrome; autism; cognitive disabilities; behavioral and emotional difficulties; health problems; and/or speech and language difficulties.

Three ministries are responsible for serving the educational needs of students with disabilities, namely: the Ministry of Education, the Ministry of National Unity and Social Development, and the Ministry of Health. The Cabinet Committee Report[9] recommended the following measures for the Ministry of Education to adopt with regard to special education: improve resources and facilities for the education of the blind; formal schooling for the deaf to commence at age six; and incorporation of remedial education into primary schools. Conversely, the Ministry of National Unity and Social Development is vested with the responsibility to safeguard the education and welfare of children with multiple and severe disabilities who are unable to be educated in government schools. These children received education and related services in early intervention and community-based rehabilitation programs. The Ministry of Health is responsible for early identification and screening of disabilities and health-related problems of children.

SPECIAL EDUCATION IN MALAYSIA

Identification and Assessment of Students with Disabilities

The Ministry of Education's Special Education Program (SEP) consists of two specific types of special schools: Special Schools for students with vision and hearing disabilities; and a Special Education Integration Program for children with learning, hearing, and vision disabilities. SEPs are provided in regular primary and secondary schools as well as in technical/vocational secondary schools that adopt the withdrawal and partially inclusive approach to teaching and learning. The Special Education Integration Program is managed by the state education department, while the Special Education Department is in charge of issues pertaining to policies and content.

The Special Education Program curriculum is used in Special Schools. The curriculum taught in the Special Education Integration Program consists of both the National Curriculum and the Alternative Curriculum. Insofar as students in special education participate in extracurricular activities with peers who are not disabled, they take the normal public examinations, while those who follow the Alternative Curriculum take the National Standard Skills test.

Special Education Rehabilitation Program

The program used is the Level One Special Education Rehabilitation Program. Students are assessed for reading, writing, and mathematics skills using the Determinant of Mastery of the 3 Rs Instrument (DM3RI). It is divided into DMRRI 1 for Year 1 primary students, DMRRI 2 for Year 2 primary students and DMRRI 3 for Year 3 students. The conditions of entry for students into the Special Education School Program are: aged no less than five for the preschool program; aged six-plus to fourteen-plus years for primary school programs; aged thirteen-plus to nineteen-plus for secondary school programs. In addition, students must be certified as disabled by a medical doctor and must be able to take care of themselves without the assistance of others. The length of primary schooling for children with special needs is six years, while secondary schooling for children with special needs is five years. The duration can be extended for a maximum of two years at any level, depending on the needs of students.

All Special Primary Schools are academic-based. Facilities provided at the primary school level include hostel facilities and free meals. Students participating in the Special Education Integration Program are given a choice to either study for the national curriculum or the alternative curriculum. Secondary education provides either academic-based or vocational-based choices.

In 1999, the government established the Special Education Services Centre for the purpose of providing one-stop specialist services to parents and students with special needs. This center functions to support agencies involved with special needs. The type of services provided by the center include audio services, sign language classes, therapy activities, parent counseling, a toy library, and resource material.

Eligibility for Enrollment into a Special Education Program

Section 3 of the School Regulations (Special Education) 1997 set out the conditions for enrollment into the special education program. Section 3(1) states that "for government and government-aided schools, pupils with special needs that are educable are eligible to attend the special education program except for the following pupils: (a) pupils with physical disability but possess the mental ability to learn like normal pupils; and, (b) pupils with various disabilities, serious physical disability, or serious mental difficulties." Section 3(2) defines "educable" pupils with special needs as those who can manage themselves without depending on the help of others and have been certified as capable of following the national education program by a panel comprised of a medical doctor, an officer from the Ministry of Education, and an officer from the Department of Social Welfare. Section 4 allows teachers to modify their teaching and learning methods, duration of classes, subjects, and teaching aids to achieve the aims and purpose of special education.

Registration Process for a Special Education Program

The process consists of eight steps.

Step 1: Commencement

Parents and teachers suspect the child of having a learning disability.

Step 2: Confirmation that the child has a disability

Certification of the child's disability by medical professionals in a government hospital, health care center, or private clinic for the purpose of obtaining placement and to receive early intervention from the Ministry of Health Malaysia.

Step 3: Registration with the state education department

Parents register their child with the state education department to receive the appropriate special education.

Step 4: Registration with the Social Welfare Department

Children are also registered with the Social Welfare Department to obtain suitable services.

Step 5: Eligibility

The state education department manages children with disabilities that have been certified as being ready for school. The children are then placed in the appropriate school. Children who have been determined as being unready for school, who have severe disabilities, or who do not fulfill the entry requirements of the Malaysia Ministry of Education's Special Education Program are referred to the Social Welfare Department to obtain suitable rehabilitation through the Community Based Rehabilitation program.

Step 6: Placement

Students will be given the opportunity for placement in either Special School or the Special Education Integration Program. Placement will be based on the nearest school or Special Education Program.

Step 7: Probation period

Students who have been placed in the Malaysian Ministry of Education's Special Education Program will be given a three-month probation period.

Step 8: Confirmation

After the probation period, students who are successful in following the Special Education Program will be confirmed in the program. Students who fail to follow the Ministry's Special Education Program will be referred back to the Social Welfare Department to receive suitable rehabilitation through Community Based Rehabilitation.[10]

Placement Issues

In the early 1990s, children with special needs were segregated and deprived of educational opportunities in regular classrooms.[11] Due to the realization that integration of students with disabilities in classrooms can contribute to the development of the full potential of children as a whole even as they are gradually integrated into the larger society, the Ministry of Education introduced the concept of inclusive education in 1995.

Inclusive education seeks to educate and provide maximum interaction between students with disabilities and their peers who are not disabled in ordinary classroom environments. School officials attempted to integrate students with disabilities into regular classrooms to bring academic and social benefits to all. Inclusion facilitates the learning of social skills that are required for interaction in society, develops positive self-esteem for acceptance in society, and shares available resources in regular classrooms.[12]

The integration or inclusive approach also addresses and responds to the diverse needs of students with disabilities through increased participation in learning and reducing exclusion within and from education. The Ministry of Education attempted to modify the content, approach, structure, and pedagogical strategy to allow students with disabilities to engage in meaningful learning. This is based on the conviction that the regular mainstream educational system is responsible for educating all children.

At the initial stage, students with disabilities are placed in special education classrooms. Later, after further assessment, principals can place students in inclusive classrooms if they are able to adapt academically and socially with their peers and on the recommendation of special education coordinators. Students are taught by both special education teachers and general education teachers. Special education teachers use adapted curricula and materials from pullout programs or resource rooms, while general education teachers use the curricula and textbooks.

The responsibility for educating children is shared by both teachers. The shared model of service delivery requires consultation, collaboration, and coteaching, unlike the traditional model of divided responsibility. Two issues that emerged are: how do teachers preserve the continuum of services provided while promoting full inclusion, and how the responsibilities of general education teachers have increased and that would lead to some resistance from the groups with the shared responsibility model of inclusion.[13] The shared responsibility model results in the development of more coherent and successful inclusion programs for students with disabilities.

Most students in inclusive classrooms have visual or hearing disabilities. These children are trained in the technical and vocational schools with the purpose of equipping them with specific skills for future employment. Unfortunately, only five schools in the country are able to provide this type of training since its implementation in 2000.[14] This may be due to limited financial support, lack of trained teachers, or parents who are unwilling to enroll their children in these schools.

Due Process Rights

The common law doctrine of in loco parentis allows teachers and school administrators to assume the authority to discipline students, including those with disabilities, while they are in schools. This is justified based on the need to maintain some modicum of discipline and order to ensure the efficient functioning of schools.

Students with disabilities in Malaysia may be disciplined by means of corporal punishment, suspensions, and expulsions after having opportunities to be heard. Suspensions must be reasonable according to the severity of the infractions, with their length depending on the severity of the misconduct and ranging from three to seven days. Expulsions and permanent removals of students from schools are serious decisions since they deprive children of the right to an education.

Regulation 4 of the Education (School Discipline) Regulations 1959 maintains that principals are responsible to their boards of governors for school discipline and have authority over students. Regulation 8 provides that principals may expel students from school whenever they believe it necessary or desirable to maintain discipline or order. Students or their parents may appeal expulsions under Regulation 10.

Due process is a legal principle that requires fairness and compliance with adequate procedures before decisions are made in Malaysia. Article 5 of the Federal Constitution established the right to fair procedures in its due process clause, which states that persons shall not be deprived of life or personal liberty save in accordance with the law. A liberty interest concerns reputation or integrity and is created when administrative actions create potential harm to future educational or job opportunities for students.

Students with disabilities, like other children, are entitled to two forms of due process: procedural and substantive. Procedural due process sets out the process or steps taken by principals and disciplinary committees in reaching their decisions. Students with disabilities have the right to hearings before disciplinary committees. These due process procedures are set out in a clear and systematic manner such that students must be given oral or written notice of the charges they face since this allows them to know what rule(s) they are accused of breaking. Further, notice must contain specific charges. Students who deny the charges against them must be allowed to explain their sides of incidents to disciplinary committees since this is a basic constitutional right. Moreover, parents must be informed of the specific charges against their children in writing and have the right to appoint counsel to represent their children at these proceedings.

Students with disabilities have a property right to receive a free public education that cannot be removed for misconduct without adherence to constitutional due process protections. As such, inclusive schools are not free from notice and hearing requirements since students with disabilities are entitled to the same oral or written notice of the charges as other pupils when they are accused of misbehaving, and if they deny the charges, to offer explanations and opportunities to present defenses.

Hearings must be conducted before impartial tribunals and must precede suspensions or expulsions since the opportunity to be heard is a fundamental right that affords a fair and impartial process while reducing the possibility of mistakes in the disciplinary process. Still, principals can remove students immediately if their presence poses an imminent danger to others. Principals cannot unilaterally exclude students with disabilities even if their misconduct is dangerous or disruptive since disciplinary committees must decide on exclusions. The failure of school officials to adhere to the rules of natural justice can lead to litigation and legislative action. Even so, students with disabilities who are suspended or expelled from school are not provided with educational services like students with disabilities in the United States.[15]

Substantive due process relates to the fairness and reasonableness of decisions. Adequate notice, how evidence is collected and applied, and the rationality of decisions are factors that courts consider in deciding whether educators adhered to substantive due process.[16] Further, substantive due process involves four principles: the rule or policy providing adequate notice of the prohibition; the legitimate educational purpose of the rule; the consequence connected to the offense; and, the equitable application of the rule.[17]

The rule of natural justice applies to students with disabilities, meaning that they have the right to know the nature of the accusations they face, to have opportunities to present their sides of the story, and to have disciplinary committees or tribunals act in good faith. Regulation 8 vests principals or the tribunals with a quasi-judicial function, allowing them to adopt their own rules of procedure as long as they are fair. On a related point, it is worth noting that the Privy Council, in *Mahadevan v. Anandarajan*,[18] ruled that in relation to administrative matters such as student expulsions, it is inappropriate to model procedure on criminal trials, meaning that lower standards can be applied. The Privy Council also reiterated that natural justice required decision makers to act fairly.

Dispute Resolution

In all matters related to special education, parents who are dissatisfied with the education of their children with disabilities are entitled to significant due process protection in the form of hearings that are often conducted in closed environments. Hearings must be conducted in the presence of fair and impartial tribunals usually comprised of teachers who are not parties to the dispute. Prior to the hearings, both parties must make full disclosure of information they have available.

Parents who disagree with the results of these proceedings may then appeal to the courts after having exhausted all administrative remedies. Courts may provide monetary damages, compensatory services, and/or costs for the litigation resolving disputes over the education of students with disabilities.

Funding and Cost Issues

The Malaysian federal government provides funding to the Ministry of Education to pay for the delivery of special education services. While local school officials may argue that the cost involved in making school environments more accessible to students with disabilities is too expensive, this contention is not legally tenable since the educational needs of students with disabilities overrides the financial considerations argument. This principle was laid down in a major case that serves as the thrust for the development of the law of special education in Malaysia, *Renner v. Scott King, Chairman of Board of Directors of the International School of Kuala Lumpur* (*Renner*).[19]

In *Renner*, the lead plaintiff suffered from a mild form of spastic dipelgia that affected his motor movements. The student studied at an international elementary school for six years and was intellectually capable of doing the work but needed a wheelchair to move about and a walking frame if he intended to walk by himself.

After the plaintiff completed elementary school, educational officials refused to allow him to continue his secondary education at the International School. The defendants argued that changing the secondary school environment to become disabled friendly to meet the plaintiff's special needs would have caused it to incur heavy financial expenditures. The plaintiff applied for an interlocutory injunction to restrain the defendants to prevent him from continuing his education at the school. The plaintiff argued that there was a serious question to be tried since he had a legitimate expectation to continue with his education and that he did not need special teaching facilities since he was fine cognitively. The plaintiff also argued that his mere presence in a school population of 1,222 did not affect its general teaching organization.

Of particular significance in *Renner* was that the education of the lead plaintiff would have suffered irreparable harm had he been denied the ability to complete his education. The court allowed the application for an injunction since it was of the opinion that school officials could not exclude the student solely on the basis of financial considerations insofar as children with disabilities have a basic right to education as a matter of law and justice. The court also examined the judicial principles governing the issuance of injunctions and actions that prevented children from attending school. In this respect, the court highlighted three important cases from the United Kingdom: *Guardians of the Poor of Gateshead Union v. Durham County Council* (*Guardians*),[20] *Bradbury v. London Borough of Enfield* (*Bradbury*)[21] and *Wilford v. County Council of the West Riding of Yorkshire* (*Wilford*).[22]

In *Guardians* a local education authority (LEA) had attempted to impose a condition that required children to pay a fee to attend elementary public schools. The Court of Appeal granted an injunction to restrain the LEA from doing so as it was inconsistent with the children's statutory right to free education. In *Bradbury* the Court of Appeal reiterated the paramount importance of the educational needs of children after parents had objected to a new policy that sought to convert the grammar school system based on selection of pupils into a uniform comprehensive school system. The court granted an injunction to keep the grammar schools in place. Further, in *Wilford* the court granted an injunction to prevent an LEA from implementing a policy that would have prevented schools from providing secular education to children in years one to three.

Justice Low Hop Bing's judgment in *Renner* further analyzed the decisions in the English case of *R v. East Sussex County Council ex p Tandy* (*Tandy*)[23] and the U.S. Supreme Court's opinion in *Cedar Rapids Community School District v. Garret F.* (*Garret F.*).[24] In *Tandy,* the House of Lords held that the financial resources of a LEA were irrelevant in determining a suitable school setting for a child with dyslexia. Similarly, in *Garret* the Supreme Court ruled that a local school board had to pay for a school nurse to accompany a student who was quadriplegic to class since he has an entitlement to such assistance under the Individuals with Disabilities Education Act.[25]

The court relied on these cases in reiterating that the educational needs of students with disabilities remain of paramount significance. The court concluded that since the legal right of children with disabilities to an education overrides the arguments of an educational provider that it is expensive to provide a friendly and safe environment for students with special needs, the school had to allow the lead plaintiff to return to the school.

Emerging Issues

Seven major issues are emerging in Malaysia with regard to the education of students with disabilities. The first issue involves the fact that there are limited numbers of schools serving the learning needs of children with disabilities in Malaysia. Thus, an issue is arising as to how educational policy makers in Malaysia can address the access rights of students to these schools. This is a challenge because many parents remain reluctant to send their children to special schools with the result that some have low enrollments. As such, the Ministry of Education needs to adopt a more effective strategy to address this issue because it is vital to have a clear and unified national strategy to include all learners in order to achieve the long-term objective of the Education for All goals by 2015.

A second emerging issue is the challenge to provide and attain high-quality, equitable education for all children with disabilities. Put another way, since inclusion can only occur when the number of places and trained teachers are adequate, in seeking to achieve the purpose of education and the Education Act of 1996 aim to develop the full potential of all children, there is a need to reexamine the weaknesses with regards to school facilities and the preparation of qualified special education teachers in Malaysia.

A third issue relates to the issue of isolation. The Salamanca conference, which focused on special needs education, concluded that special needs education cannot advance in isolation, highlighting the fact that it must form part of an overall educational strategy as well as in the new social and economic policies of both the North and South nations.[26] To this end, educational leaders and policy makers in Malaysia must undertake a major reform of regular schools in order to achieve the objective of inclusive education.

Cost represents a fourth emerging issue with regard to special education in Malaysia. While recognizing that the costs of inclusive education can strain limited national budgets and there is a lack of official development assistance, leaders must seek ways to pay for educating all children, including those with disabilities. At the same time, since parents often face difficulties in coping with the direct and indirect costs of education, leaders need to develop a more cost-efficient educational system that optimizes the use of limited resources. Further, intervention programs promoting inclusive quality education need to examine and adopt cost-effective measures to achieve the goal of Education for All.

A fifth emerging issue is how to address the problem of dropouts from school due to the perception that children with disabilities have low levels of skills and often face high rates of unemployment. One way that leaders can help to minimize this concern is to provide quality and equitable inclusive education by improving school facilities, teacher preparation programs, and support available to meet the needs of students with disabilities in Malaysian schools.

The sixth emerging issue is the Ministry of Education's responsibility to ensure the right to education for all. In welcoming diversity and fostering closer participation of parents and the community, there is the need to reorient teacher education, ensure early identification and remediation of children at risk, and encourage the use of flexible teaching and learning methods.

The final emerging issue concerns attitudinal changes through awareness programs to overcome lack of understanding and passive parental participation. In order to address these concerns, Malaysian lawmakers must enact comprehensive and clear national legislation to incorporate notions of inclusive education based on a collaborative approach to guarantee the right to education for all children.[27]

CONCLUSION

A major challenge facing Malaysian society, not just educators, is addressing the educational needs of students with disabilities. In recent years educational policy makers have become increasingly concerned over this issue, as the Ministry of Education has introduced special education programs to meet the needs of students. While these programs are more integrated in nature and are taught by trained personnel, more needs to be done to ensure that students derive maximum benefit from the programs. As such, leaders must provide regular professional development programs for all staff to help them to better understand how to serve the needs of students with disabilities. Similar informational sessions should be provided for parents and students to help ensure that they are aware of their rights. Finally, the various Malaysian ministries must not only ensure that policies and procedures relating to the delivery of special education and related services are up-to-date but also that regular monitoring occurs to meet the best interests of students with disabilities.

NOTES

1. *Federal Constitution* (2010 printing). Kuala Lumpur: International Law Book Services.
2. *Education Act 1996, Act 550*. Kuala Lumpur: International Law Book Services.
3. Ministry of Education, Malaysia (1997), School Regulations (Special Education). Kuala Lumpur.
4. UNESCO (2000). Dakar Framework for Action. Paris, UNESCO.

5. UNESCO (2006). Convention on the Rights of Persons with Disabilities. Paris, UNESCO.

6. UNESCO (2009). Policy Guidelines on Inclusive Education. Paris, UNESCO.

7. Tie, F. H. (2007). The educational rights of students in Malaysia. In Russo, C. J., Stewart, D. J. & Groof, J. D. (ed.). *The educational rights of students: International perspectives on demystifying the legal issues*. Lanham, Maryland: Rowman & Littlefield Education.

8. Teoh, H. T., & Lim, M. K. (2007). Situation of persons with learning disabilities and their families in Malaysia. Retrieved 16 March 2010. http://www.worldenable.net/shanghai2007/papermalaysia.html.

9. Cabinet Committee Report (1979). Malaysia. Kuala Lumpur.

10. The Kiwanis Disability Information and Support Centre (n.d.). *A KDISC FACTSHEET*. Retrieved 27 March 2010, http:// www.disabilitymalaysia.com.

11. Haq, Faridah S. (2000). From divided responsibility to shared responsibility: Inclusion in Malaysia. Paper presented at the International Special Education Congress 24–28 July 2000, Manchester. Retrieved 27 March 2010. Available at http://www.isec2000.org.uk/abstracts/papers_h/haq_1.htm.

12. Id.

13. Haq, Faridah S. (2000). From divided responsibility to shared responsibility: Inclusion in Malaysia. Paper presented at the International Special Education Congress 24–28 July 2000, Manchester. Retrieved 27 March 2010. Available at http://www.isec2000.org.uk/abstracts/papers_h/haq_1.htm.

14. Haq, Faridah S. (2000). From divided responsibility to shared responsibility: Inclusion in Malaysia. Paper presented at the International Special Education Congress 24–28 July 2000, Manchester. Retrieved 27 March 2010. Available at http://www.isec2000.org.uk/abstracts/papers_h/haq_1.htm.

15. Russo, C. J. (2009). *Reutter's the law of public education* (7th ed.). N.Y.: Thomson Reuters/Foundation Press.

16. Fatt Hee, Tie. (2010). *Education law in Malaysia: Principles and practice.* Selangor: Thomson, Sweet & Maxwell.

17. Stader, D. L. (2007). *Law and ethics in educational leadership*. New Jersey: Pearson Education.

18. [1974] 1 MLJ 1.

19. [2000] 5 MLJ 254.

20. [1918] 1 Ch D 146.

21. [1967] 3 All ER 434 (CA).

22. [1908] 1 KB 685.

23. [1998] 2 All ER 769.

24. 526 U.S. 66 (1999).

25. 20 U.S.C.A. ss. 1400 *et seq*. The Act is described in detail in the chapter.

26. UNESCO (1994). *The Salamanca statement and framework for action on special needs education*. Paris, UNESCO and Ministry of Education, Spain.

27. UNESCO (2009). Policy guidelines on inclusive education. Paris, UNESCO.

7

New Zealand

Kate Diesfeld and John Hancock

> The (New Zealand) Government's aim is to achieve over the next decade a world class, inclusive education system that provides learning opportunities of equal quality for all students.[1]

New Zealand's commitment to inclusive education was clearly pronounced in the governmental policy *Special Education 2000*. A stocktake is timely because the government's national evaluation, *The Review of Special Education 2010*,[2] is under way and "aims to ensure that our education system is responsive to, and effective in, providing for those students with greatest needs for support to learn."[3] Accordingly, this chapter offers an overview of New Zealand's special education law, a description and critique of its processes, and recommendations derived from legal issues faced by children and young people with special educational needs.

THE CONTEXT OF RIGHTS TO EDUCATION

New Zealand has adopted a rights-based approach to special education. According to the Human Rights Commission, education is a human right and an essential means of realising other rights.[4] The commission adds that children develop their self-worth and respect for others through education since it increases their ability to contribute to, and fully participate in, our families and communities. Moreover, education is the primary means for children and young people who have been "economically and socially disadvantaged to eventually lift themselves out of poverty, through developing skills and qualifications necessary for quality paid work."[5]

At the same time, barriers to special education consistently emerged as a significant issue in the Commission's work over many years, as noted in its benchmark 2004 report *Human Rights in New Zealand Today*.[6] The Commission's more recent 2009 report, *Disabled Children's Rights to Education*, analyzed the extent of rights-protection and enabled it to advocate more effectively for these fundamental rights.

Unfortunately, the education of students with disabilities was among the most frequent category of complaints to the Commission[7] as reflected in the high number of complaints and enquiries received by its Dispute Resolution Team (DRT). Significant issues remain in all four components of the right to education: availability; accessibility; acceptability; and adaptability. This translates into an insufficient number of inclusive educators with special education training. Further, participation and achievement rates of disabled students are disproportionately low. As a result, there are considerable variations in educational standards for students with disabilities and unsafe school environments. The Commission concluded that the education system does not reasonably accommodate students with disabilities so that they may achieve equitable outcomes in New Zealand.[8]

These findings were reflected in the complaints received by the Office of the Children's Commissioner (OCC).[9] Additionally, OCC reported that parents were asked to keep "difficult" children at home during visits by officials from the Education Review Office. Some students were not allowed to remain during lunch or attend school every day. One child was excluded unless she used a wheelchair at all times, against the written advice of her doctor and physiotherapist. Of universal concern, many children are often bullied at school. Similar complaints are received by the Families Commission, YouthLaw, IHC and the Ombudsman's Office.[10] These conditions justify scrutiny of New Zealand's special education law and its impact.

LEGAL AND CONSTITUTIONAL SOURCES OF SPECIAL EDUCATION LAW

Education Act 1989

The Education Act 1989 (the Act) is the principal piece of legislation governing New Zealand's educational system. Part 1 of the Act includes the rights of primary and secondary school students with special educational needs and the procedures for administering special education services. Despite the legal and administrative complexity of special education, the Act does not accord it with a distinct statutory Part.

Section 3 of the Act sets out a general right to a free, state-school education to all persons aged from five to nineteen and expresses the bedrock principles of the Act:

> Right to free primary and secondary education: Except as provided in this Act or the Private Schools Conditional Integration Act 1975, every person who is not a foreign student is entitled to free enrolment and free education at any state school during the period beginning on the person's 5th birthday and ending on the 1st day of January after the person's 19th birthday.

Section 8 of the Act clarifies the application of this right to persons with "special educational needs," providing for an equal right to "receive" an education:

> Equal rights to primary and secondary education (1): Except as provided in this Part of this Act, people who have special educational needs (whether because of disability or otherwise) have the same rights to enrol and receive education at state schools as people who do not.

Sections 3 and 8 are underpinned by the National Education Guidelines, as required by section 60A of the Act. The Guidelines essentially deliver the government's policy objectives through the establishment of National Education Goals and National Administration Guidelines. The Guidelines include equality of opportunity,[11] identification and removal of barriers to achievement,[12] and identification of students with special needs as well as the provision of appropriate support.[13]

Section 9 provides specialist services or entitlements while setting the basis for the delivery of "special education," defined under section 2 as "education or help from a special school, special class, special clinic or special service." Section 10 sets out procedures for review or appeal of decisions made under section 9, ostensibly where officials from the Ministry of Education rejected applications for students to receive "special education" support under section 9. This includes an internal arbitration process, facilitated by the Ministry which appoints an arbitrator, after consultation with parents. The arbitration process itself is prescribed under section 10(6) and does not confer any right of representation for the student.[14]

The High Court and the Court of Appeal in *Daniels v. Attorney General*[15] examined the relationship between sections 8, the purposive statement of intent, and 9, the parameters of special assistance. This relationship is at the heart of the debate regarding the extent of a child with a disability's "equal right to education" and whether there is an entitlement to additional support. The issue is of particular significance following the government's ratification of the United Nations Convention on the Rights of Persons with Disabilities and the 2008 amendments to the Human Rights Act 1993 regarding educational establishments.[16]

Human Rights Legislation and International Instruments

Given that New Zealand's human rights legislation does not have primacy over other legislation, the rights to freedom from discrimination conferred by the Human Rights Act 1993[17] and the New Zealand Bill of Rights Act 1990[18] sit alongside, rather than over the top of, the provisions of the Education Act 1989. To this end, the Human Rights Act 1993 defines "disability" as a prohibited ground of discrimination, either direct or indirect,[19] in broad terms,[20] including physical, psychological and intellectual impairment, physical and psychiatric illness, reliance on remedial means and loss of anatomical, psychological or psychiatric function. In application, the Act covers a spectrum from the most severely physically or intellectually disabled students through to those children with mild to moderate psychological disorders such as Attention-Deficit Hyperactivity Disorder or Asperger's Syndrome.

The rights contained in the Human Rights Act 1993 apply to state, state-integrated, and private schools and educational establishments. However, the legal tests that apply where complaints are litigated under the Act differ according to whether they are lodged against entities carrying out public or private functions. The actions of entities that carry out public functions, such state schools, are measured against the right to freedom from discrimination under the New Zealand Bill of Rights Act 1990 (NZBORA). Any limitations to those freedoms must be reasonable and able to be shown to be "demonstrably justified in a free and democratic society" per NZBORA's section 5 "justified limitations" test.[21] Entities which do not fall under this category, such as private training establishments, must rely on the prescribed limitations set out in Part 2 of the Human Rights Act 1993 under sections 57 to 60.

The government's recent ratification[22] of the United Nations Convention on the Rights of Persons with Disabilities (UNCRPD) will have added considerable weight to any post-*Daniels* interpretation of section 8 of the Education Act 1989 as analysed below. This includes the obligations under Article 24 that the government ensure:

> reasonable accommodation of the individual's requirements . . . provision of support . . . to support their effective education and effective individualized support measures that maximize academic and social development . . . consistent with the goal of full inclusion.[23]

The UNCRPD's ratification resulted in the 2008 amendment to section 60(1) of the Human Rights Act to provide that educational establishments cannot claim protection from liability under its provisions in circumstances where special services or facilities can reasonably be made available.

The United Nations Convention on the Rights of the Child (UNCRC), ratified by New Zealand over seventeen years ago, also confers an obligation on the government to provide students with disabilities under the age of eighteen with special assistance in respect of their education.[24] While neither the UNCRPD nor the UNCRC are incorporated into New Zealand's domestic legislation, they certainly go beyond mere international "window-dressing" gestures. Both the Court of Appeal and, recently, the Supreme Court affirmed the application of UNCRC in determining government policy and decision making that affects children.[25] Therefore, it is somewhat likely that the courts will accord the UNCRPD a similar status should such a point be litigated in the future.

The *Daniels* Case: The High Court Judgment

At the time of writing, *Daniels v. Attorney General*[26] remains the most significant case from New Zealand regarding the rights of students with special educational needs. It is the only case to examine the interrelationship between sections 8 and 9 of the Education Act 1989 while defining the scope of the right conferred to special education students under section 8. Also, the case is a fascinating example of judges' varying approaches to the matrix of constitutional law issues that abound in cases where government policy and objectives, human rights obligations, and nebulous legislation intersect.

The class action sought judicial review of the government's special education policy entitled *Special Education 2000* (*SE2000*) and, in particular, the disestablishment of special education units and facilities in favor of establishing resources in "conventional" schools. The plaintiffs were fourteen parents of students with special educational needs.

The essence of the claim was that *SE 2000* itself was inconsistent with sections 3, 8, and 9 of the Education Act 1989 as well as section 98(2) of the preceding Education Act 1964 and therefore unlawful. The claim also contended that the Crown's conduct in implementing the policy constituted unlawful discrimination under section 19 of the NZBORA.[27]

Section 98(2) of the Education Act 1964 provides that a Minister of Education may disestablish a special school, unit, service or facility, only if the Minister "considers that special provision is made by a similarly established special school, class, clinic or service, or by any other school or class in or reasonably near to the same locality." The provision ended up being the thorn in Crown's side and the basis on which the plaintiffs ultimately succeeded.

The case posed a number of challenging questions for the High Court, particularly since the *SE 2000* was implemented without any legislative amendment giving effect to the systemic changes it introduced. Accordingly, Baragwanath J framed the issues as follows:

- The scope of the Crown's extrastatutory authority to provide education;
- The nature and scope of the legal obligations that the Education Acts 1989 and 1964 impose on the Crown;
- Whether the Crown, in fact, breached those statutory legal obligations;
- The extent to which those statutory obligations are justiciable;
- The nature of the right to be free from discrimination; and
- Whether the Crown did unlawfully discriminate against the plaintiffs.[28]

The determination of these issues involved a complex traverse of case law and academic commentary on the sensitive constitutional ground that lies afoot when courts are called on to interpret the extent of Crown obligations in the implementation of government policy. In his judgment, Baragwanath J referred to the decision of the House of Lords in *Re S*,[29] which rejected the attempt by the Court of Appeal of England and Wales to create legal mechanisms that, in light of systemic failure in the State's care of children obligations, purported to "introduce into the working of the Children Act a range of rights and limitations not sanctioned by law."

Still, Baragwanath J did not consider that the case before him entailed any risk of judicial legislation, primarily because sections 3 and 8 of the Education Act 1989 already provided "a range of rights and limitations sanctioned by law," the issue therefore being a matter for standard statutory interpretation. To emphasise this point, His Honour stated at paragraph 135: "(I)t is the executive that has misapprehended the will of Parliament as expressed in legislation. Parliament having conferred 'entitlements' and 'rights' it is the Court's duty to determine and express such entitlements than for the executive to give in effect."

In so ruling, Baragwanath J affirmed sections 3 and 8 as providing freestanding rights to education for students with special educational needs. His Honour went so far as to map out the parameters of this right as requiring: provision of education that is regular, systematic and suitable; an individual focus on the learning needs of each child; and provision of extra assistance in proportion to the extent of the child's particular disability.[30]

Baragwanath J, thus, affirmed both the right of children with disabilities of different learning abilities to receive differential treatment and the converse obligations of the Crown to monitor its provision of education to individual students, ensure adequate provision of special education services, and not to disestablish facilities or services without first deciding that adequate alternative resources exist.[31] However, his Honour found that the failure by the Crown to provide differential services did not, in itself, constitute unlawful discrimination under the Human Rights Act or NZBORA, instead holding that this would have amounted to a contravention of the Education Act 1989. He went on to state:

> It is axiomatic that a single statutory provision cannot have inconsistent meanings in different contexts. "Discrimination" in those statutes cannot sometimes mean "failure to treat the same" and other times mean "failure to treat differently." In the NZBORA and HRA it means the former, not the latter.[32]

In conclusion, Baragwanath J noted that the evidence, in particular Dr. Cathy Wylie's 2000 report for the Crown on special education services,[33] established breaches of sections 8, 9 and 98(2) of the 1964 Act, stating (in reference to the Wylie Report):

> The former Minister could not reasonably . . . have concluded that, New Zealand wide, "sufficient provision [was] made" for the "sizable number of children with special needs [who] are missing out on the support they need to participate as much in school and class life as any other child."[34]

This outcome is supported by the fact that the Ministry paper recommending the introduction of *SE 2000* made no attempt actually to match disestablished facilities against a list of substitutes "in or reasonably near to the same locality (the language of s98[2])."[35]

Daniels: The Court of Appeal Judgment

The Crown sought further review of the decision before the Court of Appeal which reviewed the judgment on 12 and 13 November 2002. A summary of the essential issues identified by the Court of Appeal follows:

- Is there any difference between the expression of "special educational needs" in section 8 of the Act and "special education" in section 9, and what educational facilities fall within the ambit of section 9? Has *SE 2000* breached those provisions?
- What is the nature of the "equal" rights conferred to students with special educational needs under section 8 compared to those students without special education needs? Has that right been breached?
- Did the Minister comply with section 98(2) of the 1964 Act when he determined in 1998 to disestablish special units?[36]

The Court of Appeal pointed out that while the Ministry breached section 98(2) in disestablishing special units, there was no breach of sections

8 or 9 of the 1989 Act. This marked both a rejection of Baragwanath J's judgment that the decisions made under *SE2000* constituted a breach of a special right, conferred under the Act, to differential treatment and a considerable narrowing of its potential impact.

In addressing the first question, the Court of Appeal essentially drew a line between sections 8 and 9. The court maintained that section 9 accorded distinctive access to special education facilities or resources, specifically individualised Ongoing Reviewable Resource Scheme (ORRS) funding and special schools. Section 8 covered those students with special needs who did not qualify under section 9.

Most significantly, the Court of Appeal went on to reject the notion of any freestanding right to students with special educational needs under sections 3 and 8, stating:

> (W)hile there are rights under the 1989 Act that can be enforced by the Court process, those rights do not include generally, and abstractly, formulated rights of the kind stated by the Judge. . . . There is no freestanding general right, held and enforceable by each individual student under sections 3 and 8, of the kind stated.[37]

The Court of Appeal repeated this point in its judgment.[38] Additionally, the Court did not address the question of whether the policy constituted unlawful discrimination, despite the extensive submissions made by the Human Rights Commission, who appeared as Intervener in respect of this issue alone. The Commission argued that Baragwanath J's finding on this issue was an "unduly restrictive" concept of discrimination and essentially wrong in law.[39] It is notable that, in response, the Crown argued that it was unnecessary for the Court of Appeal to address the issue of discrimination, stating in their submissions that it is "unnecessary that the Court consider the proper approach to the slippery slope of discrimination in any detail."[40]

The Post-*Daniels* Landscape

The end result of *Daniels* was therefore somewhat problematic as the totality of the High Court and Court of Appeal decisions curtail a rights-based approach to special education entitlements in New Zealand. In fact, the Court of Appeal did its best to quash any notion of students with special educational needs having innate, freestanding, and enforceable rights to education under sections 3 and 8 of the Education Act 1989.

The government's more recent ratification of the UNCRPD, though, indicates its commitment to obligations in respect to the special education sector that are consistent with both Baragwanath J's interpretation of sections 8 and 9 and with the broad understanding of the antidiscrimination law sought by the Human Rights Commission. Indeed, the Commission's submissions in the *Daniels* appeal argued that New Zealand's antidiscrimination legislation "has at all times made provision for an affirmative duty to achieve equality of outcome by affording 'reasonable accommodation' where appropriate."[41] The obligation on the government to provide "reasonable accommodation of an individual's requirements" is, of course, required by Article 24.2(c) of the UNCRPD and is now reflected in section 60(1) of the Human Rights Act 1993.

The government's *Review of Special Education 2010*, which is currently drawing towards its conclusion, may well result in some reform of the Education Act 1989. Perhaps this will resolve the legal quandary left by the *Daniels* litigation and clarify the corresponding rights and obligations affirmed by the ratification of UNCRPD. Such an amendment is overdue, not just to clarify the extent of the rights of special needs students, but also to reverse current alarming systemic outcomes. For example, almost 40 percent of students excluded from New Zealand schools[42] have had special education referrals to either a Resource Teacher for Learning and Behaviour (RTLB) or the Ministry of Education Group Special Education Services.[43]

IHC New Zealand Complaint

More recently, a major advocate for inclusive education of all children with intellectual disabilities filed a complaint with the Human Rights Commission.[44] In July 2008, IHC New Zealand Inc (IHC) alleged that government practices result in discrimination under the NZBORA for children with intellectual disabilities, resulting in their exclusion from their local schools. The complaint alleged that the discrimination occurs due to factors ranging from education law to Ministry of Education policies. The complaint added that students with disabilities face situations that are not routinely faced by their peers who are not disabled. For example, the complaint charged that students' attendance was limited due to lack of teacher aide funding. It also claimed that students were excluded from classroom activities, sports, music activities, and school trips due to inadequate support and that since children were refused enrolment, suspended or expelled for behaviour attributable to impairment, in order to achieve full participation, their parents were required to contribute financially.[45]

In March 2010, the Human Rights Commission, Crown Law, and the Ministry of Education discussed the parameters of the mediation process. Depending on the outcome of the mediation, the case could proceed to the more formal Human Rights Review Tribunal. Recently, and perhaps in response to the complaint, the Ministry developed a complaint register and new information on the rights and responsibilities of parents and schools.[46]

THE RIGHTS OF STUDENTS WITH DISABILITIES

Decades of advocacy influenced reform of special education law in New Zealand. In the 1980s, the parent movement in New Zealand advocated for a rights-based approach to equal education for students with disabilities.[47] Historically, children and young adults were placed in day units operated by voluntary agencies,[48] but section 8 of the Education Act 1989 introduced the entitlement to free education at any state school from the age of five. The prevailing influences on the reform included educational leaders who promoted mainstream education, the development of articulate parents groups, and advocacy by voluntary agencies.[49]

In 2001 the government launched the *New Zealand Disability Strategy*[50] with the goal of promoting an inclusive society by adopting the social model of disability and establishing fifteen objectives. Of particular relevance, Objective 3 aims to "provide the best education for disabled people" and establishes that all children, youth and adult learners have equal opportunities to education in their local, regular education centres.[51] More specifically, the government's *SE2000* policy proclaims the commitment to "a world class inclusive education system" of equal quality to all children.[52] The key policy objectives of this movement are to:

- Improve educational opportunities and outcomes for children with special education needs in the early childhood and school sectors;
- Ensure there is a clear, consistent and predictable resourcing framework for special education;
- Provide equitable resourcing for those with similar needs irrespective of school setting or geographic location; and
- Assist schools to take ownership in meeting the full range of students' needs.[53]

Identification and Assessment

Children may qualify for special education if they have physical impairments; learning disabilities; hearing or vision difficulties (or sensory impairments); difficulties with learning, communicating, or getting along with others; and/or emotional or behavioral difficulties.[54]

The Ministry offers a range of support for special education.[55] From birth until school entrance, the Ministry Special Education Grants (SEG) offer early intervention support and other accredited services.[56] If children have not yet entered school, their parents may speak with their family doctors; Plunket nurses; educators from Parents as First Teachers; Iwi Health Authorities; or staff at their early childhood education centers. In practice, parents are usually referred to the SEG. The support spectrum includes assessment, provision of information, referral to specialist services (such as speech-language therapy), and assistance by educational support workers.

When children attend primary or secondary schools, their families may contact their teachers or principals. Assistance may be offered from specially trained teachers who work with students with learning and/or behavior difficulties (RTLBs), vision impairments, and/or hearing impairments.

According to the Ministry, most children receive special education support within their local schools, and "parents choose the school and setting their child attends."[57] Yet, children with high needs may attend special schools and/or access extra services from Ministry of Education, Special Education (GSE). This includes speech and occupational therapists, and physiotherapists; psychologists for assessment and intervention; advisors; teacher aides; and support workers. Additionally, children may receive subsidies or allowances for transportation assistance, alterations or additions to state school property, assistive technology and equipment.

Students with moderate needs may receive Special Education Grants (SEG) for extra assistance. The three principles underpinning SEG funding to schools are: the funds have to improve students' learning and/or behavior; school officials decide how the money is spent; and ownership of the process by the school is vital for it to work.[58]

Assessment is largely the responsibility of teachers and school staff, with support from specialists within other appropriate agencies.[59] Assessments should be grounded in discussions with the children and their caregivers as well as be curriculum-based. Generally assessment should occur in students' routine environments and include observations in a range of "natural and everyday settings."[60] Ideally assessments are made by those in daily contact with students rather than the previous practice by external professionals.[61] Further, assessors may administer formal standardized tests to students. Educational records, portfolios of student work and self-assessments are relevant components. Importantly, assessment should identify how children learn such as whether their optimum performance occurs when instructions are oral rather than written.

As to assessments, the Ministry declared that "New Zealand special education has taken a deliberately non-categorical approach to support for children and young people with special educational needs. This means that needs are defined in terms of support required, rather than by use of diagnostic labels."[62] The Ministry acknowledges that "effective assessment will take into account diversity of belief systems and cultural expectations." Moreover, since assessments may be stressful for families, the Ministry advises that "extra support and understanding by all those involved may ease this process."[63]

Described as a "living document,"[64] the Individual Education Program (IEP) that directs the content of the education provided for students may represent the meeting at which their needs are discussed; a document program for an individual student; or the complete cycle of assessment, planning, provision, and evaluation. It is also worth noting that students who receive ORRS funding require additional agreements linking the resourcing with their IEPs. While IEPs are usually reviewed twice per year, frequency varies according to the needs of an individual student.

IEPs are unnecessary when barriers to effective learning by students with disabilities cannot be overcome by regular classroom strategies; regular classroom planning does not provide adequate support; key transitions occur, such as changing classes or schools or preparing to leave school; and/ or changes in student circumstances such as substantial gain in skills or deterioration in health.

Ideally, the IEP process unites a collaborative team that develops a customized program[65] by identifying students' current strengths, setting short- and long-term goals and recording progress. Typically, IEPs identify the individuals responsible for implementing their specific objectives and resource requirements, with time lines. Importantly, the IEP process provides a measure of accountability[66] while demonstrating how educators fulfil their obligations under the National Educational Goals, National Administrative Guidelines, and Special Education Policy Guidelines.

In an affirming fashion, the Ministry advises that the success of the IEP process depends on a range of factors, including acknowledging that every contributor has a unique perspective and that placement decisions are central to the process. In a more blunt tone, though, the Ministry explains that the IEP is not a document commissioned from an "expert"; a lengthy meeting and enormous report; a resource "shopping list"; attended by hordes of professionals; or a disempowering, daunting and distressing experience for families.[67]

Placement Issues

Prior to 1989, the majority of students with severe disabilities were excluded from public education. Instead, these children were educated by private education trusts and voluntary agencies such as IHC.[68] Based on the normalization movement, the concept of inclusion gained acceptance during the 1970s and 1980s in New Zealand. Today the isolation of people with intellectual disabilities can be justified only under exceptional circumstances.[69] Even so, while considerable progress has been made towards inclusion in regular education, twenty-eight special schools and special classes continue to exist.[70] Special schools also run satellite schools on the grounds of regular schools. Also, some students with high needs may be supported at their local schools through mobile teaching services from the special schools or attend twenty-eight-day special schools or health schools. Five residential special schools support students with a range of educational and social needs. Additionally, two residential schools support students with hearing impairments while one supports students with vision impairments.

How Inclusive Is New Zealand's Education System?

O'Brien and Ryba report that undoubtedly New Zealand has made gains in inclusive education within regular educational settings.[71] However, arguably the use of external Ministry specialists reinforces that specialist supports are required. An alternative, ecological view is that school-based specialist staff could work beside teachers to support individual education and systemic improvements.[72] As such, O'Brien and Ryba call for greater implementation of *SE2000's* inclusion policies which were based on the social model of disability and human rights.

Ryba and Anna also observed that "for the time being, segregated programmes for students with intellectual disabilities will continue to operate alongside regular education."[73] More broadly, they report that "it would be incorrect to assume that appropriate education is now provided in state schools."[74] Despite the substantial philosophical and administrative changes recently, many students do not receive an appropriate education due to a lack of resources. The authors further report that the greatest obstacle to full participation is often the wider society's lack of acceptance and understanding of people with intellectual disabilities.

The future of inclusive education is currently being debated under the *Review of the Special Education 2010*.[75] Option A is the maintenance of the current system which offers both special schools and provision in regular schools.[76] Option B is the closure of special schools and satellites. Under this approach, all regular schools would be assisted to include all children, thereby increasing the number of schools with special units. Option C is the transformation of former special schools into resource centres to provide outreach to regular schools with an increase in the number of regular schools with special units. Former special school teachers would participate in a mobile teaching service. Option D is the maintenance of the existing system, but students would be directly enrolled in special schools without requiring prior assessment by the Ministry. This would streamline enrolment and expand the number of special schools.

A predictable division in perspectives has emerged during the consultation stage of the national review. Primary and secondary teachers want to retain the current system, while IHC proposes an entirely new system founded on principles of social inclusion and human rights.[77]

Due Process Rights and Dispute Resolution

The Ministry's webpage, Choices, Rights and Obligations, claims that parents have a range of options for school enrolment and services. It adds that dissatisfied parents may report their concerns to their key worker or obtain information regarding GSE complaints from a GSE service manager.[78] If difficulties cannot be resolved through the school's complaints process, families may contact the Ministry of Education. Parents or guardians may apply to the Ministry for formal reconsideration under section 10 of the Education Act 1989 regarding decision on enrolment, provision of education, or special services. Parents may request reconsideration within one month. Decisions regarding ORRS funding and Supplementary Learning Support are also subject to formal section 10 review.

An independent advocacy service is provided through the Office of the Children's Commissioner. One branch trains a network of community-based advocates. The other, Parents Legal Information Line, provides free legal advice, education and advocacy through the Wellington Community Law Centre.[79]

Funding and Cost Issues

According to the Ministry of Education, all special education services are provided free by the government.[80] The funding is distributed directly to GSE, GSE-accredited early intervention services and schools. Families may be asked to assist teachers to apply for two additional types of funding.

First, Ongoing and Reviewable Resource Schemes (ORRS) is available for school-age students with high special educational needs. This funding is paid to the service providers such as GSE, special schools, or other schools, while the schools receive extra teacher time. In order to qualify, students must need high levels of continuing support requiring significant adaptations of curricula as well as assistance to participate in communication and supervision with daily care and mobility. The Ministry's team of independent verifiers confirm the level of support needs. However, the former Children's Commissioner criticised the ORRS process because "parents have to navigate a complex world of entitlements," often without adequate support, skills and personal resources to access them.[81]

Second, High Health Needs Funding may be provided to schools for students with health conditions that require care and supervision for more than six weeks. This allows paraprofessionals to provide care so that student can participate at school. Still, the care does not include assistance with students' learning needs or missed schoolwork.

Over four years, the national budget allocated $51 million additional funds to ORRS and nearly $10.7 million to support students with "high health needs."[82] Yet, dissatisfaction has been reported from a number of stakeholders. For example, the Auckland Primary Principals Association (APPA) reported that the 2009 budget was inadequate because first the formula that distributes the funding must be reformed. The AAPA proposed a single funding pool for special education students, a streamlined funding process, and extension of the ORRS from the current 3 percent to 5 percent for high and very high needs.[83] Based on their daily contact with students, the AAPA concluded that principals should have greater control over funding distribution because they know students' capabilities and needs.[84]

EMERGING ISSUES

The following recommendations for dealing with emerging issues were derived from legal representation of special education students and their families in New Zealand by a national community law center, YouthLaw Tino Rangatiratanga Taitamariki. These factors were expressed in YouthLaw's submissions on Review of Special Education in March 2010.[85] YouthLaw reported that students with special needs encounter systemic barriers that prevent equitable participation and education outcomes. Many of the obstacles stem from an inadequate legal framework under the Education Act 1989 and create the following impacts.

First, students encounter difficulties in transferring between schools as the transitional processes are fragmented and in some instances nonexistent. This is particularly problematic when students progress from primary to secondary school. Successful transition largely depends on the competence of the receiving school's management in ensuring that the students' needs are identified, existing supports are maintained or reassessed and that the appropriate processes are implemented, such as convening IEP meetings. At particular risk are students who do not qualify for continuing individualised funding, including students with psychological disorders and conditions such as Autistic Spectrum Disorder or Attention-Deficit Hyperactivity Disorder. A more formalised process should be implemented through an independent service coordinator or Ministry special education caseworker. Formalisation of this role via legislation or regulation will promote consistent processes and outcomes.

Second, YouthLaw observed the need for greater intra-agency collaboration in order to serve students with disabilities. Ideally, IEP meetings should provide agreement between relevant agencies at the outset followed by comprehensive implementation. Yet, many students are excluded from schools or restricted from attendance because their IEPs were not implemented, such as the failure to follow behavioral management techniques. The resulting frustration erodes trust between parents, schools, and agencies. Again, a designated coordinator would aid communication and improve outcomes.

The third factor transcends geographical boundaries—financial resources. Of particular concern, students who fail to qualify for section 9 ORRS funding are not adequately served. Many students with severe, debilitating disabilities miss out on individualised support. Also, YouthLaw understands that ORRS does not fully expend its budget, and YouthLaw's experience suggests that the ORRS funding verification process is flawed, as illustrated by the following case.

In one case, a thirteen-year-old former orphan from Eastern Europe was adopted by a couple in New Zealand. After suffering extreme deprivation in the orphanage, the child had significant developmental delays. Without individualised support in New Zealand, the student was in no position to enjoy her right to education. Since the child's school did not have special education funding (SEG) available, her parents and school were relying on ORRS funding.

ORRS verifiers rejected the parents' first two funding applications. After arbitration, it was determined that the parents should make a third application. Although the application was well over twenty pages long, containing substantial clinical data from the student's psychologist and paediatrician, the verifiers again declined the parental request for help. Obtained under the Official Information Act, the verifiers' notes were no more than a paragraph or two. One merely stated: "An unusual child, but not an ORRS child."[86] The decision making was clearly inadequate and left a very vulnerable girl with a clinically tested, severe developmental delay without resource support, a shameful outcome for a developed country.

In other cases, the ORRS assessment did not address the relevant criteria or omitted relevant information, such as clinical or diagnostic data. Although the guidelines provide that verifiers may meet students, YouthLaw understands that this rarely occurs.[87] In YouthLaw's estimation, while it is important for decision makers to be impartial, the ORRS process excessively distances verifiers from students. Consequently, verifiers are overly detached and their opaque decisions lack rigour and accountability.[88]

Fourth, there is room for improvement in the disputes regime. Currently, the sole procedure available within the ambit of the Education Act 1989 is arbitration. Section 10 prescribes a set of procedures for reviews or appeals of decisions by the Secretary of Education under section 9. This includes entitlement to arbitration when, for example, the Ministry rejects an application for "special education" support under section 9. However, section 10 arbitration is not a truly independent process, as arbitrators are appointed by the Ministry with some input from families. Representation rights are limited and further appeal sealed off by section 10(6). YouthLaw noted that arbitrations are procedurally ad hoc and subject to the complete discretion of the arbitrator.

While High Court judicial review is available, it is beyond the means of most parents and involves legal complexities that do not necessarily fit well with the needs of students, their parents, and schools. Further, although Ombudsman investigations are thorough, the lengthy process causes educational delays and does not result in binding decisions.

YouthLaw recommends the establishment of an Independent Review Authority to ensure an appropriate degree of impartiality when considering disputes or appeals. On enrolment in schools, parents should be provided with clear information regarding review processes and support services. Other jurisdictions have adopted similar review bodies and processes. For example, in England, appeals against Local Education Authorities may be taken to Special Educational Needs Tribunals, established under the Education Act 1993 (UK).[89] Likewise, California, as part of the scheme established by the American Individuals with Disabilities Education Act,[90] has a robust alternative dispute resolution process with trained mediators. School boards in California often use mediation panels comprised of trained parents, staff, and mediators from within the special education sector, funded by the State Department of Education.[91]

More broadly, New Zealand should establish a new legal framework that reflects the government's commitments under the UNCRC and the UNCRDP. The Court of Appeal's interpretation of section 8 in *Daniels v. Attorney General* is evidence that the Act has become antiquated. The Act's lack of clarity and accountability processes is largely responsible for the types of barriers outlined above. The Act should be amended to include a new part dedicated to special education. This new section should include an interpretation clause, principles and purposive clauses, defined roles, support entitlements, detailed processes (including IEP meetings) and appeal avenues. The legislative framework should also explicitly incorporate the relevant UNCRC and UNCRPD obligations.

Of international interest, advocacy has been a recurring recommendation in New Zealand. Although the Minister reported that advocacy was essential for *SE 2000* to succeed, the Chair of the Coalition of Parents for Special Education noted that it was entirely missing.[92] Coalition-sponsored research revealed that over 60 percent of parents do not belong to any formal support group.[93] If New Zealand were to follow Australia's lead, it would have governmentally funded parent groups to inform, lobby and advocate on relevant issues. Ideally, an independent umbrella coalition of advocacy groups could "combine strength of voice and strategy to increase educational opportunities for students whose 'voice' is not audible."[94]

CONCLUSION

New Zealand's law and policy affirm the rights of students with special needs to receive appropriate and equitable education in an inclusive education system. The question remains how this will be borne out. While New Zealand has pronounced its commitment to this fundamental right for all children and young people, the evidence demonstrates that those ideals have not been fully realised. However, New Zealand's response to the current review and future enforcement of international human rights will demonstrate the extent of its genuine dedication to establishing New Zealand as a world-class provider of special education within the next decade.

NOTES

The authors appreciate the perspectives of David Hagar (Auckland Disability Law) and assistance of Yvonne Milbank and Daniel Taylor at the University of Waikato. Kate Diesfeld's sabbatical was kindly supported by Waikato Law School.

1. Ministry of Education (2010) Special Education 2000. Wellington: Ministry of Education. http://www.minedu.govt.nz/NZEducation/EducationPolicies/SpecialEducation/FormsAndGuidelines/IEPGuidelines/Introduction.aspx.

2. Ministry of Education (2010) Review of Special Education. Wellington: Ministry of Education. http://www.minedu.govt.nz/theMinistry/Consullation/ReviewOfSpecialEducation/DiscussionDocument2010.

3. Ibid. at 2.

4. Human Rights Commission te Kahui Tika Tangata (2009) Disabled Children's Right to Education. Wellington: Human Rights Commission. http://www.hrc.co.nz/home/hrc/disabledpeople/disabledchildrensrighttoeducation.php.

5. Ibid. at 4.

6. Human Rights Commission te Kahui Tika Tangata (2004) Human Rights in New Zealand Today: Nga Tika Tangata o te Mortu. Wellington: Human Rights Commission. http://www.hrc.co.nz/home/hrc/humanrightsenvironment/humanrightsinnewzealandtoday/humanrightsinnewzealandtoday.php.

Barriers to education for disabled children were also a significant priority within the Human Rights Commissions 2005–2010 New Zealand Action Plan for Human Rights: Mana kit e tangata.

http://www.hrc.co.nz/hrc_new/hrc/cms/files/documents/24-Jul-2005_21-04-32_SF_Jul_WLG_Panui_for_HR_Forum210705.ppt.

7. Supra note 4, at 4.

8. Supra note 4, at 9.

9. Carroll-Lind, J. and Rees, K. (2009) School for all: Children's rights to an inclusive education in New Zealand. Presented at Making Inclusive Education Happen: Ideas for Sustainable Change, 28-30/10/2009. Wellington, Te Papa. http://www.imaginebetter.co.nz/downloads/IE.../PR/29c_Carroll-LindPR.pdf.

10. Ibid. at 7.

11. National Administrative Guidelines Education Goal 2. Ministry of Education (2008) National Administrative Guidelines. Wellington: Ministry of Education. http://www.minedu.govt.nz/NZEducation/EducationPolicies/Special Education/PolicyAndStrategy/SpecialEducationPolicy.aspx.

12. Ibid.

13. National Education Goal 7, Ibid.

14. A right to a representative is limited to parents, who can arrange for one representative to appear on their behalf at a section 10 arbitration (section 10[6][l]). Decisions regarding the hearing duration, process of considering evidence and availability of witnesses is at the discretion of the arbitrator.

15. *LSA Daniels and ORS v. Her Majesty's Attorney-General*, M1615-SW99, High Court, Auckland, 03/04/02, per Baragwanath J; *Attorney-General v. Daniels* [2003] 2 NZLR 742 (CA).

16. Sections 9(a) and 9(b) Human Rights Amendment Act 2008 (amending section 60[1] of the Human Rights Act 1993).

17. Section 21.

18. Section 19.

19. Section 65.

20. Section 21(1)(h).

21. Section 20 (I)–(L), Human Rights Act 1993.

22. Ratification occurred on 25/9/2008. See United Nations Enable at http://www.un.org/disabilities/default.asp?id=257.

23. Articles 24.2(c)–(e).

24. Articles 23.2, 23.3.

25. *Tavita v. Minister of Immigration* [1994] 2 NZLR 257 (CA); *Ye v. Minister of Immigration* [2010] 1 NZLR 104 (SC).

26. *LSA Daniels and ORS v. Her Majesty's Attorney-General*, M1615-SW99, High Court, Auckland, 03/04/02.

27. Ibid. at para. 42.

28. Ibid. at para. 44.

29. *Re S* [2002] UKHL 10.

30. Ibid. at para. 143.

31. Ibid.

32. Ibid. at para. 97.

33. Ibid. at para. 142.

34. Ibid. at para. 143.

35. Ibid. at para. 144.

36. *Her Majesty's Attorney-General v. Daniels*, CA84/02, 19/2/03, para. 13.

37. Ibid. at para. 83.

38. Ibid. at para. 97.

39. Outline of Submissions on Behalf of Human Rights Commission, CA84/02, R Harrison QC, para. 1.

40. Referred to in Reply Submissions of Respondents in Respect of Discrimination, CA84/02, G Illingworth and I Bassett, para. 2.2.

41. Outline of Submissions on Behalf of Human Rights Commission, CA84/02, R Harrison QC, para. 20.

42. Source: V. Holm, Official Information Act request, 23/9/09.

43. See also Trainor, C. (2004) The principles of natural justice in the context of student suspension hearings and school-based restorative conferencing. In C. Breen (Ed.) *Needs, Rights and Welfare: Developing Strategies for the Whole Child in the 21st Century*. Southbank, Vic: Thomson Dunmore, 151–172.

44. IHC New Zealand Inc. (2010) What's new with IHC's education complaint to the Human Rights Commission? http://www.ihc.org.nz/Portals/0/Get%20 Information/education-complaint/Update-1209.pdf.

45. Barton, C. (2008) The red tape run-around. Auckland Down Syndrome Association. 30/7/08. http://www.adsa.org.nz/webapps/site/69075/88360/news/news-more.html?newsid=185549.

46. Supra note 44.

47. Brown, C. (1994) Special education policies for the Fourth Labour Government, 1984–1990: An interpretive analysis. Unpublished Masters thesis, Massey University, New Zealand. Cited in O'Brien, P., and Ryba, K. (2005) Policies and systems in special education. In Frazer, D., Moltzen, R. and Ryba, K. (Eds.). *Learners with Special Needs in Aotearoa New Zealand (3rd ed.)* Wellington: Thomson Dunmore Press, 22–47.

48. O'Brien, P., and Ryba, K. (2005) Policies and systems in special education. In Frazer, D., Moltzen, R. and Ryba, K. (Eds.). *Learners with Special Needs in Aotearoa New Zealand (3rd ed.)* Wellington: Thomson Dunmore Press, 22–47 at 24.

49. Ibid. at 25.

50. Ministry of Health (2001) New Zealand Disability Strategy: Making a World of Difference-Whakanui oranga. Wellington: Ministry of Health. http://www.moh .govt.nz/moh.nsf/0/820c9fc77b3e1d18cc256d8f00724755/$FILE/nzdspdf.pdf.

51. See also Neilson, W. (2005) Disability: Attitudes, history and discourses. In Frazer, D., Moltzen, R. and Ryba. K. (Eds.). *Learners with Special Needs in Aotearoa New Zealand (3rd ed.)* Wellington: Thomson Dunmore Press, 9–21.

52. Supra at note 1.

53. Ministry of Education (2003) Special Education Policy Guidelines. Wellington: Ministry of Education. http://www.minedu.govt.nz/NZEducation/EducationPolicies/SpecialEducation/FormsAndGuidelines/SpecialEducation-PolicyGuidelines.aspx.

54. Ministry of Education (2010) Special Education Services. Wellington: Ministry of Education. http://www.minedu.govt.nz/NZEducation/Education Policies/SpecialEducation.aspx.

55. Ibid.

56. Approximately 2,500 Ministry staff work in the GSE, which has sixteen district offices and employs District Maori Advisors (Pouarahi-a-Takiwa).

57. Ministry of Education (2010). Individual Education Programmes (IEP) Guidelines. Wellington: Ministry of Education. http://www.minedu.govt.nz/

NZEducation/EducationPolicies/SpecialEducation/FormsandGuidelines/IndividualEducationProgramme.

58. Ibid. at 29.

59. Supra at note 57.

60. Supra at note 57.

61. Moltzen, R. (2005) Collaborative planning for individual needs. In Frazer, D., Moltzen, R. and Ryba, K. (Eds.) *Learners with Special Needs in Aotearoa New Zealand (3rd ed.)* Wellington: Thomson Dunmore Press, 155–167, at 159.

62. Ministry of Education (2010) Special Education Services. Wellington: Ministry of Education. http://www.minedu.govt.nz/NZEducation./education Policies/SpecialEducation/Servicesandfunding/referralAssessment.

63. Ibid.

64. Supra at note 53.

65. Supra at note 61, 160.

66. Supra at note 61, 159.

67. Supra at note 57.

68. Ryba, K., and Annan, J. (2005) Students with intellectual disabilities. In Frazer, D., Moltzen, R. and Ryba, K. (Eds.) *Learners with Special Needs in Aotearoa New Zealand (3rd ed.)* Wellington: Thomson Dunmore Press, 270–293, 270.

69. Ibid. at 270.

70. Ibid. at 269.

71. Supra at note 48, 43.

72. Supra at note 48, 43.

73. Supra at note 68, 270.

74. Supra at note 68, 270.

75. Supra at note 2, 16.

76. Supra at note 2, 18.

77. Radio New Zealand (2010) IHC, unions oppose change to special education. 23/3/10. http://www.radionz.co.nz/news/stories/2010/03/23/1247f89f8cea.

78. Supra at note 62. http://www.minedu.govt.nz/Parents/YourChild/SupportForYourChild/ExtraSupport/StartingSchool/ChoicesRightsObligations.aspx.

79. Supra at note 9, 9.

80. Supra at note 62.

81. Supra at note 45.

82. Smith, J. (2009) Streamlined process for high-needs students urged. *New Zealand Herald,* 3/6/09, A2. http://www.nzherald.co.nz/nz/news/article.cfm?c_id=1&objectid=10576319.

83. Ibid.

84. Ibid.

85. YouthLaw Tino Rangatiratanga Taitamariki (2010) *Submissions on Review of Special Education Discussion Document.* Available from author at John@youthlaw.co.nz.

86. Ibid at para. 14.

87. Supra at note 45.

88. Supra at note 85, 16.

89. Tribunals Service (2010) First-Tier Tribunal (Special Educational Needs and Disability). Darlington: Special Educational Needs and Disability. http://www.sendlist.gov.uk/AboutUs/index.htm.

90. See, generally, 20 U.S.C. section 1415 (2005)

91. California Department of Education (2010) Special Education Dispute Resolution Process. Sacramento: California Department of Education. http://www.cde.ca.gov/ls/cs/k3/dispute.asp.

92. Supra at notes 48, 40.

93. Ibid.

94. Ibid.

LIST OF CASES

LSA Daniels and ORS v. Her Majesty's Attorney-General, M1615-SW99, High Court, Auckland, 03/04/02.

Attorney-General v. Daniels [2003] 2 NZLR 742 (CA).

Re S [2002] UKHL 10.

Tavita v. Minister of Immigration [1994] 2 NZLR 257 (CA).

Ye v. Minister of Immigration [2010] 1 NZLR 104 (SC).

8

Singapore

M. K. Teh

People who have been to Singapore are usually amazed that such a small country can enjoy the economic growth it does and still manage to sustain a relatively high rate of employment. Being an island of approximately 690 square kilometres[1] with no exploitable natural resources to achieve growth, Singapore has to rely essentially on "brainpower" to access the most lucrative global markets. Education is therefore a crucial concern for Singapore's leaders in the running of the country, because, alongside innovation, education is seen as a significant economy driver. Policies are thus initiated to nurture students in order that the nation has future leaders to meet the challenges of an increasingly service- and knowledge-based economy.[2] In such a high-powered environment, where do students with disabilities fit, and what are the laws and policies governing their rights?

Compulsory education was introduced in Singapore in January 2003, but it extends only to primary education.[3] Moreover, unlike some jurisdictions, where compulsory education extends to children with disabilities, section 4(1) of the Compulsory Education Act (Cap. 51, 2003) (the Act) exempts children who have any physical or intellectual disabilities from complying with its provisions.[4] In other words, if parents of children with disabilities fail to send their children to school, there is nothing in legislation to compel them to do so.

Article 23 of the United Nations Convention on the Rights of the Child (CRC) states, in part, that in "recognizing the special needs of the disabled child . . . the assistance extended . . . shall be designed to ensure that the disabled child has effective access to and receives education . . . in manner conducive of the child's achieving the fullest possible social integration and individual development."

Singapore's response to Article 23 of the CRC, and its approach to special education, is that it is a shared responsibility of the community, the government, and families. The term *Many Helping Hands* is coined by the government to depict the approach that it takes in addressing disability and special needs. Thus, this chapter gives a very unusual perspective on the "rights" of students with disabilities in Singapore since there are no legal rights as such. Instead, there are policies and initiatives to ensure that the educational needs of the students with disabilities in Singapore are not neglected.

POLICIES

Voluntary Welfare Organisations

Since its people are the so-called natural resources of the country, Singapore, in its early years of independence, concentrated on the education of mainstream learners with special education being left to volunteers. In the 1950s, special education services started with groups of volunteers founding various voluntary associations that offered educational services for children with different disabilities.[5] For example, the Spastic Children's Association was founded in 1957, the Singapore Association for Retarded Children (SARC) in 1962 and the Singapore Association for the Educationally Subnormal (AESN) in 1976.[6] SARC and AESN were subsequently changed to Movement for the Intellectually Disabled of Singapore (MINDS) and Association for Persons with Special Needs (APSN), respectively. These organisations manage the special education services, and they are known as Voluntary Welfare Organisations (VWOs).

Funding of VWOs

Special Education Schools, set up by VWOs and registered as private schools under the Education Act, are managed by voluntary School Management Committees.[7] Until 1990,[8] funding for these special education services was provided either by the National Council of Social Services (NCSS) solely, or jointly by NCSS and the Ministry of Community Development.[9] However, since 1990 funding was effected on a 50-50 basis between the Ministry of Education (MOE) and the NCSS, since the VWOs were of the view that the MOE should bear some responsibility for special education in the country.[10]

As the nation became more educated and knowledgeable, the society, systems and thinking about issues affecting lives, in particular, rights issues, underwent remarkable levels of change. "Our world has changed irrevocably . . . Singaporeans are now better educated and more informed. Their desire to be involved is much stronger," commented the then Deputy Prime Minister Lee Hsien Loong at the Harvard Club's thirty-fifth anniversary dinner on 6 January 2004.[11] It was therefore not surprising that pressure increased for the MOE to do more for children with special needs. As such, policy changes occurred in the form of the MOE not only providing funding to special education (SPED) schools for recurrent expenditure but also providing capital funding for the construction and renovation of buildings for SPED schools.[12]

Integration or Segregation

In the late 1980s, the government commissioned an advisory council to look into the needs of the disabled in the country, with the Report of the Advisory Council published in November 1988. Among the Report's many recommendations was support for the integration of children with disabilities or with special needs in the mainstream system and that such "integration should fit the disabled child to the most suitable educational environment."[13] However, in practice, since no legislation mandated the provision of special education in regular schools, the placement of special needs children depended very much on the regular schools' facilities, resources, and the needs of students. For example, students with physical disabilities will be enrolled in schools with ramps, lifts, and the like while students with moderate, severe, and profound disabilities are more likely to be enrolled in special schools. Students with milder forms of special needs are commonly integrated into the mainstream system; these include children with mild physical disabilities, visual and hearing impairment, autism and dyslexia.[14]

Identification and Assessment

When children with special needs in Singapore reach schooling age, there are no formal assessments for school and class placements. The identification of children with special needs is thus left to teachers and Special Needs Officers (SNOs) in the mainstream primary and secondary schools where educators make referrals to the professionals if they identify children who exhibit signs of learning difficulties. The assessment of children with special needs in mainstream schools is carried out by psychologists from the MOE or by clinicians in the Child Guidance Clinic at the Institute of Mental Health.[15] SNOs were introduced in 2006 to provide support and intervention for pupils diagnosed with mild to moderate special needs such as dyslexia or autistic spectrum disorder. The SNOs provide individual support for these pupils in normal classrooms in addition to training them in specific skills such as literacy or social skills in small groups.[16]

The Many Helping Hands approach means that there is no special legislation to govern due process to reevaluate or contest referrals to special schools. For example, in the past, students may have been referred to special schools for reasons such as short attention spans, behavioral problems, or emotional problems, and, as observed by Rao,[17] once these students are placed in the special education system, they have virtually no chance of returning to the mainstream system. Fortunately, with continuous pressure from parents and VWOs, growing media attention given to students with disabilities, and teachers becoming more knowledgeable in this area, instances of such haphazard referrals do not occur as often. Instead, there is a steady increase of children with special needs attending mainstream schools.[18]

Government Initiatives

From the speeches of Ministers and parliamentary debates, there is no indication of any intention to legislate or set any mandatory disability standards in the area of special education of persons with disabilities. However, there is a clear desire to provide continuous support and improved educational opportunities for this group of people.

Extensive research was carried out on the challenges faced by people with disabilities in Singapore by the Ministry of Community Development, Youth and Sports (MCYS) in the early 2000s which culminated into a report (the 2005 Report), and it was found, inter alia, that there was an urgency to bring the standard of special education to the level of mainstream education. The major areas highlighted were the qualifications of SPED teachers and the regulation of the running of SPED schools.[19] In the same report, many recommendations were put forward to address these issues, including:

- Providing funded training at the MOE and career advancement plans for SPED recruits;
- Eliminating remuneration disparity between mainstream and SPED teachers;
- Educating mainstream youths about the various disabilities so that they are equipped with the necessary knowledge and skills to interact, help and work with people with disabilities;
- Having the MOE set the standard of education for SPED schools in addition to mainstream schools;
- Requiring the MOE to take a more active role in structuring and legislating SPED schools by ensuring minimum standards, extending

professional help to the VWOs, and assisting in the recruitment of SPED teachers; and
- Including SPED children in Compulsory Attendance when the above recommendations are successfully implemented.

Following the 2005 Report, a steering committee was set up to chart a five-year roadmap for the disabled community in Singapore. In February 2007, the steering committee formulated recommendations to the government under the Enabling Masterplan 2007–2011,[20] with the main objective of helping people with disabilities to reach their full potential and to become equal, integral and contributing members of society. The committee arrived at five key findings:

- The government should take over the leadership of early intervention and education of children with special needs rather than adopting an "arms-length approach" by working through the NCSS.
- The need for clarity of options and education pathways available for children with special needs. There is no clear guidance of any post-secondary education or employment options for these children.
- The inconsistent quality of programmes and staff. For example, the special schools do not have shared frameworks for assessments, admissions, service delivery and curriculum; while in the mainstream schools, the level of professional support and individual education and transition planning for special needs children varies across schools. As pointed out by a Member of Parliament and supervisor of two special schools,[21] all of the special schools are led by different charities, each with different vision, standards, and priorities depending on the charity and school leadership. Such inconsistencies in standards are not acceptable since they impact on the education of special needs children and, probably, employment opportunities.
- The need to develop integration initiatives in the education of special needs children so that they can effectively transit into, and be better able to live and work independently in, mainstream society.
- The visible efforts from the MOE special education department and the MCYS policy team in improving the education landscape for children with special needs since 2005.

In relation to the final finding, this can be seen in the awards that MOE and NCSS have been giving out to recognize the contribution and important role SPED schools and teachers play in the education of children with special needs. Since 2007, MOE-NCSS Special Education Awards have been received by special education teachers or schools for three categories of achievement: The Outstanding SPED Teacher Award, the Innovative SPED Teacher Award, and the Innovation Award. The Innovation Award was established as an annual award to encourage SPED schools to pursue innovation and excellence. The Outstanding SPED Teacher Award recognizes teachers for their passion and commitment in teaching children with special needs.

The disabled in society have traditionally been perceived to be those who are physically or visually handicapped or those with hearing impairments and had special schools established to serve their needs. Yet, as the nation progresses and develops, there is a realisation that there are special needs such as autism, dyslexia, and Attention Deficit Hyperactivity Disorder which also have to be addressed, both in mainstream and special schools. The MOE has responded by implementing, since 2005, a Special Needs compulsory module for beginning teachers to ensure that all of those new to the profession have a basic understanding of the main types of learning disabilities in mainstream schools.[22] Since this initiative, a core group of teachers trained at a certificate level or its equivalent in special needs is placed in each school to support students with special needs.

In response to the recommendations under the Enabling Masterplan 2007–2011, the government made a commitment to address the following areas of improvement:[23]

- Greater involvement in overseeing and supporting the management of SPED schools in areas such as leadership and learning outcomes. The MOE has begun this process by:

  1. working closely with the VWOs in charge of the SPED schools in connection with the appointment of SPED school principals and school supervisors. Apart from assessing the nominations for these key posts, MOE makes recommendations where necessary;
  2. engaging the SPED schools to develop targets for the learning outcomes of their students; and
  3. developing a quality assurance framework jointly with NCSS and carrying out management audits of SPED schools periodically to ensure the accountability of the SPED schools in terms of achieving learning outcomes.

- Establishing a diverse range of educational opportunities. This can be achieved through training and recruiting more Special Needs Officers to support the schools; implementing more satellite SPED classes in mainstream partner schools;[24] locating SPED schools next to mainstream schools to facilitate interaction; and enabling children with mild disabilities in SPED schools to access prevocational training. These prevocational courses will increase the chances of special needs children contributing to the economy and becoming more independent in adulthood.

- Providing more training and professional support for SPED schools. Mainstream teachers can be prepared to teach in SPED schools, and SPED schools will be invited to be involved in mainstream school cluster activities.[25]
- Providing additional funding support for students in SPED schools. The current funding for students in SPED schools is up to four times the capitation grant for primary education. For students in SPED schools preparing for "O" or "N" levels[26] curriculum or prevocational certification, the funding formula will instead be pegged to the capitation grant for mainstream secondary education, which amounts to an increase of about 38 percent. Further, students who can benefit from additional years of education to achieve their learning outcomes or who can benefit from prevocational and vocational skills training will be funded up to twenty-one years of age instead of eighteen.

In March 2010, the MOE announced its intention to provide greater support for special education:[27]

- By providing funding to SPED schools to establish school-based awards from 2011 with each school determining the number and quantum of the awards since the profile of SPED students and the type of curriculum offered across schools differ. Schools for the hearing impaired could focus on the speech development of children while other schools might focus on the development of vocational skills or give awards based on pupils' contribution to school communities in areas such as leadership, exemplary behavior, and achievements in cocurricular activities or national events.
- By increasing the Edusave[28] Pupils Fund and Edusave Grant for special needs students from January 2011. The former can be used by SPED students to pay for school fees and enrichment programmes while the latter will be given to SPED schools to fund enrichment programmes or purchase additional resources.
- By introducing a highly structured reading programme to all SPED schools gradually. A successful pilot of "Reading Mastery, a Direct Instruction" reading programme in seven SPED schools in 2009 showed significant gains in the students' reading skills. Other Direct Instruction programmes will be piloted to support the development of oral and writing skills as well.
- By facilitating greater opportunities for integration between children from SPED and mainstream schools; for example, encouraging main-

stream schools located near SPED schools to conduct joint social and learning activities and providing resources to support the conduct of satellite classes for SPED students in mainstream schools.

- By ensuring that children with mild special needs in mainstream schools are well supported. In this regard, it is expected that by 2012, at least 10 percent of teaching staff in all primary and secondary schools are trained in special needs.

An interesting development that took place in Singapore in late 2009 was the establishment of a SNTC Trusteeship Scheme. Under this scheme, a Special Needs Trust Company (SNTC), which is non-profit-making, was set up to provide trust services for the benefit of persons with special needs. In order to understand the significance of this initiative, one must be reminded that Singapore is resource deprived such that economic development relies heavily on active labour participation with public assistance reserved only for the extremely destitute with no family to provide support.[29]

What Singapore has done, then, is to enhance the financial security and well-being of persons with special needs through the provision of a public trust service. Unlike private trusts, the SNTC is managed by the Public Trustee's Office, which means money placed there is guaranteed by the government, pays higher interest than banks, and charges a very low fixed administrative fee.[30] This initiative and the government's increased involvement in the educational needs of children with disabilities confirm the government's policy and strategy to keep its people self-sufficient and not rely on welfare. In ensuring the children with special needs receive a quality education, one that maximises their potential, there is a greater possibility that they will be able to live independently, be gainfully employed, and contribute to the community.

Another interesting development, announced on 10 March 2010, is the new Central Provident Fund (CPF)[31] scheme called the Special Needs Savings Scheme (SNSS). The SNSS is aimed at encouraging parents to save up for the long-term care needs of their children with special needs who have difficulties supporting themselves.

Under this scheme, parents can nominate their children with disabilities to draw fixed monthly payouts from their CPF savings when they are deceased until the savings are exhausted rather than paying it out as a lump sum to the beneficiaries. In order to be eligible for this scheme, both the nominating parents and persons with disability have to be Singaporeans or Singapore Permanent Residents at the time of nomination and the person with disability has to require assistance in at least one activity of daily living such as washing, dressing, feeding or toileting, or be attending a Special Education school.[32] At the time of writing this chapter, this initiative has yet to be launched and the details finalized, but one would expect that this scheme, when implemented, will complement the SNTC Trusteeship Scheme that is already in place and provide support and peace of mind to parents of children with special needs.

MOVING FORWARD

> Years ago you would not see our special children in public. These days, I am very happy to see that the public is accepting our children. They seldom receive glares from the public. The parents too have helped by taking them out instead of hiding them at home.[33]

This was the comment made by the founder of the Association for Persons with Special Needs and reflects the shifting norms in society. Many schools that were previously called "so-and-so school for retarded children" or "school for the deaf" or "school for the blind" have now been renamed "special schools." In addition, the government has recognized that the first six years of a child's life are very important, and hence has taken a commendable step of introducing a programme called the "Integrated Child Care Programmes" for special needs children. Under this programme, funding is available to selected childcare centres (run by VWOs) that provide services for children with disabilities.

One knows that providing education services for children with disabilities is not without difficulties. In fact, research carried out in 2006 with teachers training in special needs revealed that many of them were concerned about their lack of knowledge and skills to identify students with special needs in their classrooms.[34] A common reason given by countries that fail to provide for children with special educational needs is the severity of the disabilities along with the lack of facilities and trained staff.

Certainly, for a long time, Singapore relied on Voluntary Welfare Organisations to take care of children with special needs under the Many Helping Hands approach. While this approach was necessary in the developing years of the country, the time has come where "better results will only be achieved when the right hands with the right expertise and commitment are deployed."[35] Many would take the view that the Enabling Masterplan 2007–2011 is a welcome initiative and that the government needs to increase significantly its involvement in overseeing and supporting the management of SPED schools in areas such as leadership, learning outcomes and, in particular, the identification and assessment of special educational needs.

Despite initiatives to integrate children with special needs into mainstream schools and the steps taken to enhance their support, there has been no attempt to formalize this process into the education legislation or at least to give clearer guidelines on placement and special educational provision. The government argues that, if compulsory education were to include education in SPED schools, the enforcement of compulsory education may be unduly harsh on the parents of children with special needs. However, some parents do not send their children to SPED schools because of the costs. This can be overcome by making education at SPED schools free for such children, just as education is free for children in the mainstream schools. The principal objective of introducing compulsory education is to ensure that each child is given the opportunity to maximise his or her potential. If children with special needs cannot attend mainstream schools, then they should be sent to a SPED school as part of the requirement of compulsory education.

The introduction of this chapter noted that Singapore relied on the intellectual capacity of its people as a significant economy driver. It then became necessary for the country to provide special educational services for its exceptional, that is, gifted, members. In 1984, the Ministry of Education initiated the Gifted Education Programme (GEP) designed to enrich the intellectually gifted. A Gifted Education Branch was formed to identify students and teachers for the GEP, train the teachers, prepare the curriculum and monitor its progress.[36] Over the years, this programme has expanded significantly, benefiting many high-ability learners. With the government's rhetoric indicating that every Singaporean counts, and with Singapore being a progressive country, one would argue that the time has now come for the government to put equivalent, if not more, effort into the business of educating children with special needs.

CONCLUSION

Singapore's way of dealing with children with disabilities might, to some, seem discriminatory in that they are not extended the privilege of compulsorily funded education in special schools. Yet, it must be recognized that special needs children may have to be treated differently in order for their educational experience to be positive and effective. In adopting the Many Helping Hands approach, one can arguably say that the government is placing more effort and time into providing sufficient and suitable educational services for children with disabilities, rather than depleting time and resources to defend potential legal actions for unlawful discrimination, as seen in cases such as *L v. Minister for Education for the State of Queensland* (1995)[37] or *Daniels v. Attorney General* (2002).[38]

The government has recognized that not all children with disabilities will be able to attend ordinary schools. The Compulsory Education Act therefore exempts "any child who is unable to attend any national primary school due to any physical or intellectual disability."[39] While most parents will ensure some form of education for their children, some, for reasons other than costs, neglect to do so. Again, one way is to perhaps make special education compulsory. Special education could mean education for children who, due to physical or mental disabilities or learning difficulties, require educational treatment beyond that normally obtained in mainstream schools.

In many jurisdictions, an idealistic policy of the "inclusion" of children with disabilities in mainstream schools is promoted. Cases have shown that such inclusion can sometimes create significant financial and educational strain on schools. For example, disruptive and uncooperative students with disabilities in mainstream classes will affect the learning of the rest of the students while increasing the resources of staffing and costly expert support.[40] In a study of the inclusion policy and practice in England,[41] the following conclusion was drawn:

> Learning to cope with diversity was a professional plus for teachers *but* only if there was a culture and support to allow teachers to realise the benefits. There were clearly social benefits for many pupils *but* only where conditions were right and where special needs did not create resistance and resentment. Parental satisfaction was rewarding too *but* only where special needs were such that they could be met adequately within the mainstream and teachers' efforts were appreciated.[42]

The Singapore government's policy of placing children in special schools if they cannot be well educated in regular schools is probably sustainable and defensible. Yet, correctly pointed out in the Enabling Masterplan and by some academics,[43] as more knowledge and information become available, the traditional community support for children with special needs must expand into more formal services and be supported by the government. The journey will not be an easy one as most Singaporeans have grown up in an environment that segregates the disabled from the nondisabled. Still, it is a journey that will become easier as the nation "undergo[es] a journey of self-reflection; to 'deconstruct and reconstruct' their personal values and views on how they relate to and interact with others who are different,"[44] especially in the light of the recent developments and initiatives that have taken place for children with special needs in Singapore.

NOTES

Special thanks are due to Ms. Denise Phua, Member of Parliament, President, Autism Resource Centre (Singapore), and supervisor of two special schools, Pathlight School and Eden School Boards; and to Dr. Ivy Chia, Ministry of Education, Singapore. Both took time from their astonishingly busy schedules to read the draft and make helpful suggestions about improving the chapter and to also confirm the accuracy of the information presented.

1. See www.sg, Your Official Gateway to Singapore. Retrieved 18 December 2009, from http://app.www.sg/who/1/Singapore-at-a-Glance.aspx.

2. Teh, M. K. & Stott, K. (2009). Singapore. In Russo, C. J. & DeGroof, J. (2009). (Eds.) *The Employment Rights of Teachers: Exploring Education Law Worldwide.* Rowman & Littlefield Education. Lanham, Maryland.

3. Ministry of Education, Singapore: Compulsory Education. Retrieved 3 November 2009, from http://www.moe.gov.sg/initiatives/compulsory-education/.

4. Section 3, Compulsory Education (Exemption) Order, Compulsory Education Act (Cap. 51, 2003, section 4[1]).

5. Lim, L. & Nam, S. S. (2000). Special Education in Singapore. *The Journal of Special Education, 34(2):* 104–109.

6. Id., p. 104.

7. Tay, T. B. & Ng, A. (2003). Country Paper on Services for Persons with Intellectual Disability in Singapore. Retrieved 25 November 2009, from www.afid73.org/16Acmr2003 CountryReports/Cty%20Ppr.pdf.

8. Lim, L. & Nam, S. S. (2000). Special Education in Singapore. *The Journal of Special Education, 34(2):* 105.

9. The Ministry of Community Development was renamed the Ministry of Community Development, Youth and Sports in 2004.

10. Quah, M. L. (1993). Special Education in Singapore. In Quah, M. L., Gopinathan, S., & Chang, S. C. (Eds.). A Review of Practice and Research in Education for All in Singapore. *Country Report Submitted to the Southeast Asian Research, Review and Advisory Group (SEARRAG)* (pp. 89–102). Singapore: National Institute of Education.

11. Lee, H. L. (2004, January 7). I Have No Doubt Our Society Must Open Up Further. *The Straits Times, Singapore.*

12. Wong, A. (1997). Speech on Special Education. (Singapore: Ministry of Education, 31 July 1997).

13. *Report of the Advisory Council for the Disabled: Opportunities for the Disabled* (1988). (Singapore: Ministry of Community Development), p. 38.

14. Chan, S. S. (2005). 4th *Reply on Resources in Schools, Special Education, Pre-school Education and Education Hub.* (Singapore: Ministry of Education, 9 March 2005).

15. Shanmugaratnam, T. (2007). *Parliamentary Debates Singapore 11(83).*

16. Id.

17. Rao, M. S. (1999). Beliefs and Attitudes of Pre-service Teachers towards Children with Disabilities. Unpublished master's dissertation, Nanyang Technological University, Singapore. In Lim, L. & Tan, J. The Marketization of Education in Singapore: Prospects for Inclusive Education. *International Journal of Inclusive Education, 3(4)*: 339–351.

18. Basu, R. (2006, 17 November). More Kids with Special Needs Attending MOE Schools. *The Straits Times.*

19. *Report of the National Youth Council Youth Discussion Workgroups: Framework for Improving the Education, Employment and Quality of Life for Persons with Disabili-*

ties (2005). (Singapore: Ministry of Community Development, Youth and Sports). Retrieved 25 November 2009, from http://www.mcys.gov.sg/MCDSFiles/Download/Youth%20Reloaded%20-%20Disability%20Subgroup%20-%20Report.doc.

20. Enabling Masterplan 2007–2011. (Singapore: Ministry of Community Development, Youth and Sports). Retrieved on 25 November 2009, from http://www.mcys.gov.sg/enablingmasterplan/index.html.

21. In an email correspondence with Ms. Denise Phua, Member of Parliament, President, Autism Resource Centre (Singapore) and Supervisor, Pathlight School and Eden School Boards.

22. Ministry of Education. (2007). *Speech by Mr. Tharman Shanmugaratnam, Minister for Finance and Minister for Education, at the Dyslexia Association of Singapore Graduation Ceremony*. Retrieved 25 November 2009, from http://www.moe.gov.sg/media/speeches/2007/sp20071229_print.htm.

23. Ministry of Education. (2007). Press Releases. *Levelling Up Opportunities: Raising the Quality of Education for Children with Special Educational Needs.* Retrieved 3 November 2009, from http://www.moe.gov.sg/media/press/2007/pr20070307b_print.htm.

24. In 2006, a pilot scheme was implemented whereby autistic students in a mainstream school attend some classes in a SPED school, or where a group of hearing-impaired students in a SPED school crosses over to a neighbouring mainstream school to attend some lessons.

25. Singapore has a school cluster system whereby groups of schools form clusters that are overseen by superintendents who facilitate networking and collaboration among the principals of the schools in the cluster.

26. Secondary Education in Singapore places students in the Special, Express, Normal (Academic), or Normal (Technical) courses according to how they perform at the Primary School Leaving Examination. The different curricular emphases are designed to match their learning abilities and interests. Students in the Normal course follow either the Normal (Academic) or Normal (Technical) curriculum. As the terms suggest, Normal (Academic) concentrates on academic subjects while Normal (Technical) prepares the students for technical vocational education. Retrieved 31 March 2010, from http://www.moe.gov.sg/education/secondary/.

27. Ministry of Education (2010). Press Releases. *MOE to Provide Greater Support for Special Education.* Retrieved 23 March 2010, from http://www.moe.gov.sg/media/press/2010/03/moe-to-provide-greater-support.php.

28. The Edusave Scheme was started in 1993 to maximise opportunities for all Singaporean children. The Scheme rewards students who perform well or who make good progress in their academic and nonacademic work and provides students and schools with funds to pay for enrichment programmes or to purchase additional resources. The Edusave Endowment Fund is built up from government contributions. The fund is invested by the government and the interest earned is used to finance the contributions, grants and awards given to schools and students. The government contributed an initial capital sum of $1 billion to the fund in 1993, and it reached the target of $5 billion in August 1997. Retrieved 31 March 2010, from http://www.moe.gov.sg/initiatives/edusave/.

29. For a comprehensive review of Singapore's welfare system, see Ng, I.

(2004). How Unique and Sustainable Is the Singapore Welfare Model?: Evaluating Welfare Statism in Singapore in Historical and Comparative Context. *Manuscript*. Retrieved 23 February 2010, from http://sitemaker.umich.edu/ireneng/files/singapore_welfare_1005.pdf.

30. Tan, T. (2009). Govt-backed trust to help care for children with disabilities. *The Straits Times Singapore*, 30 October. For more information on the SNTC trusteeship scheme, go to http://www.specialneedstrust.org.sg/.

31. The Central Provident Fund (CPF) is a comprehensive social security savings plan that has provided many working Singaporeans with a sense of security and confidence in their old age. The overall scope and benefits of the CPF encompass retirement, health care, home ownership, family protection and asset enhancement. Working Singaporeans and their employers make mandatory monthly contributions to the CPF, and these contributions go into three accounts named the Ordinary Account (to be used to buy a home, pay for CPF insurance, investment and education), Special Account (to used for old age, contingency purposes and investment in retirement-related financial products), and Medisave Account (to be used for hospitalisation expenses and approved medical insurance). Retrieved 31 March 2010, from http://mycpf.cpf.gov.sg/CPF/About-Us/Intro/Intro.htm.

32. Ministry of Community Development, Youth and Sports (2010). Media Release: *New Initiatives to Better Support Persons with Disabilities*. Retrieved 31 March 2010, from http://www.mcys.gov.sg/MCDSFiles/Press/Articles/17-2010.pdf.

33. Wong, M. K. (undated). We Were Children Once: Our Humble Beginnings. (Association for Persons with Special Needs website). Retrieved 25 November 2009, from http://www.apsn.org.sg/.

34. Tam, K. Y. B., Seevers, R., Gardner, R. III, & Heng, M. A. (2006). Primary School Teachers' Concerns about the Integration of Students with Special Needs in Singapore. *Teaching Exceptional Children Plus, 3(2)* Article 3.

35. Enabling Masterplan 2007–2011. (Singapore: Ministry of Community Development, Youth and Sports). Retrieved on 25 November 2009, from http://www.mcys.gov.sg/enablingmasterplan/index.html, p. 3–30.

36. Ministry of Education: Gifted Education Programme: Development and Growth. Retrieved 9 February 2010, from http://www.moe.gov.sg/education/programmes/gifted-education-programme/development-and-growth/.

37. *L v. Minister for Education for the State of Queensland* (1995). Queensland Anti-discrimination Tribunal No. H39 of 1995. L's parents initiated legal action against the school authorities claiming direct discrimination within the meaning of the Anti-Discrimination Act (1991), Act No. 85 of 1991 (Queensland), when the school L was attending excluded her from the integrated school programme for behavior that was "prejudicial to the good order and discipline of the school; and heightened health and hygiene risks to other students." The Tribunal ruled that the school subjected L to discrimination, but not unlawful discrimination since her retention would cause unjustifiable hardship to other students.

38. *Daniels v. Attorney-General* (unreported) (3 April 2002). HC AK M1516/SW99, and *Attorney-General v. Daniels* (2003) 2 NZLR 742 (CA). This case involved a policy in New Zealand known as Special Education 2000, which was aimed at eventually disestablishing all existing facilities providing special education and replacing

them with a system of resources that enabled existing regular state schools to meet the requirements of special needs students. This policy was implemented without legislative change in 1998 but was quickly met with an application by parents of some special needs children to the High Court of New Zealand for judicial review. In the High Court, Baragwanath J found that there was a justiciable right to education to the extent that such education must be suitable, regular and systematic. However, the Court of Appeal held that the right of special needs students is a right to an education system, not a substantive right to education that is suitable, regular and systematic as indicated by Baragwanath J.

39. Section 3(A) Compulsory Education (Exemption) Order, Compulsory Education Act (Chapter 51, section 4 [1]).

40. See Dickson, E. (2008). The Inclusion and Exclusion of Students with Disability Related Problem Behaviour: The Contrasting Approaches of Australia and the United States of America. *The Australia & New Zealand Journal of Law & Education 13(2)*, 49–63.

41. MacBeath, J., Galton, M., Steward, S., MacBeath, A. & Page, C. (2006). The Costs of Inclusion, a *Study of Inclusion Policy and Practice in English Primary, Secondary and Special Schools.* Faculty of Education, University of Cambridge: National Union of Teachers. Retrieved 1 March 2010, from http://74.125.155.132/scholar?q=cache:ubhyKdTa_OoJ:scholar.google.com/++author:%22MacBeath%22+intitle:%22The+costs+of+inclusion%22&hl=en&as_sdt=2000.

42. Id. at p. 41.

43. Lim, L. & Nam, S. S. (2000). Special Education in Singapore. *The Journal of Special Education, 34(2):* 105.

44. Phua, D. (2008). Foreword in the book *Exploring Disability in Singapore: A Personal Learning Journey* by Lim, L., Thaver, T., and Slee, R. US: McGraw-Hill Education.

9

South Africa

Marius Smit and Petra Engelbrecht

Internationally, those involved with education have tended to identify students through notions of "normality" (Oswald, 2010). "Normal" students are supposed to be able to cope in education without additional support while students with so-called special educational needs were identified as needing special educational settings and support. In South Africa, as in other countries, this distinctive categorization has led to the development of a dominant mainstream education system for "normal" students and a secondary system of specialized education for students with "special needs," including those with disabilities.

The term *disability* in South Africa refers to any of the following: sight, hearing, communication, and physical, whether intellectual and/or emotional (Statistics South Africa, 2005). According to Howell (2007), the result has been that the term *special needs,* based on a medical model of what "special needs" are, became a catchall phrase in the 1970s and 1980s for students who were perceived as not fitting into what was seen as "mainstream education." However, increasingly, the development of an inclusive education system, based on the notions of human rights and a more general notion of social justice, became important both internationally and nationally.

The movement towards an inclusive, rather than a segregated, education system in South Africa has resulted not only from the increasing importance placed internationally on the rights of students, regardless of ability to receive an appropriate education along with their peers, but also as a result of the country becoming a democracy in 1994. Understandably, the history of legally instituted discrimination under the previous government irrevocably influenced the development of a new education system and educational policies after 1994. The result was that education policy was prioritized toward addressing the disparities and inequities of the past and characterized by a commitment to equity and redress which is apparent in all education policy documents and legislation (DoE, 1995; 1997a; SA, 1996c).

The National Commission for Special Needs in Education and Training and the National Commission on Education Support Services Commission's Report (DoE, 1997a) on the education of students with "special educational needs" suggested, in accordance with the Constitution of South Africa and its emphasis on education as a fundamental human right in the country, that education should favor an education system based on a human rights approach and a social model of disability that replaces the medical model (Engelbrecht, 2009a; Oswald, 2010). Replacing the medical discourse about disability brought forth a paradigm shift that stresses systemic change and adaptation to specific barriers to learning (see Stofile & Green, 2006) experienced by students. The Report recommended that all students should have access to a single educational system that can accommodate student diversity in meaningful ways and enable students to participate fully in society in general (DoE, 1997a). The rights of those with disabilities in South Africa were highlighted in a White Paper on an Integrated National Disability Strategy (DoE, 1997b) that gave the minority a voice and an opportunity to be included in mainstream schools.

White Paper 6: Special Needs Education: Building an Inclusive Education and Training System was published in 2001 (DoE, 2001). The *White Paper* pointed to an acceptance of difference and the need to address a broad range of learning needs in an inclusive education system. Inclusive education as defined in the *White Paper* is based on the ideal of freedom and equity as described in the Constitution and is seen as a single educational system dedicated to ensure that all individuals are enabled to become competent citizens in a democratic and diverse society (Engelbrecht, 2009b). The movement towards inclusion in South Africa is therefore characterized by the recognition and celebration of diversity, human dignity, freedom, and equality (Engelbrecht, 2006). Still, the implementation of inclusion remains a contextual challenge in South African schools.

DEVELOPMENT OF EDUCATION POLICY

White Paper 6: Policy on Inclusive Education

The movement toward inclusive education in South Africa is regulated by policy documents such as *White Paper 6* and the guidelines of the Department of Education on Strategy on Screening, Identification, Assessment and Support (DoE, 2001), which have not been enacted by the legislature.

Baxter (1984:80) defines policy, in the legal context, as a general plan of action based on political considerations of expediency and strategy to advance a collective goal, such as the administration and institutionalization of inclusive education.

The Constitution of the Republic of South Africa encompasses the separation of powers doctrine which draws a distinction between the executive and the legislature and consequently between law and policy. In terms of Schedule 4 of the Constitution, education is classified as a functional area of concurrent national and provincial legislative competence, meaning that law on inclusive or special education should be promulgated in terms of national or provincial legislation. Although the National Education Policy Act empowers the Minister of Education to determine national policy for education, sections 6 and 7 of the National Education Policy Act make it clear that national legislation, as opposed to national policy, can only be introduced after a process of extensive consultation and publication has been completed.

In *Minister of Education v. Harris* (2001) the Constitutional Court explained the context in which the National Education Policy Act (RSA, 1996b) must be understood. The Court confirmed that section 146(2)(b) of the Constitution provides for national legislation to prevail when, in order to be effective, a matter requires uniformity across the nation. The cumulative effect of the provisions of the National Education Policy Act, and those of sections 2(2) and 2(3) of the South African Schools Act, is to emphasize the distinction between the determination of guiding policy, on the one hand, and its translation into legally binding enactments, on the other. In accordance with *Harris*, policy is not law, and the present policies on inclusive education do not have the status of enactments that are legally binding.

National Strategy on Screening, Identification, Assessment and Support Guidelines

The National Strategy on Screening, Identification, Assessment, and Support (the SIAS) provides guidelines and plans to determine the proper placement and provision of additional support for students with impairments (DoE, 2008). During the first stage of the SIAS process school officials and teacher(s) gather background information of students by completing such reports as the Learner Profile, Support Needs Assessment and Diagnostic Profile (DoE, 2008:10–11). Stage two applies to students who have been identified by teachers as experiencing challenges in the learning process.

Systemic barriers to learning such as poor nutrition, family breakdown, and health issues as well as individual barriers such as physical, psychological and cerebral impairments are identified. Individual Support Plans (ISP) are developed to address the barriers to learning. The categories of support range from Level 1 (Very low frequency or once per annum intervention) to Level 5 (Very high or daily intervention by specialized staff). Stage three is managed and coordinated by District Based Support Teams, which consist of health care practitioners, social workers, nongovernment organizations, and special schools or resource centers. During this stage, students with moderate to severe impairments are placed in facilities or special schools that provide support to meet their needs. The final stage entails the implementation of action plans for support provisioning and monitoring.

For various historical and developmental reasons, South Africa does not have sufficient resources to provide health practitioners and educational psychologists at every school. In response to these challenges, the SIAS process has been developed as a measure to overcome the shortages by sharing and organizing the available resources at district level.

LEGAL DETERMINANTS OF INCLUSIVE EDUCATION AND THE RIGHTS OF STUDENTS WITH DISABILITIES

All students, including those experiencing barriers to learning with disabilities, derive their rights to education primarily from the Constitution of South Africa (SA, 1996c), the National Education Policy Act (SA, 1996a), the South African Schools Act (SA, 1996b) and case law casuistically developed by the courts.

The South African Schools Act, 1996: Cursory Reference to Special Education

The South African Schools Act (SA, 1996b) regulates the administration, governance, and management of public as well as independent schools in South Africa. Yet, South Africa lacks an enabling statute dealing with inclusive or "special" education in particular. The aim of the Schools Act was, of course, to eliminate the apartheid education system and to establish a nationally uniform system of organization, governance, and funding of all schools. As a result of the emphasis on remedying the ills of racially segregated schools, the frame of reference of the Schools Act is most prominently on mainstream public education. Regrettably, the Schools Act makes no specific reference to the concept of inclusive education and makes only cursory reference to matters concerning special education. In this regard, the special education provisions on compulsory attendance, placement of learners with special needs, provision of public schools, and ancillary matters, as contained in the Schools Act, will be discussed in the sections that follow.

Compulsory Attendance

Section 3(3) of the Schools Act provides that the national Minister of Education must, by notice in the Government Gazette, determine the ages of compulsory attendance at school for learners with special educational needs. In terms of section 3(1) of the Schools Act, parents, including guardians and custodians, must cause all children for whom they are responsible to attend school from the first school day of the year in which they reach the age of seven until the last school day of the year in which such learners reach the age of fifteen or the ninth grade, whichever occurs first. Yet, some parents who can afford the tuition choose to enroll their children with severe disabilities prior to the compulsory school attendance age. Students who have visual, hearing, communication, physical, or intellectual impairments may be admitted to special education schools as young as three years old, depending on circumstances. However, many households, particularly in the rural areas where the illiteracy rate is high and the main economic activity is subsistence farming, experience unemployment and widespread poverty. The practice is therefore that most students are initially admitted to ordinary schools during the first year of compulsory school attendance.

Minister of Education v. Harris (2001) is particularly instructive as an instance where inflexible age requirements for compulsory school attendance served as a barrier to learning. In *Harris* the Minister of Education appealed to the Constitutional Court against a decision by the High Court of Transvaal that the Age Requirements for Admission to an Independent School Policy was unconstitutional and invalid. The respondent was the mother of an underaged girl who was a prospective student at an independent school which received no public funding. The Constitutional Court upheld the High Court's decision, ruling that the national Minister of Education's notice setting out the age requirements was *ultra vires* because it purported to impose legally binding obligations on independent schools and provincial Members of Executive Councils under section 3 of the National Education Policy Act. The school in question was thus entitled to admit the underage child to Grade 1 in the 2001 school year.

Subsequently, all provincial legislatures published regulations to determine age requirements and grant more flexible provisions that enable parents to apply on behalf of their children to be admitted to schools prior to the compulsory age of attendance. Therefore, students, especially those with impairments requiring specialized care, have the right to apply for admission to schools at ages younger than the prescribed compulsory age.

Placement of Learners with Special Educational Needs

Section 5(6) of the Schools Act provides that a provincial Head of Department and school principal must take the rights and wishes of the parents of students with special education needs into account when considering their placements. This provision is obviously aimed at ensuring that parents have the right to express their preferences with regard to the placements of their children at appropriate schools in order to act in the best interest of students with special needs. Conversely, this section entails that students with special needs have the right to proper placement in accordance with their best interests and the wishes of their parents.

Provision of Public Schools

According to section 12(1) of the Schools Act, the provincial Member of the Executive Council must provide public schools, for the education of learners, out of funds appropriated for this purpose by the provincial legislature. Public schools may be ordinary public schools or public schools for learners with special education needs (SA, 1996c: section 12[3]). Section 12 refers to "ordinary" schools, without reference to the *White Paper 6* categories of mainstream, full service, and special education schools. This confirms that the Schools Act, which was promulgated before *White Paper 6,* applies the frame of reference of the outdated medical model of special needs education. In order to safeguard the rights of students who experience barriers to learning, it is essential that new legislation should be enacted to regulate the inclusive education strategy and system.

Provision of Special Needs Education at Ordinary Schools

For the purposes of this discussion, section 12(4) is the most significant and principal provision in the Schools Act that encompasses the notion of inclusive education. This subsection is phrased in peremptory language and provides that every Member of the Executive Council of a provincial education department is obliged to provide students with special education needs the opportunity for education in mainstream schools, if it is reasonably practicable. The criteria of reasonable practicability depends on the nature and extent of students' special education needs, the extent of support required, the availability of resources, proximity, and the suitability of the infrastructure of ordinary schools.

Section 12(5) also provides that the Member of the Executive Council, namely, a provincial officer, must take all reasonable measures to ensure that the physical facilities at public schools are accessible to persons with disabilities. These sections entail the essential enabling provisions that determine the implementation and application of a system of inclusive education in South Africa. In principle, therefore, the provisions of section 12 of the Schools Act confirm that students with special education needs, or learners experiencing barriers to learning, have a right to education in mainstream schools, if reasonably practicable, as well as the right to relevant educational support services.

Governance of Public Schools with Students with Special Needs

The Schools Act contains ancillary provisions regulating the governance of public schools with students with special needs. High schools are required, in terms of section 11(1), to establish representative councils for students. However, it stands to reason that this provision would not always be practically possible at high schools that serve students with severe intellectual or other impairments. Accordingly, section 11(3) makes an exception by providing that public schools for students with special education needs may be exempted from the requirement that representative councils of students should be established if it is not practically possible at the schools.

As explained above, the South African system of inclusive education entails that learners with barriers to learning may be accommodated at either ordinary schools, full service schools, or special education schools. Accordingly, the Schools Act includes provisions applicable to the unique governance for each of the three categories of schools serving students with barriers to learning or special needs. For instance, section 23(5) of the Schools Act provides that the governing bodies of ordinary public schools which provide education to learners with special needs must, where practically possible, coopt a person or persons with expertise regarding the special education needs of such learners and must establish a committee on special education needs in terms of section 30(2). In turn, special education public schools have broader membership requirements for governing bodies, while section 24 requires that persons from each of the following categories should be represented on the governing body:

(a) Parents of learners at the school, if reasonably practicable;
(b) educators at the school;
(c) members of staff at the school who are not educators;
(d) learners attending the eighth grade or higher, if reasonably practicable;
(e) representatives of sponsoring bodies, if applicable;
(f) representatives of organizations of parents of learners with special education needs, if applicable;
(g) representatives of organizations of disabled persons, if applicable;
(h) disabled persons, if applicable; and

(i) experts in appropriate fields of special needs education; and
(j) the principal in his or her official capacity.

The partnership between special schools and the stakeholders listed in section 24 enables a participatory system of local school governance that augments financial contributions and services rendered to the school. All these provisions of the Schools Act serve to ensure that students with special needs have the right to proper school governance by knowledgeable experts and representatives that have the best interest of the students at heart.

Constitution of South Africa, 1996

Section 1 of the Constitution provides that South Africa is a democratic state inter alia founded on the values of supremacy of the Constitution and the rule of law (SA, 1996c). The Constitution is the supreme law of South Africa and any law or conduct inconsistent with it is invalid, and the obligations imposed by it must be fulfilled (SA, 1996c: section 2). This implies first, that any legitimate authority to administer an inclusive education system serving the needs of students experiencing barriers to learning should be derived from the law; second, that the institutions necessary for the existence and operation of a public system of inclusive education should be created by the law (Baxter, 1984:75); third, that the rights and rules of the Constitution are binding on all branches of government as well as individuals; and fourth, that the constitutional provisions are justiciable and enforceable by the courts of law.

FUNDAMENTAL SOCIOECONOMIC RIGHTS OF STUDENTS WITH SPECIAL EDUCATIONAL NEEDS

The Bill of Rights of the Constitution of the Republic of South Africa contains provisions safeguarding the rights of students with special education needs. In particular, the Constitution provides for the traditional liberal civil and political rights that impose a "negative" duty on government to not act in a certain way, such as not to discriminate unfairly. Further, the Constitution's recognition that human rights and the social conditions of citizens are fundamentally interconnected led to the protection of socioeconomic rights which impose "positive" obligations on the government to do whatever it can to provide a basic set of social goods such as education, health care, food, water, and housing (De Waal, Currie & Erasmus, 2001:432). These socioeconomic rights of the Constitution were modeled on the International Covenant on Economic, Social and Cultural Rights

(UN, 1966), which had been ratified by South Africa (De Waal, Currie & Erasmus, 2001:437). This obliges government to refrain from undue interference with the enjoyment of these rights and, in addition, places a duty on the government to take positive steps towards fulfilling the rights such as the right to education and other socioeconomic rights of students with special needs.

The Right to Education, Section 29

While the constitutions of older democracies such as the United States of America (Russo, 2007) and Canada (Manley-Casimir and Manley-Casimir, 2009) do not include the right to education, the progressive constitution of South Africa expressly establishes the fundamental right to basic and further education. According to the relevant provisions of section 29 of the Constitution (SA, 1996c):

Education

(1) Everyone has the right—

- (a) to a basic education, including adult basic education; and
- (b) to further education, which the state, through reasonable measures, must make progressively available and accessible.

(2) . . .

(3) Everyone has the right to establish and maintain, at their own expense, independent educational institutions that—

- (a) do not discriminate on the basis of race;
- (b) are registered with the state; and
- (c) maintain standards that are not inferior to standards at comparable public educational institutions.

(4) Subsection (3) does not preclude state subsidies for independent educational institutions.

The fundamental right to education confirms that all students with special needs have an enforceable right to basic education against the state. The right to education is a general right available to every person in accordance with section 29(1)(a) of the Constitution (SA, 1996c). The meaning and extent of the concept "basic education" was considered in *Phillips v. Manser*, wherein the High Court decided that the constitutional right to basic education refers to the period of compulsory education that applies for children up to fifteen years of age or Grade 9. However, in *Phillips* the court refused an application by a seventeen-year-old Grade 11 student for readmission to a mainstream high school after he was expelled for gross misconduct. The incidents that led to the student's expulsion inter alia included an unprovoked assault of a fellow student, sniffing chloroform in class, and stabbing fellow students with a syringe filled with chemicals.

Insofar as the *ratio decidendi* in *Phillips* applies to a particular set of facts involving student ill discipline at an ordinary school, it cannot necessarily be equated with the scope and meaning of the right to basic education of students with special needs. Other considerations apply to students with special needs, such as the nature and extent of each individual's special needs coupled with a reasonable time frame for gaining training and education. Therefore, it seems more reasonable that the particular circumstances according to each student's assessment and the expected time frame of individually tailored programs should dictate a more flexible approach to the period required for attaining special needs basic education to the level of Grade 9. Section 9(2) of the Constitution provides that measures may be taken to protect or advance persons disadvantaged by unfair discrimination, such as students with disabilities, to promote the achievement of equality (SA, 1996c).

Consistent with the egalitarian design of the Constitution and the principles expounded in *Harris,* a more flexible approach to overaged students will avoid unfair discrimination against learners experiencing both disability and age as barriers to learning. This contention is further supported by the inclusion of the fundamental right to adult basic education in section 29(1) of the Constitution. This obviously implies that basic education should be provided to adults, including persons over the age of compulsory schooling, such as students with special needs, who have not had sufficient opportunity to attain basic education by the age of fifteen.

EDUCATION AS A SOCIOECONOMIC RIGHT: PROGRESSIVE AVAILABILITY AND ACCESSIBILITY

In terms of section 29(1)(b), the right to further education is limited by the state's resources and ability to make it progressively available and accessible (SA, 1996c). This implies that further education is qualified by the availability of state resources. The Constitutional Court's most significant decision on the socioeconomic rights of the Constitution is the matter of *Government of the Republic of South Africa v. Grootboom* (*Grootboom,* 2001). Although the provision of housing for homeless persons was at issue in *Grootboom,* the principles expounded by the Constitutional Court apply to socioeconomic rights such as education.

In accordance with the separation of powers doctrine the courts defer to the executive branch of government's discretion with regard to the measures adopted or the manner in which public money had been spent. However, in *Grootboom* the court held that the standard of reasonableness requires the design, adoption and implementation to realize socioeconomic rights. The mere adoption of policy or legislative measures is not enough. *Grootboom* confirmed that the egalitarian and remedial design of the Constitution requires progressive achievement of substantive equality and the protection of human dignity for the vulnerable and weakest, such as students experiencing barriers to learning in the South Africa society. The court also found that resource scarcity does not relieve the state from its duty to fulfill its "core minimum obligations." Therefore, in the education context, *Grootboom* establishes the principle that even when resources are scarce, the standard of reasonableness requires the design, adoption and implementation of the inclusive education policy to afford students who experience barriers to learning the right to basic education.

The Rights to Dignity and Equality

One of the most important challenges for the new constitutional and democratic order in South Africa is to reestablish respect for human dignity by addressing the inequities and unfair discrimination in society (De Waal et al., 2001:232). The right to equality is premised on the moral notion that every person possesses equal human dignity and is entitled to respect regardless of his or her personal characteristics or membership of groups. Unfair discrimination against students on grounds of personal attributes such as disability, language, age, or culture denies recognition of the one attribute that is common and equal to all, namely human dignity (De Waal et al., 2001:232).

Section 9 of the Constitution provides that everyone is equal before the law, has the right to equal protection and benefit of the law, and the full and equal enjoyment of all rights and freedoms (SA, 1996c). In addition, section 9(2) provides for affirmative action as a means to achieve long-term equality. Therefore, measures and programmes such as the movement toward inclusive education that is aimed at reducing current inequality of disabled students may be taken in order to promote the achievement of equality. The state may not unfairly discriminate directly or indirectly against anyone, especially against students with disabilities, on the listed grounds such as disability, age, culture, ethnic or social origin and language (SA, 1996c: section 9[3]).

Health Care, Food, Water and Social Security

Centre for Child Law v. MEC for Education, Gauteng (*Centre for Child Law*, 2008) aptly illustrates the challenges and predicaments faced by government in dealing with students coming from disadvantaged backgrounds. The Centre for Child Law, a children's rights organization based at the University of Pretoria, was concerned that the squalid conditions at the Luckhoff School infringed the schoolchildren's constitutional rights. The Luckhoff School of Industry accommodated juvenile delinquents that had been convicted of serious criminal offences.

The Centre for Child Law contended that the conditions infringed the rights of children to basic nutrition, shelter, basic health care, and social services guaranteed by section 28(1)(c) of the Bill of Rights as well as the right to human dignity (SA, 1996c: section 10) and the right not to be subjected to cruel, inhuman or degrading treatment (SA, 1996c: section 12). The Centre sought orders directing the Gauteng Department of Education province to provide each child in the school with such simple resources as sleeping bags, to put proper access control and psychological support structures in place, and to make immediate arrangements for the school to be subject to a developmental quality-assurance process.

The Gauteng Department of Education defended the matter by arguing that a remedy should not have been granted lest other schools similarly denied their rights should seek the same remedy at considerable cost to the state. The court decided that on the facts, the minimal costs or budgetary-allocation problems were far outweighed by the urgent need to advance the interests of the children in accordance with constitutional values. The court ruled that in a case such as the one at bar, where the fundamental right to dignity was central and the costs were foreseeable, manageable and containable, "leveling up" was the appropriate and desirable remedy.

The court went on to explain that the leveling-up remedy required school officials to deliver a higher standard of care than that which the parents of the children were able to provide. The court noted that Regulations to the Child Care Act (SA, 1983) specifically provide for the maintenance of appropriate standards to ensure the well-being of the children in such institutions. The court severely criticized the dilatory and lackadaisical approach of the department officials, pointing out that the bureaucratic prevarication was "equality with a vengeance." The court ordered a team of multidisciplinary experts to carry out a process of quality improvement. In addition, the court retained a supervisory role to ensure progress of this innovative remedy.

Given the lack of resources in many special education and ordinary schools have for providing inclusive education, it is probable that the principle of leveling up will be judicially applied to remedy instances where the constitutional rights of students to human dignity, basic nutrition, shelter, basic health care, and social services are infringed.

BEST INTEREST OF CHILDREN IS OF PARAMOUNT IMPORTANCE

In terms of section 28(2) of the Constitution, the best interest of children is of paramount importance (SA, 1996c). Section 28 can also be seen as an expansive response to South Africa's international obligations as a state party to the UN Convention on the Rights of the Child (UN, 1989). The four great principles of this convention which, as international currency, guided all policy in South Africa in relation to children were survival, development, protection and participation. At the heart of section 28 is the right of children to be children and to enjoy special care. Under this principle, all children have their own dignity and are constitutionally imagined as individuals with distinctive personalities who cannot be treated as mere extensions of their parents. This principle, read with the right to family care, health care, food, water, and social security requires that the interests of children who stand to be affected should receive due consideration.

In the matter of *S v. M* (2007), though, the Constitutional Court also held that the paramountcy principle was not to be applied in a way that obliterated other valuable and constitutionally protected interests. According to the Court, the "best interests" injunction was capable of limitation, and the fact that the best interests of children were paramount did not mean that they were absolute. As with all other rights in the Bill of Rights, the Court maintained that their operation had to take account of their relationship to other rights, which might require that their ambit be limited (*S v. M*). This means that the rights of some children may at times be limited if the rights of others are more important in the realm of special education.

The paramountcy principle is of particular significance for children with low to severe impairments since it emphasizes the state's responsibility to provide additional support and resources to comply with this constitutional injunction. Therefore, the comprehensive and emphatic language used in section 28(2) of the Constitution indicates that the application of the law must always be child-sensitive.

Enforcement of Rights: Just Administrative Action

The administrative process of implementation of legislation and policy with regard to special or inclusive education involves a vast range of public authorities, some at the national level and others at the provincial and local levels of government (De Waal et al., 2001:503). In terms of section 33 of the Constitution and the Promotion of Administrative Justice Act (SA, 2000), all administrative actions must be fair and reasonable.

Administrative actions which materially and adversely affect the rights or legitimate expectations of individuals must be procedurally fair and reasonable (SA, 2000: section 3). The administrative actions and implementation of legislation or policy may be enforced by judicial review if public or private interests are infringed. In the context of this chapter, it means that unfair and unreasonable action by the government with regard to the provision of special or inclusive education may be contested and reviewed by the courts.

CONCLUSION

This chapter has provided an overview of the legal determinants regulating the system of inclusive education in South Africa. As a result of historical and developmental encumbrances, South Africa does not have sufficient financial and human resources to provide special education according to the traditional medical model. However, the South African response to these challenges has been to develop and organize an intricate system of inclusive education to enable support for students with special needs as a result of individual impairments as well as support for students experiencing systemic barriers to learning.

The cursory reference to special education in the South African Schools Act is insufficient to deal with the requirements for an inclusive education system. Specific education legislation is outdated and needs to be modernized to enable proper administration and regulation of an inclusive education system. Still, South Africa has a constitutional framework that is justly regarded as one of the most advanced and progressive legal instruments in the world. The Bill of Rights accords socioeconomic rights, such as the right to basic education, basic nutrition, shelter, basic health care, and social services to students. The state further has a constitutional obligation to ensure the progressive availability of these fundamental rights. Moreover, the courts have demonstrated the willingness to enforce the implementation of these rights by means of innovative remedies in order to adhere to the principle that the best interest of children with special needs is of paramount importance.

REFERENCES

Baxter, L. (1984). *Administrative Law*. Lansdowne: Juta.

Department of Education. (1995). *White Paper on Education and Training in a Democratic South Africa*. Pretoria: Government printer.

Department of Education. (1997a). *Quality Education for All: Report of the National Commission for Special Needs in Education and Training and the National Commission on Education Support Services*. Pretoria: Government printer.

Department of Education. (1997b). *White Paper on an Integrated National Disability Strategy.* Pretoria: Government printer.

Department of Education. (2000). *A Curriculum for the 21st Century: Report of the Review Committee on Curriculum 2005.* Pretoria: Government printer.

Department of Education. (2001). *Education White Paper 6. Special Needs Education; Building an Inclusive Education and Training System.* Pretoria: Government printer.

De Waal, J., Currie, I., and Erasmus, G. (2001). *Bill of Rights Handbook.* Lansdowne: Juta.

Engelbrecht, P. (2006). The Implementation of Inclusive Education in South Africa after Ten Years of Democracy. *European Journal of Psychology of Education, XXI* (3), 253–264.

Engelbrecht, P. (2009a). Equity in Inclusive Education. Paper presented at the Forum for Inclusive Education. Stanford University, Palo Alto.

Engelbrecht, P. (2009b). Inclusive Psychology and Social Transformation: Responding to the Challenges of the New South Africa. In P. Hick, R. Kershner, & P. T. Farrell (Eds.), *Psychology for Inclusive Education: New Directions in Theory and Practice* (pp. 108–116). London: Routledge.

Howell, C. (2007). Changing public and professional discourse. In P. Engelbrecht, & C. Green (Eds.), *Responding to the Challenges of Inclusive Education in Southern Africa* (pp. 99–109). Pretoria: Van Schaik.

Manley-Casimir, M. and Manley-Casimir, K. (Eds.). 2009. *The Courts, the Charter, and the Schools.* Toronto: University of Toronto Press.

Oswald, M. M. (2010). *Teacher Learning during the Implementation of the Index for Inclusive Education in a Primary School.* Unpublished PhD Thesis, Stellenbosch University, South Africa.

Russo, C. J. (2007). *Reutter's The Law of Public Education.* Foundation Press: New York.

Statistics South Africa. (2005). Prevalence of Disability in South Africa. Pretoria: Statistics South Africa.

South Africa. (1983). Child Care Act 74 of 1983. Pretoria: Government printer.

South Africa. (1996a). National Education Policy Act 27 of 1996. Pretoria: Government printer.

South Africa. (1996b). South African Schools Act 84 of 1996. Number 86. Pretoria: Government printer.

South Africa. (1996c). Constitution of the Republic of South Africa Act 102 of 1996. Pretoria: Government printer.

South Africa. (2000). Promotion of Administrative Justice Act 1 of 2000. Pretoria: Government printer.

Stofile, S. Y. & Green, L. (2006). Inclusive Education in South Africa. In P. Engelbrecht, & C. Green (Eds.), *Responding to the Challenges of Inclusive Education in Southern Africa* (pp. 52–65). Pretoria: Van Schaik.

United Nations. 1966. *International Covenant on Economic, Social and Cultural Rights.* New York: United Nations.

United Nations. 1989. *International Convention on the Rights of the Child.* New York: United Nations.

LIST OF CASES

Minister of Education v. Harris 2001 (4) SA 1297 (CC).
Centre for Child Law and Others v. MEC for Education, Gauteng 2008 (1) SA 223 (T).
Government of the Republic of South Africa and Others v. Grootboom and Others 2001 (1) SA 46 (CC).
Phillips v. Manser and Another 1999 (1) All SA 198 (SE).
S v. M 2007(2) SARC 539 (CC).

10

United States

Charles J. Russo and Allan G. Osborne Jr.

Brown v. Board of Education (*Brown*),[1] wherein the U.S. Supreme Court struck down state-sanctioned racial segregation on the basis that officials in public schools violated students' rights to equal protection under the Fourteenth Amendment to the Constitution, is the most important case in American history on public education. In fact, *Brown* not only ushered in an era of equal educational opportunities for children of color but also, among other developments, created a movement that led to the enactment of federal laws protecting the educational rights of students with disabilities.

Aware of the tremendous changes that have taken place in the United States since the 1970s impacting the rights of children with special needs, this chapter reviews the two most significant federal statutes[2] on point, Section 504 of the Rehabilitation Act[3] and the Individuals with Disabilities Education Act (IDEA).[4] The chapter also highlights key opinions from the myriad of federal and state cases interpreting these laws. Together, these statutes, their implementing regulations, and cases interpreting them created a symbiotic relationship in setting a national standard to meet the needs of children with disabilities, since many states failed to provide equal opportunities for students with special needs until the enactment of the IDEA and Section 504.

This chapter begins with a brief overview of the legal system in the United States before examining a variety of issues governing rights of students with disabilities in American public schools.[5] Following the legal overview, the remainder of the chapter is divided into two major sections. The first, and briefer, part of the chapter examines Section 504.

The second section, which reviews the extensive provisions of the IDEA, starts with an overview before examining identification and assessment of students with disabilities; placement issues; due process and dispute resolution; remedies; discipline; funding and cost issues; and emerging issues dealing with the educational rights of students with disabilities. The chapter rounds out with a brief conclusion. In reviewing litigation, it is important to note that as litigious as Americans are, it is probably safe to say that there are more cases on special education, or most other topics for that matter, in one year in the United States than at least a decade or longer elsewhere. Thus, although the footnotes in this chapter often identify just one case, in many instances they could be replaced with multiple case citations.

THE AMERICAN LEGAL SYSTEM

Simply put, the U.S. Constitution is the law of the land. As the primary source of American law, the Constitution provides the framework within which the entire legal system operates. Accordingly, enactments of federal, state, and local governments, including state constitutions, statutes, regulations, and common law, all of which impact the law of special education, are subject to the Constitution as interpreted by the Supreme Court and lower tribunals.

As important as education is, it is not mentioned in the Constitution. Under the Tenth Amendment, according to which "[t]he powers not delegated to the United States by the Constitution, nor prohibited by it to the States, are reserved to the States respectively, or to the people," then, education is primarily the concern of individual states. Federal courts can intervene in educational disputes if a federal right is at issue, such as in *Brown v. Board of Education* (*Brown*).[6] In *Brown*, the Supreme Court struck down state-sanctioned racial segregation on the basis that officials in public school violated students' rights to equal protection under the Fourteenth Amendment to the federal Constitution rather than on the right to education per se.

Along with identifying the rights of Americans, the Constitution establishes three coequal branches of government, all of which are involved in safeguarding the rights of students with disabilities. The legislative, executive, and judicial branches of government give rise to the three other sources of law. The legislative branch "makes the law." Once bills complete the legislative process, they are signed into law by a Chief Executive such as a president or governor who has the authority to enforce them through regulations written by personnel at administrative agencies who are experts in their fields.

The fourth and final source of law is judge-made or common law. Common law requires judges to "interpret the law,"[7] examining issues that may have been overlooked in the legislative or regulatory process or that may not have been anticipated when statutes were enacted. Common law involves the concept of precedent, the notion that a majority ruling of the highest court in a given jurisdiction is binding on lower courts within its jurisdiction. A ruling of the U.S. Supreme Court is thus binding throughout the nation, while decisions of state supreme courts are binding only in given jurisdictions.

The federal judiciary and most state court systems consist of three levels: trial courts, intermediate appellate courts, and courts of last resort. In the federal system, trial courts are known as federal district courts; state trial courts use a variety of names. Each state has at least one federal district court while densely populated states, such as California and New York, have as many as four.

Trial courts typically involve a judge and a jury. The role of the judge, as trier of law, is to apply the law by deciding, for instance, whether evidence is admissible while providing direction for juries on how to apply the law to the facts of the specific cases that they are examining. There are thirteen federal intermediate appellate courts known as Circuit Courts of Appeal; state intermediate appellate courts employ a variety of names. The highest court in the United States is the Supreme Court; although most states refer to their high courts as supreme courts, a variety of titles are in use.

SECTION 504 OF THE REHABILITATION ACT OF 1973

Reauthorized partially in response to two federal cases that highlighted the rights of children with disabilities,[8] Section 504 of the Rehabilitation Act of 1973 was the first federal statute to address the needs of the disabled. According to Section 504, "[n]o otherwise qualified individual with a disability in the United States . . . shall, solely by reason of her or his disability, be excluded from the participation in, be denied the benefits of, or be subjected to discrimination under any program or activity receiving [f]ederal financial assistance. . . . "[9] Since this last phrase, "federal financial assistance," is interpreted broadly,[10] most courts agree that it applies to virtually all schools. Moreover, although Section 504 also covers employees and others in schools, this chapter focuses on the rights of children.

Section 504 defines an individual with a disability as one "who (i) has a physical or mental impairment which substantially limits one or more of such person's major life activities, (ii) has a record of such an impairment, or (iii) is regarded as having such an impairment."[11]

In order to have a record of impairment, individuals must have histories of, or been identified as having, mental or physical impairments that substantially limit one or more major life activities, "such as caring for one's self, performing manual tasks, walking, seeing, hearing, speaking, breathing, learning, and working."[12]

Once students are identified as being disabled, the next step is to evaluate whether they are "otherwise qualified." In order to be "otherwise qualified," children must be "(i) of an age during which nonhandicapped persons are provided such services, (ii) of any age during which it is mandatory under state law to provide such services to handicapped persons, or (iii) [a student] to whom a state is required to provide a free appropriate public education [under the IDEA]."[13] Students who are "otherwise qualified," meaning that they are eligible to participate in programs or activities despite the existence of impairments, must be permitted to take part in programs or activities as long they can do so by means of a "reasonable accommodation."

Reasonable accommodations may involve minor adjustments such as allowing a child to bring a service dog to school,[14] modifying a behavior policy as applied to a disruptive student with an autoimmune disease,[15] or acquiring a hearing interpreter for a student.[16] Academic modifications may include permitting students more time to complete assignments or examinations, using tutors, having teachers distribute outlines in advance, and/or permitting students to use laptop computers to record answers on examinations. In modifying facilities, school officials do not have to make every classroom and/or area of buildings accessible. When making modifications, it may be enough for educators to bring services to students such as offering keyboards for musical instruction instead of moving entire music rooms for students who wish to take piano classes.

Even if children appear to be "otherwise qualified," educators can rely on one of three defenses to avoid being charged with noncompliance of Section 504, a major difference between it and the IDEA. First, school officials can be excused from making accommodations that would result in "a fundamental alteration in the nature of [a] program."[17] The second defense allows officials to avoid compliance if a modification imposes "undue financial burden[s]."[18] The third defense is that otherwise qualified students can be excluded from programs if their presence creates a substantial risk of injury to themselves or others.[19]

Once identified, qualified students are entitled to receive an appropriate public education, regardless of the nature or severity of their disabilities. In order to guarantee that an appropriate education is made available, Section 504's regulations include due process requirements for evaluation and placement similar to those under the IDEA.[20] Finally, Section 504 requires recipients of federal financial aid to file assurances of compliance; provide notice to students and their parents that their programs are nondiscriminatory; take remedial actions in response to proven violations; enact voluntary steps to overcome the effects of conditions that resulted in limiting the participation of students with disabilities; conduct self-evaluations; designate a staff member, typically at the central office level, as compliance coordinator; and adopt grievance procedures.[21]

INDIVIDUALS WITH DISABILITIES ACT

Initially enacted in 1975 as the Education for All Handicapped Children Act, the IDEA had its name changed in 1990 and was revised in 1986, 1990, 1997, and 2004; the 2004 version of the IDEA became effective on July 1, 2005. As a condition of receiving federal funds, the IDEA and its regulations require states, through local educational agencies or school boards, to identify, assess, and serve all children with disabilities, including those in nonpublic schools,[22] regardless of the severity of their needs.

In order to be covered by the IDEA, children must meet four requirements. First, students must be between the ages of three and twenty-one;[23] students are treated as being twenty-one until the end of the academic years in which they reach the age limit. Second, children must have specifically identified disabilities.[24] Third, students must be in need of special education,[25] meaning that they need a "free appropriate public education"[26] (FAPE) in the least restrictive environments (LRE) that are directed by the contents of their Individualized Education Programs (IEPs).[27] Fourth, children must be in need of related services.[28]

The IDEA includes extensive due process protections safeguarding the rights of children[29] and their parents.[30] Among these protections, the IDEA,[31] its regulations[32] in addition to the Family Educational Rights and Privacy Act[33] and its regulations,[34] protect the confidentiality of the large amounts of information that is used in the evaluation, placement, and education of students with disabilities. Moreover, parents must be informed before consenting to initial evaluations,[35] which must occur within sixty days of when educational officials received consent to conduct them[36] and/or placements of their children[37] and have the right to take part in developing IEPs that direct the education of their children.[38]

Identification and Assessment

The IDEA directs states to establish procedures to ensure that all children with disabilities are properly identified and evaluated.[39] Testing and evaluation materials as well as procedures must be selected and administered in a manner that is neither racially nor culturally biased.[40]

Further, students whose language or other mode of communication is not English need to be evaluated in their native language or other mode of communication.[41]

Evaluation procedures for students with disabilities must be multidisciplinary such that no single test can serve as the basis for determining whether students are entitled to IDEA services.[42] Eligibility decisions are then made by teams of qualified professionals in conjunction with the parents of children who were assessed.[43] Assessments must be valid and reliable and should be administered by trained personnel in conformance with the instructions provided by their producers.[44]

School officials must undertake complete reevaluations for all children with disabilities at least every three years.[45] Evaluations can take place when officials think that they are warranted or when parents or teachers make such requests.[46]

As noted, school officials must complete all evaluations of students suspected of having disabilities within sixty days of receiving parental consent for the evaluations.[47] If state laws mandate different time frames for completing evaluations, they control. Depending on state laws, school officials may be required to conduct evaluations over summer vacation periods if necessary to complete them within the statutory time limits. The sixty-day rule does not apply if "the parent of a child repeatedly fails or refuses to produce the child for the evaluation."[48] If parents refuse to respond to requests to provide consent to initial evaluations or to services, educational officials may continue with evaluations as long as they follow the procedures outlined in the IDEA's due process provisions.[49]

Parents have the right to obtain independent evaluations of their children if they disagree with the assessments completed by their school boards[50] or if officials fail either to evaluate their children entirely[51] or in a timely manner.[52] These independent evaluations are at public expense if it can be shown that assessments conducted by board personnel were inappropriate. Parents cannot obtain independent evaluations at public expense simply to get another opinion. While parents who succeed in challenging the assessments of their children can be reimbursed for the costs of doing so, if hearing officers or courts find that board evaluations were appropriate, parents are not entitled to further testing at public expense.[53] When parents obtain independent evaluations, whether at public expense or their own cost, school personnel must consider, but are not bound by, the results of these assessments.[54]

When assessments are completed, and children are identified as being in need of IEPs, educators must convene IEP meetings within thirty calendar days.[55] Once developed, school officials must implement IEPs "[a]s soon as possible."[56] IEPs must describe students' current levels of educational performance, annual goals and short-term objectives, the specific services that they will receive, the extent to which they can take part in general education, the date services are to begin and how long they will be offered, and criteria to evaluate whether they are achieving their goals.[57] IEPs must also discuss how students' disabilities affect their ability to be involved in and progress in inclusive settings and necessary modifications to allow them to take part in the general curriculum. In addition, IEPs must detail related services that students need to benefit from their IEPs.

IEP teams must include parents in light of their right to participate actively in the development of IEPs for their children; at least one of the student's regular education teachers if the child is, or will participate, in regular education; at least one special education teacher or, if appropriate, one special education provider; a school board representative who can provide, or supervise, the delivery of special education, knowledge about general education, the board's resources, and evaluation procedures; an individual who can interpret the instructional implications of evaluation results; others, at the discretion of parents or boards, who are knowledgeable or have special expertise concerning the child; and, when appropriate, in light of age and intellectual ability, the child.[58]

Placement Issues

The IDEA requires school boards to provide a range of alternative FAPEs for all students with disabilities, from full inclusion in a regular education classroom to inclusion with help such as a personal aide to partial inclusion, partial resource room placement to an individualized placement in a resource room, to a special day school or to a hospital or homebound instruction to residential placements at no expense to their parents.[59] If parents have insurance, they can be asked to file claims to help defray costs associated with the education of their children with special needs. Even so, educators cannot refuse to provide services if parents are unwilling, or unable, to place claims with their insurance companies.[60]

As important as the "appropriate" component of FAPE is, the IDEA offers little guidance in defining this term beyond declaring that an appropriate education consists of special education and related services that is provided in conformance with an IEP.[61] Insofar as a precise definition of the term *appropriate* is not present in either the IDEA or its regulations, one must turn to judicial interpretation for further guidance on the meaning of FAPE, leading to decades of legal battles over which is more important, the appropriateness of placements of children with disabilities or their being in the least restrictive environment.

Board of Education of the Hendrick Hudson Central School District v. Rowley (*Rowley*),[62] was the Supreme Court's first case interpreting the rights of students with disabilities. *Rowley* was filed by the parents of a kindergarten student in New York who had a dispute with their school board over whether their daughter was entitled to a sign-language interpreter. Lower federal courts ordered the board to provide the interpreter on the basis that an appropriate education was one that would have allowed the child to achieve at a level commensurate with that of her peers who were not disabled.

The Supreme Court, acknowledging that the child in *Rowley* was earning passing grades and advancing from one class to the next without a sign-language interpreter, reversed in favor of the school board. The Court ruled that a FAPE was one that was formulated in accordance with all of the IDEA's procedures and is "sufficient to confer some educational benefit"[63] on a child with a disability. Insofar as the child in *Rowley* received some educational benefit without the sign-language interpreter, the Court thought that educators were not required to provide her with one even though she might have achieved at a higher level with the services.

Rowley establishes a minimum standard of what constitutes a FAPE under federal law. Since states are free to establish higher requirements, though, courts apply these more stringent standards in litigation. Courts have refined the *Rowley* standard by interpreting the "some educational benefit" criteria as requiring more than just minimal or trivial benefits.[64] Other courts have expanded the criteria by deciding that an educational benefit must be meaningful[65] or appreciable.[66] In fact, the Eleventh Circuit went so far as to maintain that student gains must be measurable to meet the *Rowley* criteria.[67] Regardless of which criteria educators apply, case law has made it clear that under the IDEA's so-called zero-reject approach, all children with disabilities must be served, regardless of cost.[68]

At the same time, the IDEA calls for students with disabilities to be educated in the least restrictive environment (LRE),[69] creating a conflict over whether this or providing children with a FAPE is more important. Starting in the late 1980s, federal appellate courts increasingly directed school boards to place students with disabilities in regular settings rather than segregated special education classrooms, ordering them to consider a variety of factors when formulating IEPs.

In *Oberti v. Board of Education of the Borough of Clementon School District*,[70] a case from New Jersey, the Third Circuit adopted a two-part test for assessing compliance with the LRE requirement.[71] The first element of the test is whether education in the regular classroom, with the use of supplementary aids and services, can be achieved satisfactorily. The second part of the test adds that if students must be placed outside regular classrooms, educators must consider whether they were mainstreamed, now referred to as full inclusion, to the maximum extent appropriate.

According to the Ninth Circuit in *Sacramento City Unified School District Board of Education v. Rachel H.*,[72] a dispute from California, educators must address four factors in making placements. These factors address the educational benefits of placing children with disabilities in regular classrooms; the nonacademic benefits of such placements; the effect that the presence of students with disabilities would have on teachers and other children in classes; and the costs of inclusionary placements.

Case law on LRE is premised on the notion that educators must make reasonable efforts to place students with disabilities in fully inclusive settings by providing them with extra aids and services to ensure their success. Even with the focus on inclusion, and in a point that many educators and parents fail to grasp, is that the IDEA does not mandate that all students with disabilities must be placed in regular education classes. Instead, inclusion is a goal rather than a right for children with disabilities. To this end, courts have approved segregated settings where educators demonstrated that students with disabilities could not function in regular classrooms or would not benefit in such settings, even with supplementary aids and services.[73]

Due Process and Dispute Resolution

One of the unique aspects of the IDEA are its extensive due process provisions that afford parents who disagree with school board actions regarding the placements of their children with an array of procedures to raise challenges, starting with mediation.[74] However, since mediation is voluntary, it may not be used to deny or delay parental requests for administrative hearings. A provision that was added to the IDEA in 2004 requires educators to conduct meetings with parents in order to attempt to resolve disputes before due process hearings are convened. These meetings must be scheduled within fifteen days of the parents' requests for hearings with a school board representative with decision-making authority. The parties may waive resolution sessions or may use the mediation process.[75]

Parents who are dissatisfied can also invoke their right to due process hearings,[76] which must be presided over by fair and impartial third-party decision makers.[77] As to the actual dispute resolution process, depending on state law, either state or local school boards may conduct due process hearings.[78] In states with two-tiered systems, if local boards conduct initial hearings, either party can appeal to the state for a final resolution.[79]

In another important addition, the IDEA now includes a two-year limitations period during which parties can request due process hearings.[80] If state laws set different limitations periods, then those periods prevail. Moreover, the IDEA stipulates that the federal statute of limitations is to be stayed if parents can show that school officials misrepresented that they resolved a disagreement or if they withheld pertinent information from the parents.[81]

Hearing officers, typically selected pursuant to state law, must be impartial, meaning that they cannot be employees of the states or school boards involved in educating students or have personal or professional interests in the outcomes.[82] In such a case, a federal trial court in Indiana refused to dismiss a parental claim that a hearing officer was biased due to a conflict of interest because he delivered a workshop for school administrators at a local university.[83] The court reiterated that individuals who otherwise qualify as hearing officers are not considered state or local board employees solely by virtue of being paid to serve in this capacity.[84] Public agencies must keep lists of hearing officers along with explanations of their qualifications.[85]

Within fifteen days of receiving parental requests for due process hearings,[86] school officials must meet with them in mandatory resolution sessions to discuss their disagreements.

If the parties are able to resolve their differences, they must execute legally binding agreements that are enforceable in state courts of competent jurisdiction or in federal trial courts.[87] The parties may void their agreements within three business days of their being executed.[88]

If parents and school officials are unable to resolve their differences within thirty days, then the due process time lines come into play.[89] Under these provisions, hearing officers must render final decisions based on the record[90] within forty-five days after the expiration of the thirty-day period,[91] but it can grant specific extensions of these time frames at the request of either party.[92] The orders of hearing officers are final unless one of the parties appeals.[93] In jurisdictions with two-tiered due process hearing systems, officials must ensure that final judgments are reached within thirty days of when a party files an appeal.[94]

In preparing for hearings, both parties must make full disclosures of data that have been compiled at least five business days in advance.[95] Hearing officers can prevent a party that fails to provide the information from introducing it without the consent of the other party.[96] Whether hearings are open to the public is a parental choice.[97]

The parties involved in due process hearings have the right to be accompanied and advised by counsel and by individuals with special knowledge or training with respect to the problems of children with disabilities;[98] the right to present evidence and confront, cross-examine, and compel the attendance of witnesses;[99] the right to written, or, at the option of the parents, electronic verbatim records of such hearings;[100] and the right to written, or, at the option of the parents, electronic findings of fact and final adjudications.[101]

Parties that are dissatisfied with the results of administrative proceedings can seek review in state or federal courts within ninety days[102] or appropriate state limitations periods.[103] However, before filing suit, an aggrieved party must exhaust all administrative remedies, meaning that it must complete the hearings processes dictated by states, unless it is futile to do so. When administrative or judicial actions are pending, under the IDEA's "stay-put" provisions, children must remain in their then current placements, meaning that school officials may not change students' placements unless they obtain parental consent,[104] orders from hearing officers[105] or judicial decrees.[106] The IDEA stays its statute of limitations if parents can prove that school officials misrepresented that they resolved a disagreement or if they withheld pertinent information from the parents.[107]

In an important preliminary matter with regard to dispute resolution, in *Schaffer ex rel. Schaffer v. Weast*,[108] a dispute from Maryland, the Supreme Court affirmed that the burden of proof rests on the party challenging IEPs. Subsequently, in refusing to distinguish between an IEP's formation and implementation, the Ninth Circuit ruled that parents who claimed that school officials failed to implement their daughter's IEP properly bore the burden of proof with regard to their allegations.[109]

Another important point with regard to who can file litigation came up with some regularity, but the lower courts were divided over the ability of parents who were not attorneys to act *pro se*, literally, "to appear on one's own behalf," in cases questioning whether educators provided their children with disabilities with a FAPE. In *Winkelman v. Parma City School District*,[110] the Supreme Court, in a case from Ohio, ruled that insofar as parents who are not lawyers have rights separate and apart from those of their children under the IDEA, they can proceed *pro se* in litigation challenging the IEPs of their children.

Once cases get to court, the judiciary has the authority to review the record of administrative proceedings, hear additional evidence,[111] and grant such relief as judges deem appropriate based on the preponderance of evidence standard.[112] Even so, the Supreme Court has advised judges not to substitute their views for those of educators.[113]

Remedies

As indicated, once parents sue their school boards over the placements of their children, the courts have the power to provide relief that they deem appropriate.[114] Arguably the most significant remedy that parents can obtain is attorney fees if they prevail in litigation against their school boards.[115] Granting such awards is based on the notion that recovering their costs would return parents to the position that they would have been in but for having had to go to court to safeguard the educational rights of their children. In modifying the IDEA by granting parents the right to recover attorney fees, Congress essentially overruled the Supreme Court's judgment in *Smith v. Robinson*[116] to the contrary. Conversely, in *Arlington Central School District v. Murphy*,[117] the Court refused to allow parents to recover fees for expert witnesses even if they prevail since they are unauthorized in the text of the IDEA. The Court reasoned that since it was not its job to amend the IDEA, any such changes had to have been made by Congress.

Another important form of relief that is available to parents who disagree with the placements of their children is that they may enroll them in nonpublic schools and try to recover tuition costs.[118] In *School Committee of the Town of Burlington v. Department of Education, Commonwealth of Massachusetts*,[119] the Supreme Court ruled that parents are entitled to tuition reimbursement if they can prove that school officials failed to offer appropriate placements and their chosen placements are appropriate. The Court later expanded on this holding in *Florence County School District Four v. Carter*,[120] deciding that parents are entitled to tuition reimbursement even if their chosen placements are not in state-approved facilities as long as the settings are otherwise appropriate. Further, courts can award compensatory services to parents for the time that children were denied services[121] even if they passed the IDEA's age limit.[122]

As important as it is, tuition reimbursement is unlikely to assist parents who cannot place their children in nonpublic schools because they cannot afford to pay for tuition. If parents lack the funds to make unilateral placements, their children may have to remain in inappropriate settings while disputes work their way through administrative and legal proceedings. If this occurs, courts can award extra educational services and prospective relief to compensate parents, and their children, for the loss of appropriate educational services.

The courts agree that compensatory services, like reimbursements, are designed to provide parents with relief for their children when school officials fail to provide them with a FAPE.[123] The IDEA permits these awards premised on the notion that compensatory services should not be available only to students whose parents can afford to pay for alternate placements while litigation is pending. On the other hand, courts ordinarily deny parental requests for monetary damages from school officials in their individual[124] or official[125] capacities for failing to provide appropriate educational placements or services for students with disabilities.

Discipline

It may be that the most challenging issue for school officials, in particular, associated with students with disabilities is discipline.[126] Surprisingly, Congress did not add specific provisions on discipline for students with disabilities until 1997.[127] Earlier, courts generally applied the IDEA's overall procedural protections to the disciplinary process. In *Honig v. Doe*,[128] the Supreme Court went so far as to declare that special education students could not be expelled for disciplinary reasons where their transgressions were manifestations of, or caused by, their disabilities.

At present, the IDEA allows school administrators to transfer students to interim alternative settings for up to forty-five days for possession of weapons or knowing possession of drugs or infliction of serious bodily injury.[129] The IDEA also makes it clear that educational services must continue during expulsion.[130] Further, the IDEA directs school officials to conduct functional behavioral assessments and develop behavior intervention plans whenever disciplinary sanctions may result in a loss of educational opportunities.[131]

All the same, the Supreme Court and the IDEA have not left educators without recourse when students with disabilities misbehave. Special education students may be suspended temporarily and are subject to other normal disciplinary sanctions that do not result in changes in their placements. If necessary, school board officials may seek intervention from hearing officers or the courts pending completion of due process hearings if they can be shown that students are dangerous and that educators cannot reach agreements with their parents over proper changes in placements.

Pursuant to the IDEA, students with disabilities cannot be excluded from school for ten or more days or expelled if their misconduct is a manifestation of, or caused by, their disabilities. Prior to changing the placements of students with disabilities for disciplinary reasons, school personnel, in conjunction with their parents, must meet as an IEP team to consider whether the (mis)behavior was a manifestation of, or caused by, their disabilities.[132] The IDEA defines a manifestation as conduct that was caused by, or had a direct and substantial relationship to, the child's disability or was the direct result of the local educational agency's failure to implement the IEP.[133] In making manifestation determinations, teams must weigh all relevant information, including evaluations and diagnostic results as well as student observations.[134]

If teams determine that offending behaviors were not manifestations of students' disabilities, they may be disciplined in the same manner as peers who do not have disabilities except that the delivery of a FAPE may not be terminated.[135] If teams interpret misconduct as either a manifestation of students' disabilities or as a result of improperly implemented IEPs, children may not be expelled or suspended for more than ten days without having IEP teams reconsider their current placements.[136]

As might have been expected, the courts have been asked to resolve disputes over manifestation determinations since parents do not always agree with IEP teams. For example, the federal trial court in Maine agreed that a manifestation was not present when a student sold marijuana at school, finding that he understood school rules and that his actions were not compulsive.[137] Three years later, the Fourth Circuit upheld a finding that a child's misconduct, persuading a peer to place a threatening note in a third student's computer file, was not a manifestation of his emotional disability.[138] The court observed that the student was aware of the consequences of his actions and even anticipated them by recruiting another student to actually place the note. More recently, a federal trial court in Virginia agreed that the behavior of a student who was involved in an incident where he and peers drove by the school three times one afternoon in order to shoot paintballs at the building and nearby vehicles in the parking lot was not a manifestation of his disabilities.[139] The court pointed out both that the student could be disciplined because the student consciously planned the incident that unfolded over several hours and that the IDEA's emphasis on parental involvement did not give his parents the right to veto or block officials' ability to act as they saw fit in punishing their son.

Funding and Cost Issues

The IDEA explicitly provides federal financial assistance to states that pass the funds on to local school boards to assist in paying for the delivery of special education services. Even though the federal government has helped to pay for the cost of delivering special education services, since federal IDEA funding is often inadequate, educators have unsuccessfully challenged the statute as an unfunded federal mandate.[140]

Aware of the need to provide assistance for state and local school officials as they pay for the costs associated with the delivery of special education services, the IDEA has set the goal of achieving its initial promise of funding 40 percent of the national average of per-pupil spending by 2011.[141] While these provisions are not mandatory, the IDEA has increased the authorized levels for funding the excess costs associated with educating students with disabilities by about $2.3 billion each year.[142]

In a related financial matter, given the high cost of caring for some children, such as those who are medically fragile,[143] the IDEA allows educators to use IDEA funds to establish and maintain "risk pools" to aid local school systems in providing high-cost services or for the unexpected enrollments of students with disabilities.[144] The IDEA also permits boards to allocate unused funds to be placed in a pool for the next fiscal year.[145]

EMERGING ISSUES

As something of a work in progress, the IDEA has undergone a variety of modifications since 1975. Some of the changes are ongoing issues, such as funding, while others emerge in light of the fact that legislators could not have anticipated the issues or the issues became evident in response to litigation.

Perhaps the most significant continuing challenge associated with the IDEA is providing adequate funding, especially at present during the economic downturn that the United States and many parts of the world economy have been facing since 2008. Put another way, the statutory promises that the U.S. government has made to provide states with adequate funds to meet the needs of students with disabilities notwithstanding, the resources have simply been inadequate.[146]

The first of two emerging issues deals with the need to assist the parents of students with disabilities who rely on expert witnesses to prevail in suits challenging their school boards. More specifically, since the Supreme Court refused to expand the IDEA by awarding expert witness fees in *Arlington*[147] because they were not authorized in the IDEA, the upshot is that parents are left in a precarious financial situation. In other words, since the use of expert witnesses can be costly, it is unclear why Congress has yet to authorize such reimbursement awards because it had previously added the attorneys' fees provision to the IDEA. Insofar as the IDEA is designed to safeguard the educational needs of students with disabilities, it would appear to make sense for Congress to provide parents with the ability to enforce the rights of their children. Since many parents may be unable to hire expert witnesses if they are unable to recover the funds that they paid for fees, it is incumbent on Congress to remedy this inequity.

As noted, since the issue of discipline can occupy a great deal of time for school officials, Congress needs to reconceptualize the procedures for excluding students with disabilities from schools for misbehavior regardless of whether it is related to their conditions. One common, troublesome occurrence is that if a student with disabilities strikes a classmate, who then hits back, it is possible that instigator is likely to be entitled to greater due process protection and subject to alternative discipline than the victim if the misbehavior was disability related, an outcome that causes a great deal of friction with parents of students who are not disabled. Further, since it is unclear how hard and fast the ten-day rule is, Congress should provide additional guidance on this and other thorny topics related to disciplining students with disabilities.

CONCLUSION

Since being enacted in 1995, the IDEA has provided students with disabilities in American schools, and their parents, with an impressive array of statutory rights safeguarding their ability to receive a FAPE. As the needs of children with special needs continue to evolve, it will be interesting to observe how the law adapts to best serve their interests.

NOTES

1. 347 U.S. 483 (1954).

2. A third statute, the Americans with Disabilities Act, 42 U.S.C. §§ 12101 *et seq.*, which extends similar protections to individuals in the private sector but has limited implications for public schools, is beyond the scope of this chapter.

3. 29 U.S.C. § 794(a). For a book on this topic, *see* Charles J. Russo & Allan G. Osborne Jr. (2009). *Section 504 of the Rehabilitation Act of 1973 and the Americans with Disabilities Act: Implications for Educational Leaders*. Thousand Oaks, CA: Corwin Press.

4. 20 U.S.C. §§ 1400 *et seq*. For a book on this topic, *see* Charles J. Russo & Allan G. Osborne Jr. (2008). *Essential Concepts and School-Based Cases in Special Education Law*. Thousand Oaks, CA: Corwin Press.

5. Since the rules applying to religiously affiliated nonpublic schools are significantly different, this chapter focuses on students in public schools. *See* Charles J. Russo, Allan G. Osborne, Joseph D. Massucci, & Gerald M. Cattaro. (2009). *The Law of Special Education and Non-Public Schools*. Lanham, MD: Rowman & Littlefield Education.

6. 347 U.S. 483 (1954).

7. For an article on the judicial process, *see* Charles J. Russo. (2009). "Judges as Umpires or Rule Makers? The Role of the Judiciary in Educational Decision Making in the United States." *Education Law Journal, Vol. 10, No. 1*, 33–47.

8. *See Pennsylvania Ass'n for Retarded Children v. Pennsylvania* 334 F. Supp. 1257 (E.D. Pa. 1971), 343 F. Supp. 279 (E.D. Pa. 1972) (finding that children who were mentally disabled could not be denied admission to public schools or subjected to changes in their placements unless their parents received procedural due process and that placements in regular school classrooms were preferable to those in more restrictive settings); *Mills v. Board of Educ. of the Dist. of Columbia*, 348 F. Supp. 866 (D.D.C. 1972) (rejecting the school board's claim that the school board lacked resources for all of its students, directing it to spend its funds equitably so that all children would have been educated in a manner consistent with their individualized needs and abilities, and holding that officials could neither deny services to children with disabilities nor exclude them from school without providing them and their parents with due process).

9. 29 U.S.C. § 794(a).

10. *See Bob Jones Univ. v. United States*, 461 U.S. 574 (1983) (upholding the revocation of tax-exempt status on the ground that it constitutes federal financial assistance).

11. 29 U.S.C. § 706(7)(B). The regulations define physical or mental impairments as including:

(A) any physiological disorder or condition, cosmetic disfigurement, or anatomical loss affecting one or more of the following body systems: neurological;

musculoskeletal; special sense organs; respiratory, including speech organs; cardiovascular; reproductive, digestive, genito-urinary; hemic and lymphatic; skin; and endocrine; or

(B) any mental or psychological disorder, such as mental retardation, organic brain syndrome, emotional or mental illness, and specific learning disorders. 34 C.F.R. § 104(j)(2)(I).

A note accompanying this list indicates that it merely provides examples of the types of impairments that are covered; it is not meant to be exhaustive.

12. 34 C.F.R. § 104.3(j)(2)(I).

13. 34 C.F.R. § 104.3(l)(2).

14. *See, e.g., Sullivan v. Vallejo City Unified Sch. Dist.*, 731 F. Supp. 947 (E.D. Cal 1990); *Gaudiello v. Delaware County Intermediate Unit*, 796 F. Supp. 849 (E.D. Pa. 1992).

15. *Thomas v. Davidson Acad.*, 662 F. Supp. 376 (M.D. Tenn. 1994).

16. *Jones v. Illinois Dep't of Rehab. Servs.*, 689 F.2d 724 (7th Cir. 1982).

17. *Southeastern Community College v. Davis*, 442 U.S. 397, 410 (1979) (upholding a nursing program's refusal to admit a student with a learning disability). *See also Alexander v. Choate*, 469 U.S. 287 (1985) (ruling that Section 504 only requires reasonable modification and not substantial changes).

18. *Davis*, *id.* at 412.

19. *See School Bd. of Nassau County v. Arline*, 480 U.S. 273, 287–88 (1987) (establishing criteria for evaluating whether, under Section 504, a teacher with tuberculosis posed a significant health risk to the school community).

20. 34 C.F.R. § 104.36.

21. 34 C.F.R. § 104.5.

22. 34 C.F.R. § 300.129. *See* Russo et al., *supra* note 5, generally, for a discussion of the rights of students in nonpublic schools.

23. 20 U.S.C. § 1412(a)(1)(A).

24. 20 U.S.C. § 1401(3)(A)(I): The term *child with a disability* means a child—(I) with mental retardation, hearing impairments (including deafness), speech or language impairments, visual impairments (including blindness), serious emotional disturbance (referred to in this chapter as "emotional disturbance"), orthopedic impairments, autism, traumatic brain injury, other health impairments, or specific learning disabilities.

25. 20 U.S.C. § 1401(3)(A)(ii).

26. U.S.C. § 1401(9).

27. 20 U.S.C. §§ 1401(11), 1414(d).

28. The IDEA, 20 U.S.C. § 1401(26)(A), defines related services as

> (26) Related services
>
> (A) In general
>
> The term "related services" means transportation, and such developmental, corrective, and other supportive services (including speech-language pathology and audiology services, interpreting services, psychological services, physical and occupational therapy, recreation, including therapeutic recreation, social work services, school nurse services designed to enable a child with a disability to receive a free appropriate public education as described

in the individualized education program of the child, counseling services, including rehabilitation counseling, orientation and mobility services, and medical services, except that such medical services shall be for diagnostic and evaluation purposes only) as may be required to assist a child with a disability to benefit from special education, and includes the early identification and assessment of disabling conditions in children.
(B) Exception
The term does not include a medical device that is surgically implanted, or the replacement of such device.

29. 20 U.S.C. § 1415.
30. The IDEA defines a *parent* as natural, adoptive, or foster parents, guardians, and individuals acting in the place of natural or adoptive parents (including grandparents, stepparents, or other relatives) with whom children live, or individuals who are legally responsible for a child's welfare. 20 U.S.C. § 1401(23).
31. 20 U.S.C. § 1417(c).
32. 34 C.F.R. §§ 300.610–627.
33. 29 U.S.C. § 1232g.
34. 34 C.F.R. §§ 99.1–99.8.
35. 20 U.S.C. § 1414(a)(1)(D)(i)(I)
36. 20 U.S.C. § 1414(a)(1)(C)(i)(I).
37. 20 U.S.C. § 1414(a)(1)(D)(I).
38. 20 U.S.C. §§ 1414(d)(1)(B)(i).
39. 20 U.S.C. § 1412(a)(3).
40. 20 U.S.C. §§ 1412(a)(6)(B), 1414(b)(3)(A)(i).
41. 20 U.S.C. §§ 1412(a)(6)(B), 1414(b)(3)(A)(ii).
42. 20 U.S.C. § 1414(b)(2)(B).
43. 20 U.S.C. § 1414(b)(4)(A).
44. 20 U.S.C. §§ 1414(b)(3)(A)(iii)–(v).
45. 20 U.S.C. § 1414(a)(2)(B)(ii).
46. 20 U.S.C. § 1414(a)(2)(A).
47. 20 U.S.C. § 1414(a)(1)(C)(i)(I).
48. 20 U.S.C. § 1414(a)(1)(C)(ii)(II).
49. 20 U.S.C. §§ 1414(a)(1)(D)(ii)(I), (II).
50. 20 U.S.C. § 1415(b)(1); 34 C.F.R. § 300.502(b).
51. *N.B. v. Hellgate Elementary Sch. Dist., ex rel. Bd. of Directors, Missoula County, Mont.*, 541 F.3d 1202 (9th Cir. 2008).
52. *Idea Public Charter Sch. v. District of Columbia*, 374 F. Supp.2d 158 (D.D.C. 2005).
53. 34 C.F.R. § 300.502(b).
54. 34 C.F.R. § 300.502(c)(1); *James and Lee Anne D. ex rel. Sarah D. v. Board of Educ. of Aptakisic-Tripp Community Consol. Sch. Dist. No. 102*, 642 F. Supp.2d 804 (N.D. Ill. 2009).
55. 34 C.F.R. § 300.323(c)(1).
56. 34 C.F.R. § 300.323(c)(2).
57. 20 U.S.C. § 1414(d)(1)(A).
58. 34 C.F.R. § 300.321(a).

59. 34 C.F.R. §§ 300.154(d)–(g).

60. 34 C.F.R. §§ 300.154(d)–(g).

61. 20 U.S.C. §§ 1402 (14), 1414 (d).

62. 458 U.S. 176 (1982).

63. *Id.* at 200.

64. *See, e.g., Hall v. Vance County Bd. of Educ.*, 774 F.2d 629 (4th Cir. 1985); *Carter v. Florence County Sch. Dist. Four*, 950 F.2d 156 (4th Cir. 1991), *aff'd on other grounds*, 510 U.S. 7 (1993).

65. *See, e.g., Board of Educ. of E. Windsor Reg'l Sch. Dist. v. Diamond*, 808 F.2d 987 (3d Cir. 1986); *Polk v. Susquehanna Intermediate Unit 16*, 853 F.2d 171 (3d Cir. 1988).

66. *See, e.g., Chris C. v. Gwinnett County Sch. Dist.*, 780 F. Supp. 804 (N.D. Ga. 1991).

67. *J.S.K. v. Hendry County Sch. Bd.*, 941 F.2d 1563 (11th Cir. 1991).

68. *See Timothy W. v. Rochester, N.H., Sch. Dist.*, 875 F.2d 954 (1st Cir. 1989), *cert. denied*, 493 U.S. 983 (1989).

69. 20 U.S.C. §§ 1406(b)(2), 1412(a)(5).

70. 995 F.2d 1204 (3d Cir. 1993).

71. An earlier version of this test emerged in *Daniel R.R. v. State Bd. of Educ.*, 874 F.2d 1036 (5th Cir. 1989).

72. 14 F.3d 1398 (9th Cir. 1994).

73. *See, e.g., Clyde K. v. Puyallup Sch. Dist. No. 3*, 35 F.3d 1396 (9th Cir. 1994).

74. 20 U.S.C. § 1415(e).

75. 20 U.S.C. § 1415(f)(1)(B)(i); 34 C.F.R. § 300.510(a).

76. 20 U.S.C. § 1415(e)(2)(B).

77. 20 U.S.C. § 1415(f).

78. 20 U.S.C. § 1415(f)(1)(A).

79. 20 U.S.C. § 1415(g).

80. 20 U.S.C. § 1415(f)(3)(c).

81. 20 U.S.C. § 1415(f)(3)(D).

82. 20 U.S.C. § 1415(f)(3)(A).

83. *H.H. ex rel. Hough v. Indiana Bd. of Special Educ. Appeals*, 501 F. Supp.2d 1188 (N.D. Ind. 2007).

84. 34 C.F.R. § 300.511(c)(2).

85. 34 C.F.R. § 300.511(c)(3).

86. 20 U.S.C. § 1415(f)(1)(B).

87. 20 U.S.C. § 1415(f)(1)(B)(iii).

88. 20 U.S.C. § 1415(f)(1)(B)(iv).

89. 20 U.S.C. § 1415(f)(1)(B)(ii).

90. 20 U.S.C. § 1415(f)(3)(E)(i)(ii).

91. 20 U.S.C. § 1415(i).

92. 34 C.F.R. § 300.515(c).

93. 20 U.S.C. § 1415(i)(1)(A).

94. 34 C.F.R. § 300.515(b).

95. 20 U.S.C. § 1415(f)(2)(A).

96. 20 U.S.C. § 1415(f)(2)(B).

97. 34 C.F.R. § 300.512(c)(2).

98. 20 U.S.C. § 1415(h)(1).
99. 20 U.S.C. § 1415(h)(2).
100. 20 U.S.C. § 1415(h)(3).
101. 20 U.S.C. § 1415(h)(4).
102. 20 U.S.C. § 1415(i)(2)(A).
103. 20 U.S.C. § 1415(i)(2)(B).
104. 20 U.S.C. § 1415(j).
105. 20 U.S.C. § 1415(k)(2).
106. *Honig v. Doe*, 484 U.S. 305 (1988).
107. 20 U.S.C. § 1415(f)(3)(D).
108. 546 U.S. 49 (2005).
109. *Van Duyn v. Baker Sch. Dist.*, 502 F.3d 811 (9th Cir. 2007).
110. 550 U.S. Ct. 516 (2007). For a commentary on this case, *see* Charles J. Russo. (2007). "The Rights of Non-Attorney Parents under the IDEA: *Winkelman v. Parma City School District.*" *221 Education Law Reporter*, 1–19 (2007).
111. 20 U.S.C. § 1415(i)(2)(C)(iii).
112. 20 U.S.C. § 1415(i)(2)(C)(iii).
113. See *Board of Educ. of Hendrick Hudson Cent. Sch. Dist. v. Rowley*, 458 U.S. 176, 208 (1982) ("We . . . have cautioned that courts lack the 'specialized knowledge and experience' necessary to resolve 'persistent and difficult questions of educational policy.' . . . once a court determines that the requirements of the Act have been met, questions of methodology are for resolution by the States [through school officials] (internal citations omitted)."
114. 20 U.S.C. § 1415(i)(2)(C)(iii).
115. 20 U.S.C. §§ 1415(i)(3)(B)(c); for limits on attorney fees, *see* 20 U.S.C. §§ 1415(i)(3)(D)–(G).
116. 468 U.S. 992 (1984).
117. 548 U.S. 291 (2006).
118. 20 U.S.C. § 1412(a)(10)(C)(ii).
119. 471 U.S. 359 (1985).
120. 510 U.S. 7 (1993).
121. *Todd D. by Robert D. v. Andrews*, 933 F.2d 1576 (11th Cir. 1991); *Birmingham v. Omaha Sch. Dist.*, 298 F.3d 731 (8th Cir. 2002).
122. *Pihl v. Massachusetts Dep't of Educ.*, 9 F.3d 184 (1st Cir. 1993); *Jones v. Schneider*, 896 F. Supp. 488 (D.V.I. 1995).
123. *Burr by Burr v. Ambach*, 863 F.2d 1071 (2d Cir. 1988), *vacated and remanded sub nom. Sobol v. Burr*, 492 U.S. 902 (1989), *re-aff'd on remand*, 888 F.2d 258 (2d Cir. 1989), *cert. denied*, 494 U.S. 1005 (1990); *Blackman v. District of Columbia*, 374 F. Supp.2d 168 (D.D.C. 2005).
124. *See, e.g., Taylor v. Altoona Area Sch. Dist.*, 513 F. Supp.2d 540 (W.D. Pa. 2007); *L.M.P. ex rel. E.P. v. School Bd. of Broward County*, 516 F. Supp.2d 1305 (S.D. Fla. 2007).
125. *See, e.g., Mark H. v. Lemahieu*, 513 F.3d 922 (9th Cir. 2008).
126. For a book on this topic, *see* Allan G. Osborne Jr. & Charles J. Russo. (2009). *Discipline of Students with Disabilities: Legal Issues*. Thousand Oaks, CA: Corwin Press.
127. 20 U.S.C. § 1415(k).

128. *Honig v. Doe*, 484 U.S. 305 (1988).
129. 20 U.S.C. § 1415(k)(1)(G).
130. 20 U.S.C. § 1415(k)(1)(D).
131. 20 U.S.C. § 1415(k)(1)(D), (E).
132. 20 U.S.C. § 1415(k)(1)(E)(I).
133. 20 U.S.C. § 1415(k)(1)(E)(I).
134. 20 U.S.C. § 1415(k)(1)(E)(I).
135. 20 U.S.C. § 1415(k)(1)(C), 20 U.S.C. § 1412(a)(1)(A).
136. 20 U.S.C. § 1415(k)(1)(C).
137. *Farrin v. Maine Sch. Admin. Dist. No. 59*, 165 F. Supp.2d 37 (D. Me. 2001).
138. *AW ex rel. Wilson v. Fairfax County Sch. Bd.*, 372 F.3d 674 (4th Cir. 2004).
139. *Fitzgerald v. Fairfax County Sch. Bd.*, 556 F. Supp.2d 543 (E.D. Va. 2008).
140. *See, e.g., City of Worcester v. The Governor*, 625 N.E.2d 1337 (Mass. 1994); *Nashua Sch. Dist. v. State*, 667 A.2d 1036 (N.H. 1995).
141. 20 U.S.C. § 1411(a)(2)(A)(ii).
142. *See* 20 U.S.C. § 1411(h)(7)(B)(i).
143. *See, e.g., Timothy W. v. Rochester, N.H., Sch. Dist.*, 875 F.2d 954 (1st Cir. 1989), *cert. denied*, 493 U.S. 983 (1989).
144. 20 U.S.C. § 1411(e)(3).
145. *Id.*
146. *See* 20 U.S.C. § 1411 (i) for projected amounts of federal appropriations for special education between 2005 and 2011.
147. For a more detailed discussion of this case and related issues, *see* Allan G. Osborne Jr. & Charles J. Russo. (2006). "The Supreme Court Rejects Parental Reimbursement for Expert Witness Fees under the IDEA: *Arlington Central School District Board of Education v. Murphy*." *213 Education Law Reporter*, 333–348.

11

Analysis and Reflections

Charles J. Russo

As discussed in the opening chapter of this volume, most nations are signatories to an array of lofty international instruments designed to meet the educational needs of all of their students in elementary and secondary schools, including those with disabilities. Yet, insofar as only forty-five countries have enacted domestic legislation designed to protect the rights of children with special needs or otherwise address their rights, there is clearly a disparity between legal theory and educational practices. Accordingly, educational and political leaders, working together, must do more to meet the needs of students with disabilities.

The need for leaders to work together is highlighted by information from the Committee on the Convention on the Rights of the Child (CRC) that is reported in the opening chapter:

> expressed concern regarding the inadequate legal protection, programmes, facilities and services for children with disabilities in South Africa; at the disparities in access to and availability of education for children with disabilities in China; that children with disabilities are not yet fully "integrated" into mainstream schools in Australia, New Zealand, Brazil and Singapore; and that children with disabilities in the UK are still unable to "fully enjoy their right to education."[1]

The reports did not directly address Canada or Malaysia; the United States is not a signatory to the CRC.

In providing comparative analysis in order to focus on areas in which nations may need to create or expand existing programming for students with disabilities, the remainder of this chapter is divided into two substantive parts. The first part relied on basically the same outline that is employed throughout this book to analyze the levels of services provided by the nations it covers. The next section of the chapter reflects on the status of the educational rights of students with disabilities. The chapter rounds out with a brief conclusion.

ANALYSIS

As an initial matter, it is worth noting that the laws of just about all of the nations reviewed in this book address the needs of students with disabilities whether by having specific, free-standing statutes (Australia, Brazil, Canada, China, England, United States), as part of more generic education laws (New Zealand, South Africa), or in regulations (Malaysia). In addition, two nations have relied on extensive internal policy papers (New Zealand and South Africa) augmenting their more general laws addressing education. Moreover, all of the nations reviewed, regardless of how their legal systems oversee the delivery of special education services, on varying degrees, support the notion of including children with disabilities in classrooms with their peers that are not disabled.

When the needs of students with disabilities are not met, the legal systems in just about all of the nations reviewed in this book afford parents the opportunity to file suit to safeguard the educational rights (Australia, Brazil, Canada, China, Great Britain, Malaysia, New Zealand, South Africa, and United States) of their children with disabilities. In order to get a better understanding of the legal rights of students with disabilities, then, the remainder of this section highlights similarities between the laws impacting their status in the nations reviewed in this volume. These brief observations focus on legal systems that share commonalities in their approaches, electing to avoid commenting on or identifying nations that do not address the various topics that are covered in other jurisdictions.

Identification, Assessment, and Placement

All of the nations that addressed the status of students with special needs include similar definitions or descriptions of disability covering a wide array of physical and emotional conditions. However, major differences begin to emerge insofar as Canada, England, and the United States employ the most highly formalized and structured systems of assessment of students with disabilities. In at least one country, Australia, most, but not all of its states and territories, have specific assessment procedures in place for identifying children with special needs. Other nations, such as Brazil, China, Malaysia, New Zealand, and South Africa, require educational officials to conduct assessments before students with disabilities can receive special services.

A unique aspect in England's system is that parents can be fined if they do not attend the examinations or assessments of their school-aged children with disabilities. In a slightly different vein, in the United States, school officials may initiate due process hearings to compel parents to have their children tested for special education, but they cannot be punished per se under federal or state special education laws. Yet, in Singapore, if parents of children with disabilities fail to send their children to school, there is nothing in legislation to compel them to do so.

All of the nations reviewed in this book promote inclusionary rather than exclusionary placements for students with disabilities at no expense to their parents. While most of the nations offer a range of placements from full inclusion to those in more restrictive settings, other than Brazil's explicitly offering funding to allow students to attend religiously affiliated nonpublic schools, the laws and policies in most of these nations make it clear that children with disabilities must attend public schools.

Once children are identified as being in need of special education, it is common for school officials to have the duty to develop written documents that are essentially contracts between educational systems and parents, or students themselves if they are old enough and legally competent, detailing the services to which their children are entitled. Two nations (Australia and the United States) allow school officials to take the opinions of students into consideration when selecting where they will attend school to the extent that doing so is practicable. In England the document overseeing the delivery of special education services is named a "statement"; this formalized agreement is identified as an "Individualized Education Program" in Brazil and New Zealand (where they are reviewed twice annually), China (even though they are not necessary for all children), and the United States; they are named "Individual Support Plans" in South Africa.

Due Process Rights, Dispute Resolution, Remedies

Insofar as the due process rights of students with disabilities and their parents, procedures for dispute resolution, and remedies not only vary greatly in terms of what they provide but also in terms of whether they are available, they are dealt with jointly under this single heading. In a preliminary matter, as pointed out earlier, almost all of the nations reviewed in this book have had parents file litigation to safeguard the educational rights (Australia, Brazil, Canada, China, Great Britain, Malaysia, New Zealand, South Africa, and United States) of their children with disabilities. While the presence of litigation, of course, reveals conflict, this must be viewed as a positive step because it affords parents the opportunity to seek final judgments about the rights of their children from fair and impartial third-party jurists.

Once again, although Canada, England, and the United States have the most well-defined procedures in place with regard to the due process rights of students with disabilities and their parents, whether through administrative processes, judicial proceedings, or alternative dispute resolution mechanisms such as arbitration and mediation, they are by no means alone in this regard. Not surprisingly, the ability of parents to challenge issues related to the placements of their children has led to significant amounts of litigation in these two countries. Even so, in contrast to the United States, where the Supreme Court only fairly recently afforded parents the opportunity to file litigation in their own names other than on behalf of their children, in England only parents have the right to file appeals, or complaints, in disability cases, not their children themselves. This can be problematic in England when students are in the care of local authorities as "looked after" children since local authorities that are potential respondents to appeal are also, in law, their "parents." Interestingly, in Canada, parents can challenge the decisions of educators with regard to the placements of their children with special needs, but likely not the services or programming that they receive.

Based on their shared British heritage, both Malaysia and New Zealand afford parents the opportunity to seek redress beyond their school systems in the event that disputes about the placements of their children with disabilities emerge. In Malaysia, parents are entitled to have their disputes resolved by fair and impartial third-party decision makers and can, like in the United States, appeal to the courts after they have exhausted administrative review. In New Zealand, on the other hand, the sole procedure available pursuant to one part of the Education Act 1989 is arbitration. Although judicial review to the High Court is available under another provision, it is beyond the means of most parents since they apparently cannot recover attorney fees for litigation.

In a related point, among the few nations explicitly addressing the rights of students with disabilities who are subjected to discipline for misbehaviors that are manifestations of, or related to their impairments, Canada, Australia, England, and the United States provide the greatest level of due process protection whether in statutes, regulations, or litigation. Unlike in the United States, students with disabilities who are suspended or expelled from school in Malaysia are not provided with educational services.

Funding and Cost Issues

The adequacy of funding aside, the two nations with the most explicit attention to the mechanism of providing financial support for educating students with special educational needs are England and the United States, with the latter forbidding direct funding for students who attend religiously affiliated nonpublic schools. In both of these nations local educational authorities or governing bodies receive varying levels of aid from both national and local levels of government. Similarly, Australia, Brazil, Malaysia, New Zealand, and Singapore (more specifically through its Ministry of Education and National Council of Social Services) provide resources through a combination of local and national resource allocation.

In Canada, for constitutional reasons, the national government provides no direct funding for education. Canada provides a mixture of provincial and local resources to pay for special education with the proportions varying from one province or territory to the next. Further, Brazil prioritizes the distribution of resources for students, focusing on children in the first through eighth grades. China offers funds for students who attend school pursuant to national compulsory attendance laws, essentially through the end of the equivalent of their attendance at elementary schools.

On a matter related to paying for special education, in the United States, students who are covered by the Individuals with Disabilities Education Act (IDEA) are entitled to services regardless of cost under what is described as the statute's "zero reject" approach. On the other hand, other nations, most notably Australia, China, England, and South Africa have adopted an approach that is similar to that of the American statute, Section 504 of the Rehabilitation Act of 1973, rather than the IDEA when dealing with students with disabilities. In other words, in varying degrees, all of these laws allow educators to take cost into account when evaluating what kind of accommodations they can make or the nature of services that they can provide to students with disabilities. However, Malaysia has explicitly rejected this perspective in case law, adopting a position closer to that of the United States under the IDEA, namely that the needs of students with disabilities are not subject to financial constraints.

REFLECTIONS

The governments of all of the nations discussed in this book have ratified various human rights instruments addressing the rights of all students, including those with disabilities. Moreover, led by England and the United States, the nations with the two most comprehensive systems for students with special needs, these countries have taken a variety of steps to enact domestic legislation safeguarding the rights of children with special needs. Some nations, such as Australia, China, Malaysia and New Zealand, have enacted laws and regulations that are not far behind in terms of their extensiveness. A third group of nations such as Brazil,

South Africa, and Singapore are stepping up their efforts to meet the educational needs of students with disabilities. At the same time, ensuring the right to education is an obligation of governments that need to translate their international commitments into constitutions and domestic legislation. Otherwise, it will be most difficult to develop and enforce policies calling for equal educational opportunities for all children.

The principles enunciated in the various international instruments that the nations in this book have signed, in addition to the views expressed in their constitutions and other domestic legal documents, need to be translated into practices conferring concrete rights on students and corresponding duties on educators, all of which are subject to protection via judicial review. When the right to education for children with special needs is reflected in national legislation, it is not automatically achieved in real terms since systemic disparities between legislation and practices often remain in place. This means that the enforcement of educational rights can sometimes be hampered. Put another way, it is difficult to prevent discrimination absent legislative or regulatory foundations establishing norms directing officials to take the necessary measures to protect the educational rights of students with special needs.

At the national, state, and local levels, governmental and educational leaders must continuously revise existing policies, or formulate new ones, to improve the quality of education for students with disabilities. Leaders must thus consider the interests, skills, knowledge, and talents of children while avoiding educational and social segregation. It is a great challenge to achieve the right to education for all. Accordingly, it is necessary to guarantee access to education for children with special needs who did not or could not complete at least their formal education in at least primary schools. In light of data, admittedly a bit dated, that the global literacy rate of adults with disabilities is 3 percent,[2] governments should adopt policies encouraging and intensifying programs to educate adults who were denied opportunities to receive an appropriate education when they were children.

Clearly, working to establish educational policy and management systems to meet the needs of students with disabilities is a daunting task. Education is a complex enterprise, particularly when dealing with special education, which tends to be significantly more expensive than regular programming, because it must represent a broad range of interests for different stakeholders including students, teachers, parents, school staff, and governing boards. Many of the stakeholders in special education are affected by the policies and decisions of what can be described as the educational enterprise. Of course, since it is not easy to anticipate the effects of policies, school officials, acting in conjunction with political leaders, must do what they can to meet the democratically agreed-to objectives of their educational systems that are grounded in domestic law and that are reflected in the appropriate international covenants. Additionally, leaders should look to international multilateral and bilateral cooperation agencies such as UNESCO that can contribute financial and/or technical support to enhance the development of programming for children with special needs.

Through national laws and policies, providing children with special needs the education necessary to afford them opportunities to participate in the economies of their countries must take concrete form in terms of educational programs and curricula. Accordingly, it is imperative that educators adapt schooling to new, emerging challenges. As difficult as change can be, as reflected by the U.S. Supreme Court's monumental decision in *Brown v. Board of Education,*[3] invalidating segregation in public schools based on race, educational systems sometimes need to be reformed in order to face social, political, cultural, and technological changes. As such, programming must reflect the needs of students with disabilities in an ever-changing world. Yet, governments remain responsible for maintaining the credibility of school curricula in terms of internal sustainability and continuity despite political, social, and institutional changes.

In order to ensure that students with disabilities receive equal educational opportunities, school officials and political leaders throughout the world should provide adequate financial support. This assumes, of course, that there are no decisive financial constraints within these countries related to educational development. However, since many governments are faced with budgetary challenges in the face of what appears to be a worldwide economic slowdown, it remains to be seen how much progress nations make in meeting the educational needs of their students with disabilities.

CONCLUSION

Human dignity is closely related to the protection of the physical and mental integrity of students with disabilities as they grow to become productive adult members of their societies. Quality education for all children, including those with disabilities, is the key to the reduction and elimination of adult illiteracy in future generations. Improvements in basic education for children with special needs are a prerequisite to sustainable personal and social development. In fact, people cannot exercise their social, civil, economic, and political rights unless they have received a basic education. Education is thus a lasting investment in the future of children, let alone society itself and sustainable development and social progress in general. Insofar as education is critical to improving the lives of people by helping them both to break the cycle of poverty and to lead lives of participation in democratic societies, it cannot be in short supply. If anything, it is an essential governmental responsibility to ensure that the educational rights of students remain protected rights that are compatible with human rights provisions.

All of the authors who contributed to this book are dedicated to achieving universal access to basic quality education for all children. In fact, we all recognize that achieving the right to basic education for all children, including those with disabilities, is one of the biggest challenges of our times. To this end, the authors hope that our collective and individual efforts in pursuit of the study of comparative education law can help to spur discussions culminating in ensuring the educational rights of all children, including those with disabilities, regardless of where they live.

NOTES

1. Byrne and Lundy, Introduction chapter.
2. Fact Sheet on UN Convention on the Rights of Persons with Disabilities (2006), citing a 1998 report from the United Nations Development Programme http://www.un.org/disabilities/convention/facts.shtml.
3. 347 U.S. 483 (1954).

Index

About the Contributors

Bronagh Byrne is a Research Fellow in Children's Rights based in the School of Education at Queen's University Belfast, Northern Ireland. She has expertise in the areas of international human rights law, children's rights, disability, equality and inclusion, and qualitative methodologies with particular focus on the application of children's rights standards to local practice. Byrne's background is in the area of young people, disability and education, in which she attained her doctorate. She previously worked as a researcher for the Centre on Human Rights for People with Disabilities and was involved in lobbying the UK government on ratification of the UN Convention on the Rights of Persons with Disabilities (CRPD). She was a member of the Northern Ireland Commissioner for Children and Young People's Children's Rights Review Advisory Group and the Northern Ireland Bill of Rights Children and Young People's Working Group.

Greg M. Dickinson, of the Bar of Ontario, is a professor in the Faculty of Education, University of Western Ontario, London, Canada, where he has specialized in education law for almost thirty years. Dickinson has also been a member in the Faculty of Law and director of the Clinical Legal Education Program. He has been the editor in chief of *Education & Law Journal* (Thomson Reuters) since 1988 and the director of The Althouse Press since 2002. Dickinson is coauthor and coeditor of several books, including *Rights, Freedoms and the Education System in Canada* (1989), *Understanding the Law* (1989, 1996), and *Beyond the Careful Parent: Tort Liability in Education* (1998), as well as numerous book chapters and articles on education law.

Kate Diesfeld is Associate Professor and Director of the National Centre for Health Law and Ethics at AUT University. In Los Angeles, she represented people with developmental disabilities through Protection and Advocacy, Inc. For eight years in Canterbury (England), she supervised students who advocated with, and on behalf of, people with disabilities through the Kent Law Clinic (Mental Health and Learning Disability) at Kent Law School. With Philip Patston, she cochaired New Zealand's first community law centre for disabled people (Auckland Disability Law). She will join Waikato Law School as Associate Professor of Social Justice in 2011.

Petra Engelbrecht is a Professor of Education, Canterbury Christ Church University in the United Kingdom. She is an acknowledged international researcher in the field of Inclusive Education and has published widely in this regard. Further recognition for research and her role in education includes, for example, awards such as a Medal of Honor in 2009 by the South African Academy of the Sciences and the Arts (SA Akademie vir Wetenskap en Kuns) for the development of educational psychology and education in general in South Africa.

John Hancock is the Senior Solicitor at YouthLaw Tino Rangatiratanga Taitamariki Inc., an Auckland-based community law centre that provides a free legal service to children and young people across New Zealand. Hancock practices as a Youth Advocate, a court-appointed lawyer for young people facing criminal charges, in the Auckland Youth Court. He also has a particular interest in law reform and legal policy issues that affect children and young people, and he has worked extensively on New Zealand's 2003 and 2010 NGO reports to the United Nations on the UN Convention on the Rights of the Child.

Neville Harris is Professor of Law and Research Director–elect at the University of Manchester School of Law. He is the general editor of *Education Law Journal* and the *Journal of Social Security Law* and Senior Editor of the *Education Law Reports*. His books include *Law and Education: Regulation, Consumerism and the Education System* (Sweet & Maxwell, 1993), *The Law Relating to Schools* (Tolley, 1995); *Special Educational Needs and Access to Justice* (Jordans, 1997), *Social Security Law in Context* (with others) (Oxford University Press, 2000); *Challenges to School Exclusion* (with Eden) (Routledge Falmer, 2000); and *Education, Law and Diversity* (Hart, 2007). He has worked on a wide range of funded research projects, the latest of which was funded by the Economic and Social Research Council in the UK, and he has examined the resolution of disputes concerning special educational needs.

Jim Jackson is College Director, Kaplan Singapore. He joined Kaplan in February 2010. Prior to that, he was Chair of the Academic Board at Southern Cross University, Lismore, Australia, and Professor of Law. He remains Emeritus Professor at Southern Cross University. He has held positions in commerce and/or law schools at the Darling Downs Institute of Advanced Education, the University of Wollongong, and was Associate Professor, School of Law, Bond University, before moving to Southern Cross University in 1991 to establish the law school as its Foundation Dean. Jackson has written widely on higher education law, including papers on governance, dismissal processes, compulsory student unionism, marketing law, academic freedom, legal rights of international students, speech rights, and fiduciary obligations of university governing bodies. He has jointly written "Law for Educators: School and University Law in Australia," LexisNexis 2007. More recently he led a team that gained an ALTC grant to examine student grievance and discipline issues in Australian universities. He has written in the area of school law, especially in relation to disability, the right to education and linguistic rights in education.

Laura Lundy is a Professor of Education Law and Children's Rights in the School of Education, Queen's University, Belfast, and a Barrister at Law. She is the Director of the School of Education's Research Cluster on Children's Rights and Participation and the universitywide Research Forum for the Child (www.qub.ac.uk/child). She is the author of *Education Law Policy and Practice in Northern Ireland* and has published widely on education law and children's rights. She has extensive experience of sociolegal and interdisciplinary research projects in the area of childhood studies, with a particular focus on education. While Lundy's expertise is in law and human rights, she has worked in research teams with psychologists, sociologists, and criminologists as well as academics in the health sciences, including nursing, pharmacy and medicine. She has been a principal investigator or coresearcher in large, interdisciplinary research projects funded by the ESRC, public bodies such as the Northern Ireland Commissioner for Children and Young People and leading charitable foundations such as The Wellcome Trust and Barnardo's. She was the Chair of the Northern Ireland Human Rights Commission's working party on education rights for the Northern Ireland Bill of Rights and is a former Equal Opportunities Commissioner for Northern Ireland.

Allan G. Osborne Jr. is the retired principal of the Snug Harbor Community School in Quincy, Massachusetts. He received his doctorate in educational leadership from Boston College. Allan Osborne has authored or coauthored numerous articles, monographs, textbooks, and textbook chapters on special education law, along with textbooks on other aspects of special education. A past president of the Education Law Association (ELA), he has been a frequent presenter at ELA conferences and writes the "Students with Disabilities" chapter of the *Yearbook of Education Law,* which is published by ELA. Allan Osborne is on the Editorial Advisory Committee of *West's Education Law Reporter* and is coeditor of the "Education Law into Practice" section of that journal. He also serves as an editorial consultant for many other publications in education law and special education.

Nina Ranieri is an Associate Professor in the Department of State Law of the Faculty of Law of the University of São Paulo (USP). Currently she is Deputy Secretary of Higher Education of the São Paulo State and member of the State of São Paulo Education Board. She is the author of the following books: *Autonomia Universitária (University Autonomy), Educação Superior, Direito e Estado (Higher Education, Law and the State),* and the organizer of *Autonomia Universitária na USP, de 1934 a 2004 (University Autonomy at USP from 1934 to 2004),* among others. She has also written several articles in the areas of public law and education law, and has contributed to law journals and other publications.

Charles J. Russo is the Joseph Panzer Chair in Education in the School of Education and Allied Professions and Adjunct Professor in the School of Law at the University of Dayton, Ohio. The 1998–1999 president of the Education Law Association and 2002 winner of its McGhehey (Lifetime Achievement) Award, he is the author of more than two hundred articles in peer-reviewed journals and the author, coauthor, editor, or coeditor of thirty-nine books. He has been the editor of the *Yearbook of Education Law* for the Education Law Association since 1995 and has written or coauthored in excess of 750 publications; he is also the editor of two academic journals and serves as a member of more than a dozen editorial boards. Russo has spoken and taught extensively on issues in education law in the United States and in twenty-one other nations on all six inhabited continents. In recognition of his work in Education Law in other countries, he received an honorary PhD from Potchefstroom University, now the Potchefstroom Campus of North-West University, in Potchefstroom, South Africa, in May 2004.

Marius Smit, an attorney and a qualified educator, is an Associate Professor in Education Law at the Faculty for Education Sciences at North-West University, Potchefstroom campus, South Africa. He has published several articles in refereed journals and professional publications and has coauthored eight books in the field of education law. Smit serves as a member of the school governing body of Potchefstroom Gimnasium High School, a member of the provincial committee of the Federation of Governing Bodies of South African Schools (FEDSAS) and of the national executive of the South African Education Law Association.

M. K. Teh is both a lawyer and an educator. She is a qualified Barrister-at-Law in London, and qualified as an Advocate and Solicitor of the Supreme Court of Singapore in 1996. She was a lawyer in Singapore before moving to Australia. Earlier in her career, Kim was both a teacher and a head of department in Singapore schools. Kim was the recipient of the inaugural Dr. Ann Shorten Doctoral Thesis Prize 2009, awarded by the Australia and New Zealand Education Law Association for the most outstanding PhD thesis in education law research and its contribution to education law and practice. She is currently based at the University of Southern Queensland in Hervey Bay, where she lectures in law.

Fatt Hee Tie is an associate professor at the University of Malaya in Kuala Lumpur, Malaysia. He was admitted as an advocate and solicitor to the High Court of Malaya in 1994. He has taught in two secondary schools and a teacher training college for more than ten years before joining the university. At the university, he taught education law for more than fifteen years. He has published in the *Australia and New Zealand Education Law Journal, Education and Law Journal, International Journal for Education Law and Policy,* and *Education Law Journal.* He has also contributed a number of chapters in education law books. His latest book is *Education Law in Malaysia: Principles and Practice,* due for publication by Thomson Sweet and Maxwell in November 2010.

Sally Varnham is an Associate Professor with the Faculty of Law at the University of Technology, Sydney. She was admitted to the New Zealand Bar and practised law in Wellington and in London before beginning her teaching career. She taught Business Law for the College of Business at Massey University in New Zealand before joining the Faculty of Law at UTS in 2007. Her main research interest is in legal issues arising in compulsory and higher education, and her theses for LLM (VUW) and PhD (UNSW) are in this area. She is widely published in Australia, New Zealand, the UK and Europe and regularly presents at national and international conferences.

Ran Zhang is an Assistant Professor of Educational Law in the Graduate School of Education, Peking University, China. She has published articles and book chapters on Chinese or American educational law and coedited two special issues of *Chinese Education and Society* on new trends in educational litigation in China. She has received research grants from the U.S. National Science Foundation and the state government of China to study the legal-rights consciousness of Chinese college students. Her research interests include educational law, comparative education, and research methodology.